Stories
from
Hispano
New Mexico

A New Mexico Federal Writers' Project Book

Stories
from
Hispano
New Mexico

A New Mexico Federal Writers' Project Book

*Compiled and Edited
by*
Ann Lacy and Anne Valley-Fox

SANTA FE

© 2012 by Ann Lacy and Anne Valley-Fox.
All Rights Reserved.

No part of this book may be reproduced in any form or by any electronic or mechanical means including information storage and retrieval systems without permission in writing from the publisher, except by a reviewer who may quote brief passages in a review.

Sunstone books may be purchased for educational, business, or sales promotional use. For information please write: Special Markets Department, Sunstone Press, P.O. Box 2321, Santa Fe, New Mexico 87504-2321.

Book and Cover design › Vicki Ahl
Body typeface › Palatino Linotype
Printed on acid-free paper
∞

Library of Congress Cataloging-in-Publication Data

Stories from Hispano New Mexico : a New Mexico Federal Writers' Project book / compiled and edited by Ann Lacy and Anne Valley-Fox.
    pages cm
Includes bibliographical references.
ISBN 978-0-86534-885-1 (softcover : alk. paper)
 1. Hispanic Americans--New Mexico--History--Anecdotes. 2. Hispanic Americans--New Mexico--Social life and customs--Anecdotes. 3. New Mexico--History--1848---Anecdotes. 4. New Mexico--Social life and customs--Anecdotes. I. Lacy, Ann, 1945-, compiler, editor. II. Fox, Anne Valley, compiler, editor. III. Federal Writers' Project. New Mexico.
 F805.S75S76 2012
 305.86'80730789--dc23
                    2012011395

WWW.SUNSTONEPRESS.COM
SUNSTONE PRESS / POST OFFICE BOX 2321 / SANTA FE, NM 87504-2321 /USA
(505) 988-4418 / ORDERS ONLY (800) 243-5644 / FAX (505) 988-1025

Dedicated to the people of New Mexico

CONTENTS

Acknowledgements 11
Editors' Preface 13
About the New Mexico Federal Writers' Project . . . 15
Foreword by Nasario García, PhD 17
Map of the Territory of New Mexico, ca. 1857 22

VILLAGE LIFE

Don José Miguel Archuleta, A Character of Old Taos:
    La Bajada de la Santa Cruz by Lorin W. Brown 25
Early Days and Customs in Agua Fria by Lorin W. Brown 29
Nuestra Señora de Dolores by Lorin W. Brown 32
The Bell Marianna by Lorin W. Brown 34
Victorio by L. W. Brown 38
Old Timers Dictionary in Detail: Mrs. Deonicio Álvarez,
    Spanish Wedding Custom by Marie Carter 40
Old Timers Stories: Bertha Mandell Candler by Marie Carter 44
Old Timers Stories: Mrs. Juan Valdéz by Marie Carter 48
Old Timers Stories: Nemecio Provincio (Wife: Anita Provincio)
    by Marie Carter 50
The Biography of Guadalupe Lupita Gallegos (I) by Bright Lynn . . 55
A Second Ananias by Reyes N. Martínez 59
A Sheepherd at Work in Taos County by Reyes Nicanor Martínez . . 63
Cooperation by Reyes Martínez 70
Social Life by Reyes N. Martínez 73
The Weaver of Talpa by Reyes N. Martínez 76
Early Life in Questa as Told by Frank V. García by L. Raines 78
Slavery by L. Raines 80

NARRATIVES

Canuteros and the Death of Colonel Means by Lorin W. Brown . . . 83
El Adivino Casual "A Fortune-Teller by Accident" by Lorin W. Brown 88
El Leoncito by Lorin W. Brown 92
Los Comanches by Lorin Brown 93
The Ambuscade by Lorin W. Brown 100
The Mexican War at Reserve by H. P. Collier 104

Pioneer Story: Mrs. Lorencita Miranda by Edith L. Crawford 107
Pioneer Story: Rumaldo Águilar Durán by Edith L. Crawford 109
Padre Antonio José Martínez of Taos, New Mexico by Luis Martínez . . 112
The Taos Massacre—1847 by Luis Martínez 119
Hallucinations and a Wildcat Venture by Reyes Martínez 125
Wamsley's Crossing by Reyes N. Martínez 128
The Masons by L. Raines 130
Old Days in Socorro, New Mexico by N. Howard Thorp 132
Mexican Boy Captured by Apache Indians by Clay W. Vaden 137

WITCHCRAFT & GHOST STORIES

New Mexico Folklore: Goblins of Truchas by Manuel Berg 141
New Mexico Witchcraft: A Magical Cure by Manuel Berg 143
New Mexico Witchcraft: The Dancing Light by Manuel Berg 144
New Mexico Witchcraft: The Flying Brujas by Manuel Berg 145
New Mexico Witchcraft: The Hanging Tongue by Manuel Berg 147
New Mexico Witchcraft: The Magic Ointment by Manuel Berg 149
New Mexico Witchcraft: Victims of a Bruja by Manuel Berg 151
The Trunk by Manuel Berg 154
A Witch Story by Lorin W. Brown 157
Flight to Mexico by Lorin W. Brown 159
Tales of the Moccasin Maker of Córdova: Witchcraft by Lorin W. Brown . 164
Ghostly Revenge by Genevieve Chapin 168
The Witch of Arroyo Hondo by Reyes Martínez 171

BILLY THE KID

Billy the Kid by Edith L. Crawford 195
Billy the Kid Story: Donicino Molina by Edith L. Crawford 201
Billy the Kid Story: Francisco Gómez by Edith L. Crawford 202
Reminiscences of Billy the Kid by Edith L. Crawford 203
Reminiscences of Billy the Kid as Told by Sam Farmer, Hijinio Salazar,
    Apolónio Sedillo, Gregorio Ventura by Edith L. Crawford 204
Story of Billy the Kid by Edith L. Crawford 207
What I Know About Billy the Kid as Told by Francisco Gómez
    by E. L. Crawford 208
The Biography of Guadalupe Lupita Gallegos (II) by Bright Lynn 209
About Billy the Kid as Told by Ismael Valdéz by L. Raines 213
Interview with José García y Trujillo by Janet Smith 214
Early Days in Lincoln County as Told by Josh Brent by Frances E. Totty . 219

TALES OF LAS PLACITAS

Dos Hombres Sabios de Las Placitas "The Wise Men of Las Placitas"
   by Lou Sage Batchen 223
El Platero "The Silversmith" by Lou Sage Batchen. 228
How the Civil War Reached Las Placitas by Lou Sage Batchen. . . . 231
Las Huertas by Lou Sage Batchen 237
La Madera "The Timber" by Lou Sage Batchen 242
The Good Samaritan of La Madera as Told by Rumaldita Gurulé
   by Lou Sage Batchen 244
La Cita de Las Brujas "Rendezvous of the Witches" as Told by
   Rumaldita Gurulé, Teresita Gallegos de Baca, and Catalina Gurulé
   by Lou Sage Batchen 245
El Misterio "The Enigma" as Told by Catalina Gurulé
   by Lou Sage Batchen 247
El Hombre Alegre "The Jolly Man" as Told by Rumaldita Gurulé
   by Lou Sage Batchen 249
Luxuries Come to La Madera as Told by Rumaldita Gurulé
   by Lou Sage Batchen 251
Ojo de la Casa "House of the Spring" by Lou Sage Batchen. . . . 253
El Inocentón "The Innocent" as Told by Teresita Gallegos de Baca
   by Lou Sage Batchen 259
El Ojo "The Eye" as Told by Teresita Gallegos de Baca
   by Lou Sage Batchen 260
Luz de la Luna "Moonlight" as Told by Teresita Gallegos de Baca
   by Lou Sage Batchen 261
Old Houses of Placitas by Lou Sage Batchen 262
Tejón by Lou Sage Batchen. 266
The Fury of 1869 by Lou Sage Batchen 272
The Panic of 1862 by Lou Sage Batchen. 278
Tiempo de Pasqua "Easter Tide" 1863 by Lou Sage Batchen . . . 285

PLACE

Alto Huachin by Lorin W. Brown 293
The Salt Traffic from the Estancia Salt Lakes to Mexico
   by Lorin W. Brown 294
Manzano by Jean Cady 295
Gallegos: Quay County by Genevieve Chapin 296
Mountains and Peaks: Rabbit Ears by Manville Chapman. 300

Points of Interest in Taos County: The Las Trampas Mission
   by B. C. Grant 302
Las Vegas by Bright Lynn 303
Lea County Plains—Once a Hunting Ground by Mrs. Benton Mosley . . 305
Los Torres by L. Raines 307
San Augustine by Lester Raines. 308
San Miguel del Bado by L. Raines 311
Starvation Peak by Lester Raines 313
Tecolotito by Lester Raines. 314
Roswell by Georgia B. Redfield 315
Estancia in Tradition by N. S. Rose 316
History of Arroyo Seco, New Mexico by Simeon Tejada 317
La Capilla de San Juan "The Chapel of St. John" by Thorp and Adams . . 319
How Apache Creek Got Its Name by Clay W. Vaden 320

List of Illustrations 321
Bibliography of New Mexico Federal Writers' Project Documents 323
Names Index. 328

Acknowledgments

We wish to thank the New Mexico State Records Center and Archives, the Museum of New Mexico Palace of the Governors Photo Archives and the Fray Angélico Chávez History Library, Santa Fe, New Mexico for the use of their collections.

We are grateful to the archivists at the NMSRCA for their able assistance with our research.

Special thanks to Daniel Kosharek, Palace of the Governors Photo Archivist.

We greatly appreciate Project Crossroads and Elise Rymer for her inspiration and steadfast support.

Editors' Preface

Stories from Hispano New Mexico is the fourth volume in the New Mexico Federal Writers' Project Book series. The first, *Outlaws & Desperados*, was published in 2008 to mark the 75th anniversary of the New Deal; *Frontier Stories* followed in 2010 and *Lost Treasures and Old Mines* in 2011. *Stories from Hispano New Mexico* celebrates New Mexico's one hundred years of statehood in 2012.

Although we can well imagine the dramatic pull of land, climate and vying traditions on those who lived here, there were no written histories of the area until Spanish conquistadors and Franciscan priests came clanging into the Southwest in the 16th century. With the exception of *La Relación* — Alvar Nuñez Cabeza de Vaca's narrative of his crew's shipwreck off the coast of Florida in 1528 and his eight-year trek into the Southwest — the first known recorded history of New Mexico was *Historia de la Nuevo México*, a verse narrative by Spanish soldier-poet Gaspar Pérez de Villagrá published in 1610. Since then, New Mexico's evocative landscape, culture and history have inspired thousands of books of poetry and prose.

From 1936 to 1940, the New Deal's Federal Writers' Project was in full swing in all 48 states of the union. The dual goal of Franklin Delano Roosevelt's project was to gainfully employ local writers while collecting archival documents related to the state's history and culture. In New Mexico, field writers fanned out around the state collecting regional documents and recording the stories, pecked out on old upright typewriters, of old-timers who remembered New Mexico's vanishing past.

Most of the oral histories collected by New Mexico field writers refer to events in the mid to late Territorial Period, approximately 1880 to 1910. Though the stories target a thirty-year timespan — a time in which ranchers, farmers, sheepherders, miners, prospectors, outlaws and settlers alike were battling forces of nature and man to tame the territory — they are evocative of a long and enduring way of life that still flavors life in New Mexico.

Although the tales collected here are wonderfully various, they are far from inclusive: appreciative readers must read between the lines to fill in missing voices and viewpoints. Of particular significance, Native American populations were rarely interviewed and no Native Americans were represented in NMFWP's stable of writers. Women, too, most often appear as secondary figures within the narratives.

In editing this series, we have attempted to stay true to the voices of the oral history informants and to uphold the dedication and veracity exhibited by the project writers in their manuscripts. From the start, our editorial policy has been minimalist in intent: we have changed punctuation and corrected spelling only when necessary for readability and clarity. Our policy has been to edit the material sparingly so that the richness of the "told and retold" stories reflects the relevant time and place and tells something of the storytellers (who were sometimes also the protagonists). Our hope is that each manuscript retains a sense of the writer's creative expression and preserves the authentic storytelling voice of the informant.

Stories from Hispano New Mexico presented a new challenge to us as editors. In previous volumes, most of the oral histories were told in English and transcribed in English; in this volume, many of the tales were told in Spanish and later transcribed into English—often without the aid of a translator. Although two of the field writers, Reyes Nicanor Martínez and Lorin W. Brown, were bilingual, many knew little Spanish. Consequently, a number of Spanish words in the manuscripts were misspelled; in some cases, the word use was simply incorrect. In this collection, in addition to correcting obvious misspellings, we have added accent marks to Spanish words where sometimes none were indicated in the typed manuscripts. Attentive readers may notice inconsistencies from one document to the next, as we made editing decisions one word at a time. We hope that the manuscripts retain the authenticity of their original versions and at the same time conform to proper written Spanish.

We have greatly enjoyed assembling this volume of oral histories and stories, which gives voice to New Mexico's remarkable Hispano settlers and their enduring legacy.

—Ann Lacy and Anne Valley-Fox
Santa Fe, New Mexico
Winter, 2012

About the New Mexico Federal Writers' Project

The Great Depression that came on the heels of the stock market crash of 1929 threw the country's financial institutions into chaos and put many people across the nation out of work. In 1933, President Franklin Delano Roosevelt inaugurated his New Deal administration, a comprehensive program designed to stimulate the country's economy while lending a hand to the unemployed.

At a time when many people were down on their luck during the Great Depression, the New Deal's New Mexico Federal Writers' Project (NMFWP) employed writers around the state to record the extraordinary history and lore of New Mexico. The Federal Writers' Project was one of a number of white-collar relief projects of the Works Progress Administration (WPA) that put Americans back to work. In addition to the Federal Writers' Project (FWP), the projects included the Federal Art Project, the Federal Music Project, the Federal Theater Project and the Historical Records Survey.

The New Mexico Federal Writers' Project was officially launched on August 2, 1935, under the direction of poet and writer Ina Sizer Cassidy. Between October, 1935, and August, 1939, a cadre of field writers wrote stories, collected articles, conducted interviews and transposed documents for the public record. Although each of the forty-eight states across the nation launched their own Federal Writers' Project, New Mexico was seen as geographically and culturally unique. From his office in Washington, DC, the national director of the Federal Writers' Project, Henry G. Alsberg, urged New Mexico project writers to emphasize the state's visual, scenic and human interest subjects in the project's guide, *New Mexico: A Guide to the Colorful State*. "Try to make the readers see the white midsummer haze, the dust that rises in unpaved New Mexican streets, the slithery red earth roads of winter, the purple shadows of later afternoon...," he told them.

New Mexico field writers apparently felt a similar enthusiasm, as they created hundreds of documents to preserve the state's vivid lore, scenic locale and colorful past for future generations. Their subjects ranged from the colonial New Mexico days of the 1600s and 1700s to the beginnings of the

1900s—from horse-drawn cart to car. Their many lively selections included firsthand oral accounts and remembrances by settlers and residents who lived to tell the story of New Mexico's Territorial days.

In 1939, under the WPA's reorganization, the New Mexico Federal Writers' Project became the Writers' Program. By that time, Aileen O'Bryan Nussbaum had replaced Ina Sizer Cassidy as project director. In Washington, DC, Charles Ethrige Minton supervised the New Mexico Writers Program until its closure in 1943. Through its tenure, the New Mexico program produced *Calendar of Events,* written by project writers and illustrated by Federal New Mexico Art Project artists, as well as *Over the Turquoise Trail* and *The Turquoise Trail,* two anthologies of New Mexican poems, stories, and folklore. A major achievement of the FWP was an American Guide Series publication entitled *New Mexico: A Guide to the Colorful State,* first published in 1940.

Project writers in New Mexico had a wealth of sources to draw upon and they mined them well. They collected tales from colorful old-timers as well as reports from early explorers, diarists and journalists, poets and artists, miners, ranchers and cowboys, farmers and merchants, lawmen and outlaws, anthropologists and folklorists. These are the voices of the many travelers—*paso por aqui*—who animate New Mexico history.

The efforts of the NMFWP field workers have left us a rich compilation of documents stored in various collections in New Mexico, including the New Mexico State Records Center and Archives and museum and university collections. The Library of Congress in Washington, DC also holds copies of many of the manuscripts. Now, seventy-nine years after FDR launched the New Deal, the New Mexico Federal Writers' Project book series moves a substantial number of these readings out of archival folders and into print for the public's enjoyment.

Foreword

by Nasario García

I grew up in Guadalupe (aka Ojo del Padre), New Mexico on the Río Puerco Valley southeast of Chaco Canyon. Of the various components comprising folklore that I was exposed to as a small boy, to wit, riddles, wedding songs (*entriegas*), ballads (*corridos*) love quatrains (*chiquiaos*), and hymns (*alaba[d]os*), the ubiquitous folk sayings (*dichos*) undoubtedly were the most popular among parents and grandparents. No child was spared from hearing them at the dinner table or out in the cornfields. *Dichos* were, in a manner of speaking, the order of the day in the upbringing of children. My father, who quit school in the fifth grade to help his parents eke out an existence, could neither read nor write in his native Spanish, but he possessed a reservoir of folk sayings at the tip of his tongue. He was a walking Sancho Panza.

But when it came to an evening's entertainment in the hinterland long before the days of television, no folklore genre galvanized more interest among family, relatives, or friends than the short story, *el cuento*. Gathered by the potbelly stove on a cold winter night, seated at the kitchen table in the summer, or huddled around the campfire during autumn cattle roundups, storytelling was magical. The mere mention of a *cuento* or an *historia*—the latter a popular term among Hispanic old-timers—evoked the sound of joy and perked up children's ears. Grownups did not stand on ceremony either; they, too, joined in the jubilation. I know. I was there more than once.

The preponderance of folklore stories that reached New Mexican villages starting with colonial times originated in Spain, *la patria grande*, the motherland, but others came via Spain from neighboring countries like Italy and Germany. Some popular tales portraying royalty, such as the wise servant advising the king, were fashioned after *Bertoldo, Bertoldino, and Cacaseno*, penned by the Italian writer Giulio Cesare della Croce (1550–1609), a contemporary of Miguel de Cervantes. Others with "happily-ever-after" denouements came from Christopher (Cristóbal) von Schmid (1768–1854) who wrote about Genoveva from Brabant(e), the queen accused falsely of adultery.

On the other hand, the more popular stories that cut a path across our state were related to adventure, pathos, wisdom, demons, ogres, and witchcraft and the supernatural. Narratives with a moral underpinning (*de escarmiento*) typical in Medieval Spain, also left their mark, but no stories were more widespread than the disobedient son and the evil eye (*el mal ojo*), the latter a superstition found around the globe in countries like Iraq, Greece (*B[V]askania*), Italy (*mal' ochio*), and Mexico (*ojo de venado*), although the evil eye purportedly is of Basque origin.

With the advent of the Great Depression, a massive undertaking was launched under the auspices of the Workers Progress Administration, the WPA or Diablo a Pie (the Devil on Foot), a linguistic mimicking of the acronym. Its goal, a daunting but successful enterprise, was to rescue from oblivion hundreds of time-honored stories along with those born in New Mexico during the territorial era and early statehood days of 1912. A unified cadre of dedicated field workers hit the road, heard, interpreted, and recreated, at times in impressionistic fashion, the voices of our ancestors. The informants featured in *Stories from Hispano New Mexico* take the reader on a multiplicity of vicarious mini journeys throughout different corners of the state.

The cornucopia of oral stories regarding our Land of Enchantment are as diverse thematically as they are geographically, but edifying nonetheless. They encompass fascinating topics—some not readily found in books—central to the understanding and appreciation of New Mexico history. Among them are slavery, witchcraft and the supernatural, kidnapping, racial relations, fortunetellers, patron saints, family games, and buffalo hunting in the Llano Estacado.

In New Mexico, those of us of Indo-Hispano descent can speak proudly of *la patria chica*, that is, our towns and villages where we were born, reared and lived until becoming acculturated or urbanized. In the process, we have allowed our language and culture, two inextricably bound entities, to slip from our grasp into seeming obscurity. What characterized each locale, and consequently gave identity to villagers and their *modus vivendi*, were language (Spanish), customs and traditions that we espoused and honored for generations.

Such richness, which began to wane following World War I, today for the most part is etched only in memory and ghost towns. With the passing of the *viejitos*, old-timers, the standard bearers of our heritage, we have interred with them a rich cultural and linguistic past. As one of the WPA writers, Lester Raines, pointed out in his story "San Agustín," "[Villagers] are happier to stay in their own little domain and live their daily lives as did their ancestors before them."

People in their respective *patria chica* were prone—and proud—to accentuate local color without looking askance at the foibles of human nature. A select group of poignant stories that typifies a *patria chica*, are "Tales of Las Placitas" (Tumbleweed Press published Las Placitas in 1972 with some of the same entries) by Lou Sage Batchen. Placitas, once a small Hispanic community, is nestled at the foothills northwest of the majestic Sandía Mountains north of Albuquerque. Adding to its breathtaking scenery were places nearby like La Madera. The wise elders, love affairs and weddings, bewitchment, craftsmen, and camaraderie that Batchen describes breathed life into Placitas.

Originally an Indian settlement where some of my relatives were born, lived, and are buried, Placitas fifty-plus years ago symbolized the quintessence of an Hispano village. Today it is an affluent community with high-tech energy efficient homes, but only the name and a few Hispanics remain as testimony to its rich historical past.

My father was not prone to tittle-tattle, hence, he disliked hearsay. *"No me vengan aquí con chismes"* (Don't come to me with idle talk), he would tell my siblings and me. His admonition was thought-provoking; it packed a strong punch. Then again, I often overheard grown men in my village say to one another, "*¿Qué no supo compadre . . . ?*" ("Didn't you hear compadre . . . ?"), or "*¿Qué me cuenta, compadre?*" ("What's new, compadre?") a more forthright way of eliciting gossip.

Yet gossip, intrigue, and exaggeration constitute an integral part of the storytelling tradition in New Mexico. Ironically, falsehoods and hyperbole could well be placed at the hands of a 16th century churchman named Fray Marcos de Niza (ca. 1495–1558) who lauded the legendary

Seven Cities of Gold. However, without his glorifying reports of gold, precious jewels, and silver other fortune seekers or explorers would have been less inspired to venture to what became known as the Land of Enchantment. Therefore, one could say, without any disrespect to other less flamboyant chroniclers, that the short story, *el cuento* or *historia*, had its roots in *mitote*, lodged in history.

To be sure, no storyteller worth his salt rivaled the roving mailman or *correo* as he was called long ago in scores of New Mexican villages. He was the purveyor of good and bad tidings, but the spreading of a spicy story hinged on him as he rode on horseback or drove a horse carriage from one hamlet to another. A typical scene while the men worked in the fields or tended to their livestock was to see a group of elderly women scurrying to hear the mailman relate the latest gossip from neighboring villages. Old men basking in the sun (*resolaneros*) perked up their ears to partake of the same *mitote*. The mailman, through no fault of his own, and a recondite figure in folklore annals, became the Number One *mitotero* (gossiper), but in the eyes of his admirers he was a dandy about the villages, an unsung hero, and an entertainer for all seasons.

Whatever the circumstances, whoever the person or persons at the heart of chitchat, the mailman's story was planted and sallied forth from village to village. Along the way one could bank on embellishment and exaggeration. Each story was skewed and thus evolved into something different, more enticing and scintillating, perhaps even dramatic or hilarious, depending on the raconteur's personality and knack for retelling a story. Though recycling was hardly a term in vogue at the time, that is precisely what people did with their stories.

The epitome of exaggeration and twisting of the truth is beautifully illustrated by Reyes Nicanor Martínez in the WPA story "A Second Ananias" contained in the present volume. The central character, a veritable rogue and teller of tall tales who hails from San Cristóbal north of Taos, is the charismatic Ramón Roybal. He is reminiscent of the picaresque character Pedro de Urdemalas, a popular figure in New Mexico folklore. Roybal's whopping fishing stories leave the reader laughing but not scratching his head. Humor, after all, is an intrinsic part of the Latino-Hispanic character.

The WPA writers' charm, passion, unabashed style, and mode of recreating a story are stamped on every page of their stories. And no matter how assiduous a collector-turned-writer might be in retelling an informant's tale from written notes or memory, it is virtually impossible to replicate verbatim the spoken word. When embellishing or romanticizing a story, the writer is just as vulnerable as the informant. If a writer in reconstructing a story says, "Nature had on her holiday attire," then it behooves the reader to look beyond lyrical words like these—hardly typical of the *viejitos'* lexicon—to glean what truly lurks behind them.

The eminent Spanish philosopher Miguel de Unamuno (1864–1936) once said, "The truth [lies] in life and life [lies] in truth." Whether lodged in truth, fiction or a combination of both, the ensuing compendium of captivating and entertaining WPA stories honoring our forefathers will leave an indelible impression on the reader's psyche for a long time to come.

—Nasario García, PhD
Professor Emeritus of Hispanic Languages and Literatures
Santa Fe, New Mexico

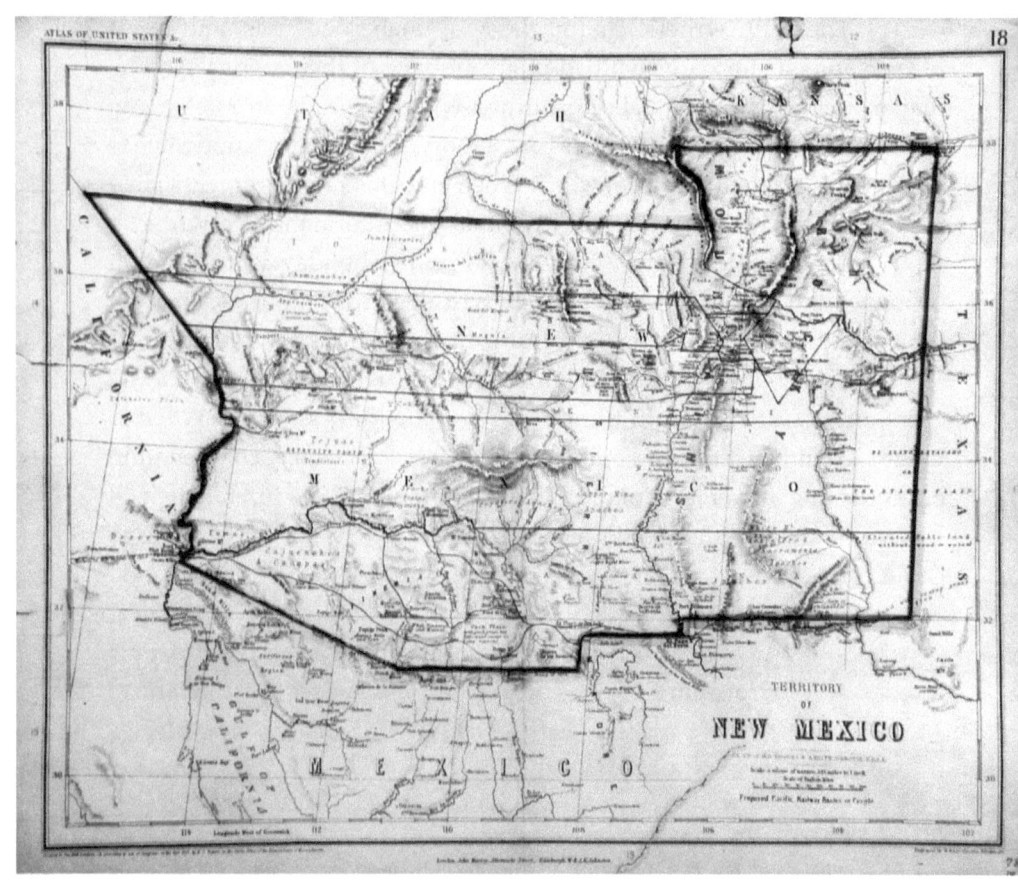

A. D. Rogers, A. Keith Johnston, *Territory of New Mexico*,
Fray Angélico Chávez History Library, Map Collection (78.9) ca. 1857

VILLAGE LIFE

"'Sometimes we would go to bed hoping to rest after a hard day's work,' Nemecio said, 'only to be wakened by the lap, lap, of water at our doors; sometimes around our beds. It had a voice, Señora, that we grew to hate—a voice that struck terror to our hearts and souls; it was there in the rising river, increasing in volume as the water rose, submerging our land, stealing our seed, quite often our homes, leaving us nothing—nothing. The newcomers can't begin to realize the hardships of the early pioneers.'"

From "Old Timers Stories: Nemecio Provincio (Wife: Anita Provincio)" by Marie Carter

Don José Miguel Archuleta, A Character of Old Taos:
La Bajada de la Santa Cruz

by Lorin W. Brown

Around the year 1837 the citizens of Taos had been having trouble with the Taos Indians with regard to the actual boundaries of the original grant of land to the village by the Indians. To avoid serious trouble with the Taos pueblo the citizens held a public meeting called by the Alcalde to decide what measures to take. Here it was decided to send two men to Mexico City to procure the actual measurements from the Federal Archives. This undertaking called for men of experience, education or at least the ability to read and write, and not the least requirement, courage, because of the many dangers which threatened on a long journey in those days.

The men chosen were Don José Gabriel Vigil and Don José Miguel Archuleta, men whom everybody felt embodied the necessary qualifications and who were the unanimous choices, so great was the general confidence in their ability.

Don José Gabriel Vigil, the elder of the two men, was a man of influence in Taos, who made a study of the law and was very much in demand when legal questions came up before the alcalde. He was well off for those times, owning ranches in El Prado and elsewhere. His town residence was located on the present site of the Bond-McCarthy store on the northwest corner of the present plaza.

Don José Miguel Archuleta, though not well off, was a much respected citizen. He was one of the first school teachers in Taos, holding school in his own home and in the old original courthouse. A very pious gentleman also, he was very active in all religious observances of the community, leading the prayers on all public occasions such as the feast of Nuestra Señora de Guadalupe, Santa Cruz Day and throughout Lent. He was always ready to pray for the dying and at the wakes to lead the prayers for the welfare of the souls of the deceased. He also manifested great interest in civic matters, lending the weight of his knowledge in all discussions concerning the public welfare.

So it was that no two better men could have been chosen for this mission. Funds having been raised to defray their expenses the whole village took a personal interest in their departure and successful return. After farewells to their families and prayers to the Saints for their protection the two men set out on their arduous trip. Each rode a mule and led another loaded with the necessary equipment and clothing for the trip and for their stay in Mexico City. They were gone for several months and one can imagine the anxiety with which news was awaited regarding their safe arrival and the progress of their mission.

Their final return was ample excuse for a season of feasting. They were the heroes of the day, feasted and honored wherever they went. Accounts of the trip, the trials and narrow escapes were listened to with interest and recounted throughout northern New Mexico.

They were enthusiastic in their accounts of Mexico City, their gracious treatment at the hands of the president and his wife and the other functionaries of the Mexican Government, the fetes and corridas they attended and all the other wonders which they saw there and on the way. From accounts handed down, Mexico City was described as being built on a lake but no mention survives of the name of the Mexican president who was in power at the time. Also they were proud of the magnificent gifts given them by the president of Mexico and other officials of that government.

Their mission was accomplished in that an authoritative description of the boundaries of the village of Taos as described in the Federal Archives, and brought back by these men, was the basis for a subsequent survey. This survey, a subject of general interest, definitely fixed the disputed boundaries and happily resolved a troublous question to the satisfaction of both the Indians and the Taoseños.

One ceremony which was observed by them while in Mexico impressed Don José Miguel Archuleta, the religious enthusiast, and which ceremony he introduced in Taos. This ceremony was called La Bajada de la Santa Cruz and Don José Miguel instituted its observance and made himself its sponsor. This ceremony began eight days before Santa Cruz day (May 3rd) and was carried on before an altar of a pyramidal shape consisting of eight steps. On the first day the altar would be elaborately decorated with flowers and lighted tapers. On each day after prayers and hymns pertaining to this ceremonial the cross was lowered to the next lower step until it rested on the lowest step on May 3rd or Día de la Santa Cruz. When the cross reached this final resting place the point was reached which was called, "El Desempeño de la Santa Cruz" or The Redemption of the Holy Cross.

At this time it was that the "mayordomos" or sponsors of the annual fiesta of Santa Cruz were set free of their obligations in respect to the observance of the feast day and new ones were installed. Being named mayordomo was considered a great honor. These men were entrusted with all the preparation for the feast day, to collect money for the mass to be said, to supervise and arrange for the procession, to secure the music for the baile and to provide other amusements. It was fortunate they were given a year's time in which to prepare, because usually this honorary position entailed considerable expenditure of both means and energy.

On the day of the feast each mayordomo held open house. Here was spread the most elaborate and plentiful festal board, as these men were in honor bound to receive all outside guests and visitors. Courteously they and their families would seek out and escort all comers to partake of their hospitality. In every house a feast was spread to which the friends of the household were invited. So that no one was overlooked and feasting and merriment was the order of the day.

There was a nice element of reciprocity in all this for the hosts of one village feast would be the guests of the neighboring villages when they celebrated the feast of their patron saint and the erstwhile hosts would be received and feted in their turn. Since there are many saints in the calendar and nearly as many villages as saints, one could by arranging his itinerary pass from village to village enjoying a continuous round of feasting and amusement.

La Bajada de la Santa Cruz was not observed in Taos very long after the death of Don José Miguel who died in 1880 or thereabouts at the age of ninety-five. Throughout his life he was a respected and venerated member of the community and towards the last enjoyed the affectionate title of "Tata" José Miguel or Father José Miguel. He enjoyed full mental vigor in his last years and when he died Taos lost a representative citizen, who through his piety, public service and honorable life fully merited that distinction.

A personal description of Don José Miguel, received from one who knew him in his later years, gives us a picture of a tall, slim gentleman with a fine face, the most prominent feature of which was a fine long nose, slightly hooked and large eyes topped by a full intelligent forehead. This description tallies with the character of one whose memory lived so long in the minds of his contemporaries and their descendants.

Early Days and Customs in Agua Fria

by Lorin W. Brown

I had stopped for a drink of water from a well in the patio of a group of houses in lower Agua Fria. While drinking I reflected how well named the little village had been. For the water from its springs and wells is very cold and refreshing and I could visualize how grateful man and beast must have been in those days of slow travel. The magnificent grove of large cottonwoods made an ideal camping spot for travelers on the way from Santa Fe to La Bajada and other points in Río Abajo or the lower Río Grande.

While still at the well, Nicolás López approached, leading a pair of small horses. After greetings I helped him draw water for his thirsty team. "Qué calor, amiquito, if it would only rain so that we would be sure of saving our beans and corn. But the good God knows what he is doing, there is no use in worrying. He will not fail us. Let us go into my house where it is cool." Entering the cool earthen-floored room I was offered a chair.

From Don Nicolás' conversation I gathered a picture of a much different life in Agua Fria, the life of my host's boyhood. Very meager opportunity for education was his lot. "The teacher was very good at punishing and our textbook was the Catechism and our arithmetic problems were worked on the surface of the school house door with charcoal. I was not allowed to go to school long. My father took some cattle to herd on the shares from Bishop Lamy and the Sisters of Charity. That was the last of my schooling. For a month at a time I would be gone from home, taking care of the cattle, sometimes towards Las Tetillas, other times in the Arroyo Hondo, wherever the grass was best. I will tell you the truth, that when I left the school I stole a catechism and while alone in camp I studied this book until it fell to pieces. Before it did fall to pieces it was so greasy and dirty you would have laughed to have seen it. And you would have laughed to have seen me when I would come home after a month or more in camp. I would have a head of hair like a buffalo and my clothes would be all torn and in a very sorry state. My father would shear me like I was a sheep.

"After two days at home I would go back with provisions on my burros for another month or two. A very lonely life I am telling you for a boy.

"I used to like to come home when the folks were boiling out syrup from the sugar cane. There used to be two miles here. Everybody would bring their cane to the presses and while the syrup was boiling or while the cane was being crushed, there would be dancing in the patio. Our musician was an Indian captive Antonio Domínguez who was very good on the violin. We had very good times then dancing nearly all might and telling tales while the syrup boiled out. The children enjoyed it too because they were the ones who rode the cross beam which operated the pestle. There high up in the air they would rock back and forth shouting and laughing and fighting for their turn to ride.

"There were great times and I was always glad to be back at those times and I would try to stay as long as I could enjoying myself, eating too much syrup and candy because in camp I tasted no sweets except when I could find wild honey."

"Why don't you raise any more cane now? Why have the times changed so; I don't see that they raise many crops here any more?" I asked.

"Oh, then we had all the water we wanted. Now the water company has all the water which used to belong to us. You would not believe it but this dry river bed used to have willows growing along its banks from Santa Fe to Ciénega. We had good ditches to carry water to all these lands.

"We raised much corn and wheat. Oh, we lived well then from the land but now that is all past. Only if God is willing to send us rain do we raise anything now. Todo pasa en este mundo. Everything passes in this world.

"Now we have very much work trying to find a little wood to sell in town. Soon we will have to move into town to find work and abandon our lands. My boys are all in town working now, that is why you find me here alone with my daughters-in-law and my grandchildren. I am getting too old to do any work except feed our 'animalitos' and see that they get water.

"But I do not have many years left and the good God willing, I want to die here in my home where I was born."

Source of Information: Nicolás López of Agua Fria.

Nuestra Señora de Dolores

by Lorin W. Brown

In the old church in the pueblo of Taos there used to be a very large image of Nuestra Señora de Dolores. Nuestra Señora de Dolores was the patron saint of the village to the east of Taos, known as El Cañon de Taos, where the people possessed a small image of the patron saint, but nothing as large and as handsome as the one which the Indians had in their church.

For many years the people of the above mentioned community had observed the following custom: sometime during the late summer or early fall they would send a delegation to the Taos pueblo to ask for the loan of the Indian's image of Nuestra Señora de Dolores. The Indians having agreed and a day having been fixed the delegation would return to their village with their report.

On the morning of the day agreed upon, all of the villagers of el Cañón de Taos who could possibly leave, would set out for the Taos pueblo, in wagons, buggies, on horseback—even afoot. In the lead there would be a small group, carrying their image of Nuestra Señora de Dolores, to the accompaniment of hymns sung in her praise. This group would be relieved from time to time by others of the procession, eager to render this service of devotion to their patron saint.

Upon reaching the church at the pueblo, the larger image and the object of this pilgrimage would be ceremoniously carried out of the church and now with both images in the lead, the procession would repair to a secluded corner of the large communal grazing grounds of the pueblo, close to the river.

Here under a leafy bower or shrine, both images would be enshrined, beloved objects of adoration throughout the ensuing ceremony or vigil, which lasted all night. The crowd of devotees would alternate in singing "alavados" (religious hymns) and in praying during the duration of the vigil.

At midnight a plentiful meal was served to all present. The food, prepared beforehand and brought thither in the wagons, as well as meat roasted over the fires surrounding the shrine, would be more than sufficient to feed the throng.

Although the greater number of the crowd at the ceremony would attend with a purely religious motive, there were many, especially amongst the younger folks, who were attracted by the social side of this observance. Many Indians attended also.

Whether or not this custom is still observed I cannot say.

The Bell Marianna

by Lorin W. Brown

There was great excitement in the little hill village of Quemado or El Pueblo Quemado to give it its full name and now known as Córdova. On the morrow, the new bell donated by Don Pedro would be christened, and after a procession around the church, would be hung in the bell tower. There was a great stir of preparation; smoke from the many bake ovens rose into the air to mingle with the smoke from the banked fires where whole beeves, sheep and deer were roasting. Savory odors from both these sources were carried by the breeze to the young goat-herds who kept their flocks close to the village and, sniffing the breeze, hungrily anticipated the feast to come.

The priest had already arrived and was lodged at Don Pedro's home. Don Pedro was the "rico" of the village. Owner of all of the tillable lands of the little valley in which Quemado was located and of the land grant to the East, he virtually controlled the destinies of the rest of the inhabitants. He was the "patron" to whom all looked for their material welfare. His large establishment swarmed with all kinds of help, villagers as well as several Indian slaves. Although a seeming confusion, there was a well-ordered division of labor. In the kitchen Indian women were continually busy, some as "tortilleras" with no other task than to round out and bake tortillas; others were kept busy bringing water from the river, grinding meal, etc., while yet others, the more reliable, were the actual cooks and had supervision of the lesser help. As for the men, some had charge of the planting and harvesting of crops, others of the herds of cattle and sheep and yet others were continually arriving or leaving on trading trips to Ranchos de Taos or Taos, driving herds of fat steers before them which they would trade for grain in that fertile valley.

A hard worker himself, Don Pedro saw to it that everybody else was kept busy. To those to whom he paid wages he was very liberal, not confining himself strictly to the wages earned but giving them additional help as needed. Wages in those times were an "almud" of cornmeal for a week's work and a fat mutton for two weeks' labor. Enough for the simple needs of that time and which could always be supplemented with game, which was plentiful. All in all, Don Pedro was considered a good "patron" and his people found a certain measure of security in the plenty which was his.

In his many years of trading and barter Don Pedro accumulated a certain amount of gold and silver coin until, legend has it, he measured it in "almuds" (approximately a peck). However it may be he undoubtedly gathered a large amount which was well nigh useless to him, as all of his material wants were supplied from the produce of his lands and herds or acquired through barter.

Not long before the time of this account the village had celebrated the completion of their church of which they were very proud. Don Pedro had been largely instrumental in its building, donating the labor of his people towards the making of adobes, raising the walls, and his oxen had dragged the heavy beams down from the hills for the roof.

Now, three years afterwards, Don Pedro conceived the idea of having a bell made for the church. To this end he secured the services of one Francisco Martínez from La Puebla, a little settlement in the lower Chimayó valley. This Francisco Martínez had followed in his father's footsteps as a maker or caster of bells. His father had brought knowledge of this art with him from Mexico.

Towards the making of the bell Don Pedro donated thirty gold escudos and some silver coin. These were added to the baser metals to give the bell a clear tone. The mold was made of clay and the bell was cast in Don Pedro's patio just outside his private room. When the metal had cooled and success was assured, a date was set for the christening and installation of this addition to the church.

The news of this event traveled far and wide and a week before the day people began to arrive, some on foot, others on horseback and others in the noisy, complaining carretas or ox carts. An occasion like this was a wonderful chance for trading, gossip and general enjoyment. On the evening before the christening Don Pedro and the padre were seated in the "patrons" private room taking their evening meal. This room, about sixteen feet high and larger than the average, had only one door and this led to the outside. Off from it was a small kitchen where Don Pedro's meals were prepared and passed into his room through an opening in the wall. Here they were received by a lone servant who served his master as he dined in solitary state. On this occasion Don Pedro and his guest, the padre, sat at supper, a succession of courses of the most valued and choicest dishes and delicacies of that time. Wines carefully packed in from Río Abajo and Mexico were drunk during the progress of the meal and its conclusion as a toast to the christening of the next day.

Early the next morning everything was in readiness for the ceremony. The bell had been placed on a gaily decorated litter or platform so that it could be borne by four men in the procession to the church. Don Pedro and Doña Ramona followed close and the rest of the gaily dressed crowd fell in behind. Entering the church it was carried up to the altar where Don Pedro and his wife, as sponsors or as "padrino" and "madrina," made known the name they had chosen for the christening. The padre sprinkled the bell with holy water and christened it Marianna, the name chosen by its sponsors.

After this ceremony Marianna was carried in triumph around the church following the image of San Antonio, the patron saint of the village. An alavado of thanksgiving was sung and muskets were discharged as the procession wound its way around the church. Successfully hoisted to the roof, the bell was suspended in the bell tower. Don Pedro struck the first notes from it using a stone, as the bell had no clapper. Its tones rang out pure and clear, echoing back from the hills but not entirely drowning out the cries of admiration and delight which rose from the crowd below. So it was to be heard for many years after its padrino and madrina had been sleeping in the camposanto below it.

Now the real festivities began. Groups gathered around the great fires where the different kinds of roast meat were to be had and helped themselves to the bread which was piled high in one corner of the long portal. Long tables held the rest of the feast and everybody was welcome to help himself and eat his fill. In the crowd were some Apache Indians, notorious gluttons, who did not need a second bidding and who soon rendered themselves easy victims for a scalping knife if the laws of hospitality could have been suspended.

Horse racing and horse trading and other amusements took up the afternoon. And in the evening the baile in the long hall was well attended by an ever changing crowd; dance awhile, eat a while and back to dance again. Fine straw spread on the earthen floor created a cloud of dust which the many candles tried to dissipate with little success. No matter if it wasn't a brilliantly lighted ballroom with waxed floors, the polka, the valse redondo, the cuna and the other dances of the period were danced with a light hearted enjoyment and the extempore couplets sung by the guitar player in honor of Marianna. Don Pedro and his wife and everybody else in turn were heartily applauded and cheerfully rewarded. Now and then there would be a sudden commotion, two jealous young men, hot words; then a thrust for outdoors, hands on knife hilt. There in the dark their differences would be settled in a manner satisfactory to both or of no more moment to one.

The feast and the merriment continued far into the next day. Don Pedro, with a few favored guests and relatives, feasted apart overlooking the tumult from his portal which commanded a view of most of the village.

And today Marianna still sends her clear tones ringing out through the hills calling Don Pedro's descendants to mass or announcing yet another addition to the already crowded Campo Santo. The yellow metal gleams brightly, the thirty "escudos" imparting their unmistakable "color" as the sun hits the battered spots where the stones in the hands of the ringer strike.

Victorio

by L. W. Brown

An incident related by Andrés Alvarado, with regard to the early life of Victorio, the Apache chief. He says that Victorio was captured as a child by the Apaches from somewhere in the vicinity of Chihuahua, Mexico. He made his escape and went home to rejoin his family. Contrary to his joyful expectations, his family refused to recognize him and, embittered, he set out to rejoin the Indians.

Near Ojinaga he entered into the employ of a man by the name of Bruges or Burgess (Alvarado's pronunciation of the name was too indefinite to make out just what it could have been), but known locally to the natives as "Broches" (brooch or fastener).

Broches was a trader employing his many mule teams and wagons in a varied trade according to the local demand and the seasons. He employed Victorio as a teamster and a guide as well because of his knowledge of the country and the Indians.

On one trip to some salt mines, a considerable caravan of wagons taking part, Victorio rejoined the Indians under the following circumstances. After the caravan had left the settlements, they were aware that they were being followed by a large number of Indians. Reaching a point where a defense could best be made, Victorio suggested that the wagons be drawn up into a square, with the stock enclosed within. Soon, according to Andrés, an Indian was seen on top of a nearby hill, who started to pregonar (harangue). Victorio mounted one of the wagons and talked back to him. Then he announced that he must go to the Indian and try to induce them to refrain from attacking the wagon train. He remarked that if he were not back that night or early the following morning that they must sell their lives as dearly as possible because that would be a sign that he had failed in his negotiations for peace. Fortunately, Victorio was successful, returning late that night with the assurance that all would be well with the Indians, that in fact he had prevailed on them to guard the train until they had returned safely with their load of salt.

However Victorio was a changed man, seeming to brood over some secret sorrow. What this could be was not known until, once again at Ojinaga, he turned over his mule team to "Broches" saying, "Here is your team and wagon. I have tried to be a man amongst my own people. But the Indians consented only to not attack us if I would return to them after a period of eight days after arriving here. I must keep my promise, it was the only way to have saved you all from being killed."

Andrés said that "Broches," full of gratitude and grief also at losing Victorio, said, "Victorio, drink, dance and enjoy yourself until your time is up; Broches will pay for everything."

Victorio took advantage of "Broches'" offer and at the expiration of the eight days, took his leave of his friends, embittered by the repudiation of his family, to become the noted Apache chief of history, one of the most daring and elusive of them all.

Source of Information: Andrés Alvarado, of Presidio, Texas and Ojinaga, Mexico.

Old Timers Dictionary in Detail: Mrs. Deonicio Álvarez, Spanish Wedding Custom

by Marie Carter

*T*he day was Sunday. I recall it quite well. Because the neighbor's little girl woke me up to tell me that my cat had had kittens in her barn. Just why I selected that particular day to go to La Union, in search of a former resident of Anthony, is something I cannot explain.

When I knocked at the front door of the woman I sought, there was no response, so I meandered around to the back door, unaware that she was sick in bed. The maid came to the door and opened her mouth to tell me, I feel quite sure, now that I recall her expression, that the doctor did not permit her mistress to see anyone. But just as she was about to utter the fatal words, a tall elderly man shoved her aside and invited me to enter.

Having preceded me as far as the bedroom door, he stepped aside and bowed me into the presence of Cecilia Richards Álvarez, who favored me with a beautiful smile and inquired:

"What is it you wish?"

"Information."

"Regarding whom?"

"You."

"Oh!"

"It isn't anything to be alarmed about," I assured her. "I merely want to know how long you have been in the Southwest and the year in which you arrived?"

"Well, I can tell you that in a few words," she said. "I came here with my parents when I was sixteen years of age."

"Here?"

"Yes, to La Union. But in a few months we moved to Anthony," she explained.

"Oh, I see. What year was that?"

"1890. I was born in Fort Stockton, Texas," she added.

"Do you mind telling me the year?"

"Not at all," was her gracious reply. "January 25, 1874."

"Now we're going places!" I exclaimed.

Her expression was quizzical as she softly murmured: "Ah, you are young."

"Not as young as I sound," was my retort.

Mrs. Álvarez laughed and came right back at me with: "You'll do."

"Would you like to know who sent me to see you?" I asked.

"Very much. You see," she added, "curiosity is one of my faults."

"I must be afflicted the same way," I said, "or I wouldn't be here today. But then, I'm drifting away from my main object. I believe I was going to tell you—"

"Who sent you to La Union," she supplied.

"Thanks. Well, it was a former neighbor of yours—Mrs. Pat Coleman."

"Oh, was it?" Her soft low voice throbbed with a note of pleasure.

"You must have known Charley Miller, too," I observed.

"Yes, I knew him very well. Mr. Miller, Mrs. Story and I were in business on the same street."

"I believe that was old main street?"

"Yes, west of the Santa Fe tracks. The present main street was a mere wagon road. Anthony was a stopping place for travelers. Mr. Royal Jackman was the station agent. A man by the name of Scott was the first postmaster; he carried the mail on horseback. Charley Miller ran a store and a flour mill. And the Pat Colemans had a sheep ranch."

"I suppose farming was the chief occupation?"

"Yes, but the farmers were often discouraged. The Río Grande was muy furioso." She lapsed into Spanish; then continued in perfect English: "There was a flood almost every spring. The Mexicans were very brave though and patiently rebuilt their farms and homes over and over again. We used to ford the river or cross on crude rafts."

"Didn't the people ever try to build a bridge?" I asked.

"Oh, yes, but the river would rise and wash them away. The year after I was married the flood damaged our ranch to the amount of five thousand dollars."

"Did you marry someone in Anthony?" I quizzed.

"No. I married Mr. Álvarez, a rancher of La Union."

"If you don't mind telling me, I should like to hear about your engagement and wedding. For I think the old Spanish engagements were very romantic."

"You refer to the prendorio, or engagement announcement. I think we took marriage more seriously in the old days. As no doubt you know, there are slight variations in the old customs of every country. So it was with the prendorio. Some families discarded the letter, but my family, or to be exact, the boy's family, adopted it. The parents of my future husband wrote a letter to my parents which they presented in person, asking them for their consent to the marriage of their son to me. Fifteen days later my parents wrote a similar letter, which they presented in person to the boy's parents, in which they gave their consent."

"Did your parents give a reception?"

"Oh, yes, and it lasted all day. While my parents received their guests I remained hidden in another room. And during the reception, refreshments were served. When it came time for the boy's parents to enter, they left their son outside. Finally they called me in; then they called the boy in."

"Were you embarrassed?"

"Very much," she replied. "If my face was as red as my ears felt, I am sure that it was the color of a poinsettia."

"Did the boy bring you a gift?"

"Sí, Señora, la cajita bonita!" she said.

"A pretty little box, eh? Well, what did it contain? Now you have me curious."

"No more so than I was," she laughed. "Upon opening that pretty little box I fairly gasped with surprise. Of course I expected jewelry, but not so beautiful as the pieces I received; they were family heirlooms. Accepting the gift was accepting the boy, so he placed a diamond engagement ring on my finger. Then, after my father announced our engagement to the guests, congratulations followed. The ladies remained inside but the men went outside and celebrated by shooting off guns in our honor."

Cecilia Richards: Born in Fort Stockton, Texas, January 25, 1874; moved to Pecos with parents; moved from Pecos to La Union; moved from La Union to Anthony, New Mexico, 1890. Attended Loretta Academy, Las Cruces, New Mexico; Father was English, mother Spanish. Married Deonicio (Dennis) Álvarez. Husband born in La Union, which used to be called "Amoles," after the roots of the palm plant from which the natives made soap. Mrs. Álvarez is the mother of Cruz Richards Álvarez, Attorney of Old Mesilla; Joe Richards Álvarez of La Union; Edward Richards Álvarez of La Union; Estella Richards Álvarez, who is now Mrs. Paul Scharman, Country Club, El Paso.

Amoles: roots of the Spanish palm, a fungus from which soap can be made. Can also be used for soap in its raw state by soaking it in water for about an hour, after which time it forms a lather. Mexicans liked it better than any other kind of soap for washing wool blankets. Furioso: furious, and la cajita bonita, pretty little box. Prendorio: engagement announcement.

Old Timers Stories: Bertha Mandell Candler

by Marie Carter

When I called on Mrs. Bertha Mandell Candler, principal of the La Mesa grade school, she was taking her vacation at home with Jeff Candler and the three little Candlers.

"I love to be at home with Jeff and the kiddies," she said. "It beats going to California, the mountains or anywhere else."

"How long have you lived in New Mexico?" I inquired.

"Why all my life," she said, "I was born in old Mesilla. My parents came from Santa Ana, California in a covered wagon in 1874. My grandfather was Thomas Casad, the man responsible for the first mowing machine in the valley. In 1876 he built the first flouring mill at Mesilla. The building is still standing, though no longer used for milling purposes; it was operated by water. My grandfather was the first farmer to attempt to grow fruit on a commercial scale in the valley. He set out about forty acres in apples, pears, peaches and grapes. About the time the trees began to bear the coddling worm arrived and destroyed the whole orchard.

"Grandfather also introduced the first purebred Angora goats and the first registered Poland-China hogs into this region. He drove the goats from El Mora, New Mexico and hauled the hogs in wagons. He was so successful as a livestock man that he followed that business the rest of his life. He raised the Mexicans' wages from twenty-five to fifty cents, and in 1874 he planted the first field of alfalfa in the valley.

"The first school I attended was at Mesilla Park; a cousin to May Bailey, or Mrs. Royal Jackman, was my teacher. I finished my education at State College and then taught school, a profession I have continued to follow for almost twenty years. My first venture in teaching was at La Union in 1911. With the exception of one or two, my pupils were all Spanish American children. I had over seventy pupils in half of my schoolroom and my sister Jessie had as many more in the other half. I taught the primer, first and second grades while she taught the third and fourth grades. We had practically no equipment with which to work, and the common drinking pail containing a tin dipper stood on a box in the corner. My wages were fifty dollars per month out of which I paid for board and room. We stayed at the home of Mrs. Álvarez. Cruz, Estella and Eduardo Álvarez were my pupils.

"I have always liked the Spanish American children and their parents. They were always very nice to us and easy to get along with. Mrs. Álvarez and Mrs. Valdéz were always doing something for us. Robert Valdéz was also one of my pupils. And my pupils always felt grieved if 'teacher,' as they called me, didn't share their candy. Every morning my desk was fairly loaded with donations of all sorts. They were generous to a fault, but I loved every one of them and never gave up a school without shedding bushels of tears.

"I seldom found a Spanish child lacking in artistic ability. Every one of them could sing, dance, recite or draw, and they were invariably good in penmanship. On San José day they would take the little Santo, or statue of their patron saint and visit every house where they had a son by the name of José. We always went along and were offered refreshments of wine and other good things to eat and drink. They celebrate here in La Mesa too, but they only parade around the church. The La Mesa mission, which bears the name of San José was built in 1853, a year before the Gadsden Purchase was signed. The walls are eight feet thick at the base, and it is pretty well peppered with bullet holes, for in the early days it was used as a fort. This house we live in was also built in 1853. Whenever you see adobe walls as thick as ours and the ceilings made with latillas and vigas, you will always know that they are very old.

"In the old days there were no bridges across the Río Grande so we paid the Mexicans to ferry us across in their skiffs, which they kept ready for that purpose. If, however, we were going to a party or a dance somewhere, we would ford it with a horse and buggy. One evening a young man offered to take us girls to a dance over at Anthony. We made it across without any trouble, arrived at the dance in good order, and had a good time. Following the dance we discovered that the river had come up. None of us wanted to remain in Anthony all night so we decided to risk the Río Grande. Now I wonder how we happened to escape with our lives, for the old buggy was cradling us from one side to the other and it was all we could do to hold on and keep from slipping into the water. The poor old horse finally struggled through it however, and landed us safely on the western bank.

"I taught at La Union for a year and then went to Las Cruces to teach at the Central school where I remained from 1912 to 1916. In the latter part of 1916 I was married, but not to the boy I loved. We had a quarrel and Jeff went away. I thought he wasn't coming back so I accepted the other fellow. But I wasn't happy and I don't think he was. Finally we were divorced and I was free again. Then my childhood sweetheart returned and we were married. I have been very happy with Jeff Candler and we have three healthy children. His father was a cattleman and Jeff was brought up on a cattle ranch. At the present time he's working on the Corralitas ranch sixteen miles west of Las Cruces. The Corralitas has three hundred and thirteen sections. Harvey Bissell, Jeff's boss, just paid twenty-eight thousand for some new stock. Jeff's people are from Georgia and related to Asa Candler the Coca Cola man.

"After I was married I continued to teach because I enjoy it. But following my second marriage I rested for two years. From 1919 to 1924 I taught at Mesilla Park. Then I returned to Las Cruces where I taught from 1924 to 1927. In 1928-29-30, I taught at Fair Acres, a suburb of Las Cruces. Then I came to La Mesa where I am the principal.

"This spring the teachers called at the homes of the school children to get acquainted and to cement a better understanding between the parents and teachers. The American mothers were very gracious, but the Spanish American mothers were delighted, extended us a hearty welcome and if they happened to be cooking, gave us a pressing invitation to dine with them. Their homes were remarkably clean and quite comfortable. We found two families in need of assistance but they were from Oklahoma.

"The Mexican people take an optimistic view of life. A little thing like a national debt or how the future generation is going to pay it wouldn't bother them like it does the average American. They are great for credit; they like the system of paying a little bit at a time on their bills. Sometimes a newcomer in business will have a fit because some native runs a bill on him and fails to pay up in a hurry. They soon learn, however, that the Mexican is born an installment man, that he doesn't mind paying a little each week or month, but to pay it all at once in a lump sum to any merchant seems like highway robbery. I have always noticed that they have a way of stating their troubles in a matter-of-fact way, with no self pity. They are always ready to help, sympathize and grieve over others, but as far as their own personal affairs are concerned, well, today may be sad but there is always a brighter tomorrow—a mañana or poco tiempo!

"Many things happen in a schoolroom to break the monotony. One day I asked the children how many of them owned a toothbrush? So many hands were held up that I was amazed.

"'Well, Roberto,' I said to a large boy in the front row, 'why don't you hold up your hand?'

"'I no got wan brush,' he replied.

"The next day I noticed that Roberto was elated over something so I said:

"'Well, Roberto did you get a brush?'

"The teeth he exposed for my inspection were gleaming white, and I was proud to think that I had something to do with the transformation. His next words, however, brought me down from the clouds where I'd been floating, with a jolt.

"'I no buy the brush,' he explained, 'eet belong to my beeg brother.'"

Bertha Mandell Candler was born in Old Mesilla, New Mexico, December 16, 1890; mother was Sara Van Winkle Casad, daughter of Thomas Casad, pioneer farmer of the Mesilla Valley, who brought his family overland in a covered wagon from Santa Ana, California and located in Old Mesilla in 1874; they were not attacked by Indians but saw numerous fresh graves of people whom they had murdered; Bertha Mandell Candler has taught school in Doña Ana County for the past twenty years; one of her former pupils is Robert Valdéz, a member of the Governor's staff at Santa Fe; she was educated in the public schools of Doña Ana County and finished her education at State College; Bertha Mandell Candler is the principal of La Mesa School; she is the wife of Jeff Candler and the mother of three healthy children. Interview: June 27, 1937.

Old Timers Stories: Mrs. Juan Valdéz

by Marie Carter

Juliana Valdéz, or Mrs. Juan Valdéz, smiled as she informed me with a slight accent: "I was born in La Union, Señora; my childhood, girlhood and womanhood have been spent at the old Mission, La Union. You see, Señora, that is what they called it in the old days when the first settlers colonized this valley. La Union is the foundation of the Refugio Grant."

Juan Valdéz affirmed Juliana's statement with a nod, and smiled as she resumed: "I was born in 1879 on the 9th day of January. That is a long time, Señora. My father was Jesús Enríquez; my mother was Luz Noriego de Enríquez. They immigrated to the United States from Juárez, Chihuahua, Mexico; then up the Río Grande Valley to La Union. They, my parents, were very fine people," she volunteered with pride.

In speaking of her husband, Juliana said: "Juan was born in Mason, Texas, 1880 on the 5th day of February. Then, Señora, he came to La Union to fall in love, and has been here ever since. You see how he sits and watches me? Well, he did that before we were married. One day I said 'Juan, why do you watch me all the time?'

"'Juliana,' he said, 'I can't help it; I want to marry you.'

"'Bueno!' I said, 'let's get married. Maybe you will stop watching me.' But it didn't work, Señora. All these years he has done nothing else."

Including the whole country with a wave of her hand, Juliana continued: "When my parents came here that was all bosque, or woodland. Many people left Chihuahua when they learned that they could get plenty of free land in New Mexico. My father was one of the commissioners for the Refugio Corporation. Some of the Americans called their grants 'terrenas' but the correct name is terreno. Instead of a terreno being fifty-four acres, as some of them thought, it was between thirty-six or thirty-seven acres. And a vara, by which the colonists measured the land, was not a yard of thirty-six inches, but thirty-three inches."

Juliana didn't have any more respect for the ruthless Río Grande of the past than her neighbors, for she referred to it as: "The big fussy river. Señora," she said, "it was never still, for there was nothing to hold it back. Sometimes it would suddenly dry up; then our crops would dry up. Then we would worry and pray for water, and bah, a flood would come and almost destroy us. Ah, Señora, I know this country well. I am part of it. I have spent the best part of my life helping to make it what it is today. Fighting the wind, turning the soil, hating and loving the river, planting the seed, watching it grow. Sí, Señora. I, like the rest, have suffered, but I think it is a pretty fine country."

Juliana, or Mrs. Juan Valdéz, was born in La Union, New Mexico, Doña Ana County, January 9, 1878, Juan Valdéz, Sr. was born in Mason, Texas, Mason County, February 5, 1880, and went to La Union, New Mexico in 1900. Jesús Enríquez, who immigrated from Juárez, Chihuahua, Mexico to La Union, New Mexico in 1877, was the father of Mrs. Juan Valdéz, Sr., Mrs. Luz Noriego de Enríquez, wife of Jesús Enríquez, who immigrated from Juárez, Chihuahua, Mexico in 1877, was the mother of Mrs. Juan Valdéz, Sr.

Mr. and Mrs. Juan Valdéz are the parents of: Robert, Juan Jr., Magadelena and David Valdéz. Robert Valdéz, who was a teacher and principal of the La Union school for several years, is now the State Corporation Commissioner for New Mexico. He was recently appointed Chairman of the New Mexico State Corporation Commission by Gov. Clyde Tingley, to represent New Mexico at the Juárez-Chihuahua Road meet to boost for the Juárez-Chihuahua-Mexico City Highway, May 14, 1937. Robert Valdéz married Nellie Navárez of Las Cruces, New Mexico. Mr. and Mrs. Robert Valdéz live in Santa Fe, New Mexico.

Juan Valdéz, Jr., second son of Mr. and Mrs. Juan Valdéz, Sr., is a farmer of La Union, New Mexico. Juan married Katy Medena of Las Cruces, New Mexico. Magadelena Valdéz is at home with her parents. David Valdéz, who graduated from the Union Valley High School in the class of 1935 and attended the A & M State College of New Mexico in 1936, married Annie Marie Ames of Las Cruces. David is associated with his father in farming at the home ranch in La Union, New Mexico.

Interview: May 18,1937.

Old Timers Stories: Nemecio Provincio (Wife: Anita Provincio)

by Marie Carter

*T*he outstanding feature of the Provincio family is their innate refinement and courtesy. When I called at their Spanish Mission ranch home, two miles northwest of Anthony, Mr. Provincio said:

"I have lived in New Mexico all my life. I was born in the town of Old Mesilla, October 31, 1872. My parents moved their family to Chamberino in 1882. But the Río Grande, which was more powerful than man, forced them to higher ground; so they built their home a short distance above the town, at Ojito, or little spring. They continued to plant their crops on the lower land, but they didn't take chances of living there, for they never knew when the river was going to rise and flood them out."

The Provincio boys were brought up fighting the river. "It was the big bad wolf of our lives," Nemecio said. "The Elephant Butte Dam was a God-send, Señora. Before the dam came there was no way to control it; it was never still; always rushing, rising and overflowing. Finally, in the year of 1892, we pulled up stakes and moved to the Anthony district."

Mr. Provincia, his brother Victor, and his father Agapito, all settled on adjoining Terrenas. "A terrene," Nemecio explained, "is 36 acres. Each settler was permitted to have a solar or building site in town if he wished it, and an ortaliza in back, or an extra piece of land thrown in. We were the first to settle on this land. It was all bosque or woodland, and no ditches of any kind. We worked from early morning till dark, days, weeks and months, cutting down trees, clearing the ground, building our homes, plowing, planting and fighting the Río Grande."

It seems that the Río Grande had a habit of taking toll at the most unexpected times. "Sometimes we would go to bed hoping to rest after a hard day's work," Nemecio said, "only to be wakened by the lap, lap, of water at our doors; sometimes around our beds. It had a voice, Señora, that we grew to hate—a voice that struck terror to our hearts and souls; it was there in the rising river, increasing in volume as the water rose, submerging our land, stealing our seed, quite often our homes, leaving us nothing—nothing. The newcomers can't begin to realize the hardships of the early pioneers."

Mr. Provincio paused a moment, then resumed: "The greatest surprise of the early days was the morning we awoke and found our land an Island in the center of an ocean of water. The river had come up in the night and submerged the whole country. For several days we went to town in row boats. We made the first request for an irrigation ditch, and when we received it, more people began to settle on the land near us. Very often I had to assist people across the Río Grande, by swimming and leading their horses or teams. I used to breed horses and kept a herd up in the Franklin mountains east of Anthony. Sometimes I would bring several in to the ranch and when I was ready to ford the Río Grande, I would link them with a rope and swim across leading the whole group. I was forced to do this to keep from losing them, for sometimes the current was so strong that it would take a single horse two or three miles downstream before I could rescue him.

Charley Miller was a good friend to the early settlers; he was also a good business man. "Charley never lost anything in a trade," Mr. Provincio said. "If we borrowed one pound of seed from him he got two in return. He built the first store on the old business street west of the Santa Fe tracks. Savina López, who built the little white chapel northeast of Anthony, in honor of San José, traded quite a bit of her land at Charley's store for groceries. At one time she owned a hundred and sixty acres in Anthony."

In speaking of schools Mr. Provincio said: "We didn't have any schools. Somebody started a private school, which I attended for awhile. That is, until it closed, for money was scarce. I used to hire out to other farmers and work all day for fifty cents. Once I was paid as much as a dollar and fifty cents laying railroad track for the Southern Pacific, and I thought I was pretty rich."

In referring to the Pool ranch west of Anthony, Mr. Provincio observed: "Mr. Pool has some very fine land, but in the early days it sold at a very low price. Will Snow bought it for three dollars an acre; then Mr. Snow transferred it to his wife, who sold it to S. P. Miller, brother-in-law of

Mrs. O. C. Story, for forty dollars an acre; S. P. Miller sold it to J. W. Brooks for eighty dollars an acre; J. W. Brooks sold it to Mr. J. Pool for a hundred dollars an acre, and to-day it is worth three hundred dollars an acre."

In speaking of the original land owners in his vicinity Mr. Provincio said: "I am the only one left—Guerra, Arias, Gómez, Téllez and Márquez—all had the same amount of land I have today—but they sold it for almost nothing. Many people have offered to buy my land. Always, they tell me, it is very beautiful. And I feel like telling them that they can't realize how hard I worked to make it beautiful. Every time I cut down a tree I have made it a rule to put the date on it. There is one outside dated 1884."

Mr. Provincio's ranch is in that strip of land known as the "Refugio Grant," which borders the Río Grande. "This grant," he said, "originated at the Mission La Union. When we came here there was a corporation in charge with a change of commissioners every two years. The commissioners at that time were Jesús Ochoa, Jesús Enríques, and Jacinto Perea. These men were authorized to divide the land into terrenas, or thirty-six acres to a settler."

Farming was a tedious task in the old days. "The farmers," Mr. Provincia said, "had very few implements. We ploughed with a small hand plough, and we cut our wheat with a scythe. We planted wheat, corn, frijoles (beans) and alfalfa to feed our horses. Sometimes I would take a load of alfalfa to El Paso to sell. The trip usually took three days. Now, with a good truck, I can make it in three hours."

In the course of his conversation Mr. Provincio said: "My distant cousin, Eulogio Provincio, used to like to go camping. He usually went to the Robleros, the mountains northwest of us. One day when he returned from one of these trips I noticed that he looked very odd—others noticed it too. I guess I was more curious than anyone else, for I kept urging Eulogio to tell me why he acted so mysterious. But he tightened his lips and would tell me nothing."

Mr. Provincio paused, then resumed: "Finally Eulogio took a man into his confidence, and they both went to the Robleros. When they returned I noticed that their faces wore a look of disappointment. Señora, I am telling the truth when I say, I wanted to know their secret so much that

I almost burned to a cinder. But Eulogio was that way, you could burn and be-damn, but he wouldn't tell what he thought was nobody's business."

Suddenly Eulogio decided to enlighten Nemecio, who confided: "I didn't know whether to believe him or not when he told me that he had found a treasure chest in the Robleros. I was so surprised I hardly knew what to say. My lips went dry and I had to moisten them with my tongue before I could speak, but finally managed to ask him how he knew it was a treasure chest? He stared at me a moment, then exclaimed: 'Válgame Dios! Don't you think I know a treasure chest when I see it? This chest was heavy—so heavy I couldn't move it. Some day, I kept telling myself, I will take tools to the Robleros and open it. But I kept putting it off and keeping my secret. Then I thought, maybe I will tell somebody about it and just as quick I thought I would, I changed my mind and kept still. I think I was poco loco. Then I got so I couldn't sleep thinking about that treasure chest. As you know, at last I couldn't keep the secret any longer, so I took Ramón to the Robleros with me telling him only that I wished to show him something.'

"'Yes, I know about that,' I said, impatient to hear more about the chest. 'Then what did you do?'

"'Well, we kept on going, leading our pack burros up the mountain path. I guess Ramón was a little afraid of me for I kept talking to myself about gold and how rich I was going to be, and I know that he was very glad when I told him that we had come to the place where I had left the chest. Then I told him to leave the burros and follow me, for you see, I had to climb a little higher, where the chest was concealed behind a clump of mesquite, which I grabbed hold of to pull myself up. When Ramón followed my example and reached my side, he found me standing but shaking like a sick man with chills, and staring at the imprint of many coins in the wet sand. That and nothing more. My treasure chest was gone.'"

Nemecio Provincio was born in Old Mesilla, New Mexico, Oct. 31, 1872; he moved with his parents from Old Mesilla to Chamberino, New Mexico, in 1882; moved from Chamberino to Anthony, New Mexico, in 1892, where, with his brother Victor and father Agapito, he settled on a terrene, or thirty-six acres adjoining the land of his brother and father, two miles northwest of Anthony, in the strip of land that borders the Río Grande and which is known as the "Refugio Grant."

The Provincios were the first land owners to ask for an irrigation ditch, which, when granted, was the means of bringing other settlers to this district. They cleared the land, which was all bosque, felled the trees and built their own homes.

In 1896 Nemecio Provincio married Jesusita López of Chamberino, New Mexico, who was the daughter of a Civil war veteran of the Union army. By this marriage there was one son, Fidel Provincio, who is a farmer. Mrs. Provincio died in 1899.

In 1901 Nemecio Provincio married Anita Martínez of El Paso, Texas, who bore him five boys and two girls. The children are: Louis, Raymundo, Emilio, Otellio, Anita, Ramiro and Henry. Raymundo was dragged and killed by his own horses while working on his father's ranch in 1930, an accident which shocked and grieved the whole community.

Otellio has been a teacher in the Anthony Grade School for the past eight years, and Anita, who is a very fine dancer, has been teaching in the Alta Vista School for two years. Louis Provincio, who is a farmer, owns his own ranch. His wife was the former Alvino Geck, who taught in the Anthony Grade School prior to her marriage. Emilio is also a farmer who owns his own ranch, and is serving his second term as County Commissioner. Emilio married Fay Dutchover, who prior to her marriage, was private secretary to Charles O'Hara of Anthony. Ramiro and Henry Provincio are pupils in the Valley High School. And Mrs. Nemecio Provincio, the mother of this commendable family, is a housewife who finds time, in addition to her other duties, to grow and cultivate some of the most beautiful flowers in the valley.

Date of Interview: May 9, 1937.

The Biography of Guadalupe Lupita Gallegos (I)

by Bright Lynn

In the face of Guadalupe Lupita Gallegos is written the story of a long and interesting life—a life that has more than its share of heartaches and happiness. It is a kind, intelligent face and devout.

She dresses in unrelieved black. On her head is worn a tight-fitting cap with ribbons tied under her chin in a bow. Around her slender shoulders is wrapped a black Spanish shawl. Her blouse and skirt are black and on her feet she wears tiny, patent-leather shoes.

When asked a question about some incident of long ago there flashes in her eyes the look of a girl; she smiles half-wistfully, and begins:—

"I was born in Las Vegas, New Mexico on December 12, 1853. I was baptized by Father Pinal, a French Priest.

"My parents, Severo Baca and María Ignacia, were wealthy, owning several farms, many cattle and sheep, and much money and jewelry. My great grandfather, Santiago Ulibarrí, had several children but I was his only great grand-daughter and so I was his pet. Mr. Ulibarrí was tall, blond, and green-eyed, and very wealthy.

"His home was Spanish with all the windows opening on the placita, a large yard in the middle. This house was very dark and gloomy and was open to no one except a few Spanish friends. When one entered one of those old Spanish houses it seemed as if one were entering a tomb, so cold and uninviting were they. Several families would live in these houses: the owners' children, their husbands and wives, and their children.

"We lived there shut away from the rest of the world. Mr. Ulibarrí was the head of his household and he knew it. He was virtually the dictator of his family. The women were never allowed on the streets without someone trustworthy to escort them. We obeyed Mr. Ulibarrí in everything. Only that which he dictated was done.

"Since it was considered such a disgrace for a lady of the upper class to be seen on the street unescorted, we spent most of our time sewing, and playing the piano. We never dreamed of soiling our hands in the kitchen cooking or cleaning.

"In front of Mr. Ulibarrí we were always very dignified and well-behaved, but when he was not present we were often silly, as most girls are. I was the only one of the girls who was permitted to go with Mr. Ulibarrí very often. He would have chocolate in bed about eleven o'clock, arise later and have his regular breakfast. Then he would say to the servants in a commanding voice, 'Louisiana, my cape, my cane, and my hat.'

"The servants would rush to do his bidding. Then he would say, 'Lupita, come with me.'

"'Oh! No! No!' protested the servants, 'she is all dirty. Let us wash her.'

"'You wash yourself. Leave her alone,' Mr. Ulibarrí would say in a very patient voice.

Then he would go to different stores with little Lupita holding his hand. Immediately upon entering a store, Lupita would go to the candy counter and help herself.

One day when Mr. Ulibarrí was away all the women got together. They had heard of a strange new toy that had just come to Andrés Dol store. They were very anxious to see it. The new toy was a jack-in-the-box. The women had a good time at the store and when they returned home they made Lupita promise not to tell on them.

Later in the afternoon Mr. Ulibarrí returned home looking very pleased. He called all of his children, servants, and relatives together and told them he had a surprise for them. He laid a large box on the table and told one of the girls to open it. When she opened the box out jumped the jack-in-the-box. Of course everyone was surprised. Only Lupita was unimpressed, "Oh! I have seen it already!" she blurted out.

"What? My child?" asked her great grandfather. Before she had a chance to answer, Lupita was carried away to another room and scolded.

Lupita had a Negro nurse who was called Lorenza. She had been brought to Las Vegas by Mr. Ulibarrí who had bought her from the Comanche Indians when she was only seven years old. It is believed that she was the first Negress brought into Las Vegas. People from far and near came to see her. Lupita says it was very pleasant to kiss Lorenza because of her soft, thick lips.

Governor Manuel Armijo was María Ignacia's father's first cousin. He sent word one day from Tecolote that he was coming to Las Vegas to visit his cousin and that he wanted the family to have some delicious hot tamales ready when he arrived.

The Governor was in Tecolote already! The house was in an uproar. Servants set to work cleaning the house and cooking chili.

María Ignacia was in the kitchen when Governor Armijo arrived. She had never seen a governor before and she was anxious to see what one looked like. She took a bag of tobacco and ran into the room. "Mother, here's your tobacco!"

Her mother was embarrassed, "Go and wash yourself," she said.

"Oh, no!" said Governor Armijo, "don't send her away. Come to me, my child."

María Ignacia ran to him and jumped upon his lap, spilling the cup of chocolate which he held in his hand all over his trousers. María Ignacia's mother was very embarrassed, but the Governor only laughed.

When Lupita was eight years old Santiago Ulibarrí died and left her an inheritance.

When the Civil War broke out Lupita was sick with fever and her father wanted to take her south, but her mother refused, because the sympathies of the New Mexicans were with the North.

In her home, Lupita was a regular princess. She was the only child and had everything she desired. At noon the servants would come to dress her. Then she would come downstairs, roam through the yard, or play with her toys, or go visiting with her parents.

She had an old tutor who taught her to read, write, and to work out problems in arithmetic. When she was ten years old she attended the Loretto Academy in Santa Fe. She had been there only seven months when a fever epidemic broke out, and her parents sent for her at once. She was taught to embroider, to play the piano, and only such things that would make a lady of her.

Lupita's mother, María Ignacia, was just a little girl when General Kearny came to Las Vegas to take possession of the territory. María

Ignacia's father got up unusually early and went for a walk. Where the Normal University now stands he saw many cannons all pointing toward the town. Immediately he rushed to town to spread the news. The town was in an uproar. Everyone, it seemed, was screaming and crying. None wanted to become Americans; all wanted to remain under the Mexican flag.

María Ignacia's father refused at first to become an American. He left everything he owned and went to Mexico. All his land confiscated, his stock was killed to feed the troops, and only his house remained to him.

The family which Mr. Ulibarrí had been the head of for so many happy years moved to San Miguel. After a year Illario Gonzales, head of the family, came back to Las Vegas. He made friends with Kearny, regained some of his possessions and moved into his house where some of the troops had been lodged. Gonzales sent to San Miguel for his family and when they arrived General Kearny, his wife and their six year old daughter, moved in with them. The little girl was pretty, having fair hair and blue eyes. General Kearny's men were fed on the cows, sheep, and other stock belonging to Illario Gonzales.

Source of Information: Mrs. Guadalupe Gallegos.

A Second Ananias

by Reyes N. Martínez

*I*n the little settlement of San Cristóbal, sixteen miles north of Taos, resided Ramón Roybal, artful and cunning, always devising some means whereby to make an easy living. In a small, low-roofed house on the outskirts of the settlement he managed to keep a family of five children and his wife, Toña, (Tonia) who, through some malformation of the larynx, could never speak above a low whisper. Throughout spring and summer he passed his days along the banks of the Río Grande or Red River, with rod, hook and bait in his favorite occupation, fishing, and there never was a better fisherman in these parts than Ramón Roybal. His daily catch of trout would amply supply his table and, also, furnish other necessities for the family in exchange from the store at Arroyo Hondo.

His chief characteristic was his utter disregard for the truth, which coupled with a keen sense of humor added a mystical charm to his personality. Of medium height and somewhat stocky build, with big, staring eyes similar to those of a hypnotist, long mustache and long, flowing beard, he presented a man of unique appearance. Fishermen like to tell whoppers about the size of the ones that got away, etc., but Ramón was a real enthusiast of high caliber in his profession and everything connected therewith. He always brought the biggest specimens to the shore, a dozen or more real beauties on every trip. His tales at the country store related in his own highly inimitable way fascinated store-keeper, clerks and customers. On such occasions trade remained at a stand-still, the catch on display on the counter, all two, three pounds and over in weight, and the accumulating crowd held entranced by his narrative of adventures of the day.

On one occasion, he related, he took along with him on one of his trips to the river his young son, Andrés, to count the fish as he drew them out. Starting to count, "One" with the first fish his father pulled out of the stream, the boy continued the count in rapid succession, "Two, three," etc., etc., as the fish flew out of the water, till he shouted "Fifty." "Not fifty but sixty," said Ramón, having pulled out more fish than the boy had been able to count. His exaggeration was always natural and spontaneous.

In another of his stories of his fishing trips to the Río Grande, he sat on the bank of the river smoking calmly a hand-rolled cigarette (he was an inveterate smoker) when he suddenly felt a heavy pull on his line. Believing he had hooked a big specimen, perhaps an eel, he began maneuvering with all his expert skill, pulling and tugging first in one direction then in another in an endeavor to bring the fish into a favorable position to land it. Unable to bring the object at the end of his line close to the surface, he began to lose faith in his ability as a fisherman and he let the line drag close to the bottom of the river. The pull became stronger and stronger till he was obliged to follow along the shore in order to avoid breaking the line. Confused by the strange occurrence, he paced along, walking rapidly, almost at a trot, downstream, when to his amazement, the line was drawn obliquely towards the shore and a horned head protruded out of the water followed immediately by the rest of the body, bringing into view a big, white buck-goat carrying, entangled on its horns, the hook and line. It was the goat of Nieves Anaya, owner of a large herd, which had disappeared several miles up the stream the year before and had supposedly drowned.

During the winter months he used to bring to the store the chamois he made from the hides of deer that he killed. In those days chamois was a staple article of merchandise at country stores and commanded a high price, being sold at twenty-five cents an inch in width, cut lengthwise.

It was a cold winter day during the Christmas holidays that brought Ramón on his horse at his usual trot-trot gait to the store at Arroyo Hondo with a couple of chamois skins and some jewelry that he had made at home, for he was a fairly good jeweler and made rings and brooches of copper and silver which he sold or traded among the folk of the community.

A larger crowd than usual was at the store that day. Displaying the jewelry to prospective customers he remarked that they were made from Aztec silver that he had brought from old Mexico, in his younger days with trading expeditions, and no one dared to express doubt of his assertion. Mention of Old Mexico always struck a chord of happy reminiscence, and he never let the occasion pass without relating some occurrence incident to his travels in that country. On this occasion he related a story of a trip he made to the City of Guadalajara. That city is noted for its numerous churches and a visit to them is always included by the sightseer. Ramón and a companion took advantage of their visit. Entering one of the churches, they knelt in prayer for a few moments in the usual Christian custom, then arose and walked about the edifice observing the artistically carved altars and the many priceless images. Retracing towards the entrance, they noticed a stairway that led down to the basement. Wishing to satisfy their curiosity fully, they walked down. The sight that met their eyes was truly awe-inspiring. All around the basement, in niches in the walls, stood what they supposed to be life-size statues of saints. The two visitors knelt down reverently in front of one of them making the sign of the cross and intoning a fervent prayer. While thus engaged in religious fervor, an attendant approached them and, tugging at their coat sleeves, said: "Señores, qué hacen? Estos son cuerpos embalsa mados de difuntos." (Sirs, what are you doing? These are embalmed corpses of dead persons.) The biggest joke ever played on them had never provoked such uncontrollable outburst of laughter as the one these two young men let out as they stumbled over each other up the steps on their way out of that church.

Ramón Roybal was born in "La Villa de Santa Fe," as the capital of the State was called then, in the year 1850, and came to Arroyo Hondo while yet a young man, marrying later and settling in San Cristóbal. He died about the year 1920.

He was such an expert in the fabrication of false and untrue tales and the exaggeration of true occurrences, that his name is still mentioned in connection with any humorous incident related to the fishing pastime. The fish that got away from him were always the size of a "ten-year old boy."

Proof of his adeptness at the false and untrue is furnished in the case of the murder of Antonio María Martínez, in 1914, one of the most brutal murders in the history of Taos County. Evidence pointed almost unequivocally against Ramón, but by expert maneuvering with the officers of the law he managed to turn States' Evidence and thereby absolve himself of all blame and perhaps saved himself from the gallows or life imprisonment.

Source of Information: The writer was a clerk in the store at Arroyo Hondo covering the period embraced in this narrative and was intimately acquainted with Ramón Roybal.

A Sheephered at Work in Taos County, New Mexico

by Reyes Nicanor Martínez

*I*t was the first week in May of the year 1896, when the writer, while yet a small boy, was taken by his father to "Las Cuchillas," the country immediately west of Tres Piedras, in Taos County, to help him lamb his sheep.

It was there that I first became familiar with the life that a sheepherder leads in this part of the state.

In those days, the public domain was used as free range for grazing sheep. No restrictions, as those now imposed by Forest Service regulations were then in force, although by common agreement among themselves, each owner of a flock of sheep reserved a certain section of the range for lambing. These lambing places came to be known, as time passed, by the name of the owner of the sheep that were first lambed there, and those names serve to designate the places to the present day.

Las Cuchillas is a low range of mountains, or what might be termed an extension of the foothills of the Chama range. This extension spreads out eastward, like a wide fringe, in the direction of the Río Grande river. Narrow valleys cut the surface and afford good grazing at lambing time; and the wooded section affords protection to the new-born lambs from the cold and sleet that sometimes comes unexpectedly over that section at that season of the year.

Eastward of Las Cuchillas, as far as the Río Grande river, spreads an extensive plain, dotted here and there by "cerros," as those high, wooded, individual hills are called. This is the dry section of Taos County, as no rivers course through it, and it is almost uninhabited.

That part which lies east of the Río Grande river is the irrigated and inhabited section, where lie all its villages (except Ojo Caliente) and its rivers. This is the farming section of the county, and there is very little land between the villages and the farms that can be used for grazing livestock, except that part of the Sangre de Cristo range which borders the county on the east, where many sheep are grazed in summer.

The extreme southern part of the county consists of more rugged mountainous country, and includes two or three land grants, which also afford summer grazing for a large number of sheep.

In this section of the country the sheepherder of Taos County plies his vocation, and a vocation it is, because a great part of the adult male population of Taos County chose or adopted, since many years past, sheep-herding as their calling or main occupation, in which kind of work they became very proficient, so much so that even to this day preference is shown by the big sheep-raisers of the states of Colorado and Wyoming for men from Taos County to tend their sheep. (In this connection, a story is told of a man who came to love the work so much, that he spent several years in succession tending sheep, without ever visiting a human settlement in all that length of time. His whole interest and attention so centered in his job that it became part of his very existence; and it is said that when he returned to his native village, his gait was indicative of the mode of walking of a sheep, straight forward, head lowered, and looking only at the ground and some people used to say that when walking alone, he would even bleat, in an undertone, like a sheep.)

The life of the sheepherder is very solitary and monotonous. The same routine is the order, day after day. He gets up at dawn in order to prepare and eat his breakfast before the flock begins to stir in the "mojada" (the sleeping-ground). No late staying in bed is permissible, as the sheep, once they begin to stir, soon "string out" (the habitual way of sheep to follow one another in "strings" or rows) of the sleeping-ground and spread out to graze, and, if not followed immediately by the herder, many of them stray away in bunches from the main flock, and a "corta" (a bunch of sheep that cut away from the main flock and wander away, sometimes for days without being found) is the result. After eating his breakfast, he makes a bundle of some lunch for his noonday meal, and throws his rifle over his shoulder and, with the aid of his dog, he drives the sheep out of the sleeping-ground to graze for the day.

Having nothing to do but watch that the sheep do not scatter too far apart, or that some hungry coyote does not strike the flock, he sits at some convenient spot, his dog beside him, changing once in a while to other points to suit his fancy, and meditates all day long. Occasionally he sends out his dog to gather the sheep when they have spread out too far. At dusk he returns to camp, driving the flock to the sleeping-ground. Then he prepares and eats his evening meal, not forgetting to throw a piece of meat to his dog, and retires for the night.

A cook-stove is a luxury that the sheepherder does not enjoy, except at lambing and sharing time, when the greatly increased number of men employed on those occasions requires the cooking of food in much larger quantities. Winter or summer, the herder cooks his meals on an open fire in front of his tent.

A sheepherder's bed usually consists of two or three sheep-pelts and from one to three blankets (depending on the season of the year), housed in a one-pole tent. In the tent he also keeps his supplies of food, matches and other necessaries.

A flock of sheep usually numbers, at the most, fifteen hundred head, and includes several goats; the larger the number of sheep, usually the more goats in the flock. These goats are very useful in leading the sheep across rivers, into corrals and other places where the sheep by themselves would be loath to go.

Sometimes two men send a flock. In this instance, one of the men is the "mayordomo" and the other one, the herder. The duty of the mayordomo is to prepare the meals for both, to seek fresh grazing-grounds, to move camp, to care for the pack-burros, and to watch the flock at night. To avoid disturbance by hungry coyotes and, on some occasions, by lions or bears, he places lighted lanterns at suitable places about the sleeping-ground, although this precaution does not always assure freedom from attack. The barking of the ever-watchful dog many a time arouses the mayordomo from his sleep, and he has to get up and, rifle in hand, go after the predatory nocturnal visitors. Many instances are related in which a lion or bear has driven off part of a flock from its sleeping-grounds in the night and slaughtered most of the sheep, eating only part of the carcasses and leaving the remainder strewn all over the ground. It is said that these predatory beasts have a habit of killing as many sheep as they can, before starting to eat the flesh.

A curious and interesting part of a mayordomo's job is that of loading camp on the burros, preparatory to moving it to another location. These beasts of burden quickly learn to obey the command of the mayordomo; and when he has to load the tent and the rest of the camp-outfit on them, he taps them gently on the shins with a stick, saying, at the same time, "íncate, íncate" (kneel, kneel). The burro kneels down on its front legs and then the man puts the load on its back with little difficulty.

The sheepherder gains much experience in telling changes in the weather. He watches the heavens and the behavior of wild animals for signs which, although not always accurate, in the great majority of cases indicate that his judgment has been right. Thus it is that when a new moon first appears in the evening above the western horizon, if it is "colgada" (hanging), that is, if its points appear in a line perpendicular, or nearly so, to the earth's surface, it is going to let all the water run out, and the succeeding four weeks will be a rainy period; but if its ends appear in a line horizontal or parallel, (or nearly so) to earth's surface, like an upturned saucer, it is going to hold all the water, and the ensuing period, throughout all its phases, is going to be dry. An "ojo de buey" (ox's eye), a patch in the sky resembling a small segment of a rainbow, indicates an unusually rainy period. In winter, when the coyotes howl vehemently at night, a storm is brewing.

All these signs make the sheepherder cautious, and he prepares to meet all these expected changes in the weather by taking his raincoat along in summer, or his overcoat and sheep-lined mittens and plenty of matches in winter.

Before forest reserves were established, herders used to burn the old, dead grass every spring, in April, and the new grass would then make quicker growth for lambing time.

Lambing the flock is the most laborious part of a sheepherder's job. At this time, the owner of the sheep employs four or five more men than during the rest of the year, with the exception of shearing time. The work requires good knowledge of the job, and experienced hands are very necessary at this time.

First, "el primal" (the cousins), the yearlings, are separated from "el prenado," the ewes that are to bear lambs, into a separate flock, and a camp is set for them at a distance away from the lambing grounds. The ewes that are to bear lambs are then divided into two or three flocks, each of a size more convenient to handle. As the lambs begin to arrive, all those born on the same day, together with their mothers, are held apart for two or three days, a lighted lantern being placed at their sleeping ground every night; then these small flocks that have come in sequence during each week are joined into a larger flock, till at the end of the lambing period, usually three weeks, all the lambs born and their mothers are joined into one large flock till shearing time. After shearing, the flock is divided into two smaller flocks till the fall of the year, when the lambs are sold and delivered to the buyer, or shipped to market.

Many a time, during lambing time, the herder has to play the role of midwife and assist some mother-ewe to give birth to its lamb, as otherwise many a ewe dies in the act.

Some ewes sometimes give birth to their lambs and go away and leave them, forsake them without even giving them their first feeding. When this happens, the herder catches the ewe and marks it and holds it while the lamb sucks its first meal. He places a similar mark on the lamb. In the evening, when he drives the flock to its sleeping-ground, he carries the lamb with him and there shuts it up with the mother in a small, narrow pen, the size of which does not allow the ewe to turn about. In this manner, the lamb is able to suck and feed itself. Usually, the ewe "takes" her lamb again within two or three days. But when the ewe is obstinate in taking her lamb, the herder has to take the trouble, every day, to hold the ewe so as to give the lamb a chance to suck the milk and feed itself, till it is able to rustle for itself. Some lambs that are born on very cold days get so benumbed by the cold that they are unable to suck. These lambs are taken by the herder and warmed by the fireside and then left with the mother to feed themselves. Some of these lose their instinct to suck and become helpless cases and soon die of hunger.

"Pencos" (lambs whose mothers die) are common at this time, as are also ewes whose lambs die. When a new-born lamb dies, the herder takes off its pelt as soon thereafter as possible, and saves it. If a ewe dies within a day or two thereafter, leaving her lamb a penco, the herder puts the pelt which he saved from the dead lamb, over the penco, making it fast by tying it with strings about the neck and the mid section. (It is a well known fact that ewes recognize their offspring by its scent, as well as by its bleat). The herder then places the mother of the lamb that died, together with the penco that wears her lamb's pelt, in a pen. If not immediately, at the most by the next day, the ewe adopts as its own the motherless lamb.

After lambing comes the shearing of the sheep. The herder has no special task at this time, other than to help in driving the sheep that are to be sheared into the corrals and the pens. Here his dog is of great help, as the sheep are very loath to enter the corrals at this time, even though led by the goats, which at other times readily follow. The dog running here and there, barking and biting gently at the legs of some of the sheep, scares them and causes them to push forward into the corral.

After the sheep are sheared, they are driven to the higher altitudes, either to the Chama range or to the Sangre de Cristo range, there to remain till the latter part of September or the first week in October, when the lambs are sold and delivered, or shipped to market.

Life in summer is much more cheerful for the sheepherder than during the cold months of the year. High up on the mountain ranges he passes, rather loafs, most of his time in the shade beneath the aspens or the evergreens. He bathes and fishes in the mountain streams, and eats of the ripe berries that abound there in summer. But there he has to contend with another problem. Bears are numerous in the mountains, and the herder has to be ever watchful in order to stave off their attacks, either upon himself or his flock. His dog serves him very usefully there, as the sheep sometimes spread through the forests, over ground which the herder finds it difficult to overtake them. The dog does the job for him and drives them down to where the herder wants them to be.

In winter, the same daily monotony is his daily lot. He packs himself in two to three pairs of trousers and about the same number of shirts, besides his overcoat and sheep-lined mittens, in order to keep warm. The days are short and the sheep do not move out of the sleeping-ground till a late hour in the morning. The sagebrush of the plains between the Sangre de Cristo range and Las Cuchillas, where the sheep are wintered, provides ample feed for the flock, excepting the old ewes, which have to be cared for at the home-ranch. On these plains, a well-trained dog does most of the work.

A sheepherder's dog learns to obey its master if it is trained while it is young, and obeys his every command explicitly. And the help afforded by these dogs has made sheep-herding an especially appealing job to many persons who, even today, spend the major part of their lives tending sheep, living only two or three months of each year with their families.

When the sheep spread out too far, the herder sends his dog to gather them. The dog goes out and stops at intervals to watch for signs which the herder makes with his arms, indicating to the dog in which direction to round up the sheep, or whether to drive them toward him, and when to stop and come back to him. This saves many a step to the meditating herder.

In years gone by, the sheepherder led quite a shabby existence. He used to go without changing his garments, without shaving and cutting his hair, for long intervals of time, till he visited the village. And his visits to the village used to cause much merriment, as he walked through the village in his uncouth appearance, driving his burros ahead of him.

The life of the sheepherder has changed but little since those early days, with the exception that he now is afforded some conveniences which he did not enjoy in those days. He leads a cleaner existence now and, all in all, the job has now a stronger appeal to the man who likes that kind of existence than ever before.

There is a poem, written in Spanish, entitled "Así Es Como Va Pasando El Pobre Pastor La Vida" (This is the way the poor sheepherder spends his life), which very aptly describes the sheepherder's job and existence in the early days. This poem was written by Escolástico Martínez, a native of Taos County, who, although uneducated, had great ability for composing poetry.

All in all, a sheepherder's life is one of peace and contentment. The hurry and annoyance of modern life are far away from him.

Cooperation

by Reyes Martínez

The year 1900 seems to have been an imaginary dividing line between the old and the new in Taos County. Many of the old customs seem to have gone with the turn of the century. The modern supplanted the ancient with a suddenness, almost imperceptible at that time, but now clearly perceived by those casting a retrospective glance to that date—1900 A. D.

The modern inventions that have revolutionized modes of travel, farming, etc., have also effected changes in the relationship of people towards one another. In no other respect has this change been more marked than in the lack of neighborly cooperation among the present-day inhabitants of the very same villages, where the people of that former era worked together at their daily tasks. Now money is the primary consideration in all matters where the employment of labor is concerned. In those times, neighbor helped neighbor, without a money consideration between them. This spirit of cooperation developed from the times of the first settlers, when it became essential, almost imperative, for the preservation of their very existence against the hostile tribes of Indians that inhabited the region. This cooperation custom was strikingly demonstrated during the harvest season, when as many as twenty men gathered, each with his sickle, at the field of a neighbor, to help him reap his wheat, oats, or other similar grain. Each man took a "melgo" (a narrow strip of land on the field, designated by a shallow ditch on each side to afford easier irrigation and conservation of the soil) the full length of the field. There were some very fast reapers. These soon cut deep swaths into the field and finished their strips far ahead of the others, then turned back and uttered a loud shout of triumph and returned to the other end of the field for a rest and a leisurely smoke of a cigarette, rolled from native-raised tobacco (Mexican "punche") in long corn husks commonly used at the time for cigarette paper, while the others finished their strips.

At the house, the preparation of the meals required the help of several women (wives of some of the men in the field), and the noon hour found a tempting menu spread before the hungry workmen.

The reaping at this particular field was finished in short order; then the men went to the field of the next man whose field was ready to be reaped, then on to the other succeeding fields, till all their grain was stacked, ready to be threshed. At threshing time the grain was hauled in sacks, on the backs of the men, sometimes a mile or more from the fields to their bins at home.

Other work in which they cooperated was the cleaning, carding (combing) and spinning of wool, the plastering of their houses, the washing, at the river, of their blankets and mattresses (twice a year—in the spring and in the fall), when the spread of colored blankets formed a curious display on the fences of the village. These jobs were done by the women. The making of syrup from cornstalks was also a cooperation job, done by the men and the women, working together. This was always an interesting event, to both adults and children.

During the latter part of August or the first part of September, the cornstalks were cut and gathered in from the fields by the men. The stalk was cut just above the highest ear of corn (a plant produced, usually, one or two ears, and many plants produced no ears), so as to allow the grain to mature fully, later, on the remaining part of the plant. The stalks gathered were then stripped of all leaves, washed and placed in a deep trough made from a large, hollowed-out pine-log, where they were pounded with long-handled wooden mallets, to a pulp. For the purpose of pressing the juice out of the pulp, an apparatus called "La viga-prensa," was used. This consisted of a round receptacle, about three or four feet high, made from a section of the log from which the trough was made, open at the top, with a hole at the side adjacent to the bottom, and a long pole, to which was attached a solid, round block of wood that fitted into the receptacle with a leeway of one-half inch all around. The receptacle was fixed upon a platform.

The pole was attached at one end, from some strong, fixed object, six feet or so, opposite the wooden receptacle, in a way that permitted it to be raised so as to allow the solid cylinder of wood to be inserted into the receptacle. A quantity of the pulp was placed into the receptacle, to within a few inches from the top, the solid block of wood lowered upon it, then the apparatus was ready for pressing out the juice. Here the youngsters of the village had their fun. A string of boys and young men would climb on the long horizontal pole, holding with their hands from a rope stretched lengthwise above them, between two upright poles, and would swing up and down with it, in this manner pressing out the juice from the pulp, the juice running out through the hole near the bottom of the receptacle into pans, basins and other utensils. Once in a while one of them in the noisy merriment would let go of the rope, or was pushed off the pole, and would fall to the ground. The women poured the juice from the utensils into copper kettles to boil to the desired sweetness and consistency. During the boiling process the scum was gathered and taken off as it arose to the surface. The boiling juice required close watching to prevent boiling over. The pressing out and boiling of the juice was done at night in the open, starting at dusk and continuing throughout most of the night. The flare of two or three wood fires furnished the necessary light.

As soon as the first batch of syrup was made, and at intervals thereafter, the young men were treated to a spread of it on slices of bread, as an incentive to swing on the viga-prenso throughout the night, when necessary. One night and sometimes two or three nights were required to put out the product of one owner; then the rest of those who had any cornstalks for syrup would take their turn.

Gone forever are those days of mutual cooperation, and the trend of modern times now requires every man to hustle for himself, or pay for all the labor that he employs.

Source of Information: Personal knowledge of writer.

Social Life

by Reyes N. Martínez

At the beginning, social intercourse was limited to visits among the neighbors. Later, as conditions became more settled, games and dances were engaged in. Their games were of the simplest form. Most frequently engaged in was "Pelota," or hockey; sides being chosen, the opposing groups of players spread out in rows facing each other, "chuecos," hockey-clubs, in hand, ready for the contest. The captains of each team "fought" the ball as it was tossed into the air by the umpire, or referee, and the game got into full swing. And it really was "swing," the ball speeding along the ground at each blow from the chuecos, sometimes forward, at other times backward, the fastest runners having the advantage. Spectators lined the way in the open fields where the game was being played. Exciting moments were when the ball "grounded" on a stretch of soft ground and both groups closed in. The high swinging and clicking of the chuecos indicated to the observers that a heated contest was in progress. Sometimes out of the scuffle a real fight resulted, as someone of the players was accidentally struck by a club which drew blood. It was a serious matter then. Some of the onlookers would join the melee, and the final result was the ending of the game after most of the players had been disabled by severe beating with the clubs, some lying unconscious on the ground, the remaining few reaching a truce and disbanding. Most of them had gone into the game sporting white dress shirts and wearing colored silk handkerchiefs around their necks. Their coming back was an even more "colored" affair, their white shirts blotched with blood and some of the handkerchiefs tied around their heads covering wounds, mementoes of an overheated contest. However, games did not always end in this gory manner, and when a more sporting spirit prevailed and the game was played to conclusion, it was a very enjoyable pastime for players and spectators alike. Played "hasta metesol," till sunset, the deciding factor was the location of the ball with respect to the starting point, the ball lying on the losers' side of the field at sunset. Sometimes the game was played between teams from neighboring towns and keen rivalry developed, most of the population of each town attending the game; the course of the game then being the distance between the towns, miles in extent. The stake of the game was a dance to be given by the losing side to the victorious team in their home town. On account of its frequently gory aspect, the game was finally outlawed by the territorial legislature.

Another popular game was "carrera de gallo," race with the rooster. The game was played on certain feast days only, such as Día de San Juan, Saint John's day, on June 24th and Día de Santiago, Saint James' day, on July 25th. The game was played on horseback. The custom was to bury a live rooster in a small mound of earth, its legs tied together with a string and protruding upwards. The players arranged themselves about twenty-five yards away from it. The game was started by the players making a swift run, one at a time, towards the rooster, and when opposite, making a lurch downward in an effort to snatch it up by the legs. The successful one became the "leader," and would keep on the run as fast as the horse could carry him, the others following behind trying to overtake him, and, as each one came up alongside of him, he would strike at him with the live fowl, and the other in turn would try to snatch it away from him, using the bridle-reins held in both hands to loop the fowl and pull it away from him. The one succeeding in pulling it away would then be "leader," and also would keep on the run. This was kept up until the rooster was beaten to a pulp and its body pulled apart. The players would then contribute to buy another rooster, which would undergo the same process. The game lasted all day till late in the evening. The "galleros," as they were called, raced swiftly through the streets of the village, while the rest of the men not engaged in the game and the women and the children enjoyed the sight, being careful to keep off the streets, as the galleros had the right-of-way all that day.

After laying in all their crops in the Fall, the rest of the time was "playtime," or continued merry-making, till planting time arrived the following Spring; their only other occupation being hunting, as wild game was very abundant; and this was considered sport and not work.

Festivity had its way throughout the cold weather season. Dances, particularly, were enjoyed very frequently then. Most weddings took place during the winter and were occasions of sumptuous feasting and dancing. When a young man made known his intention to wed, it was customary for his parents to recommend to him for selection as prospective bride a number of young ladies from good, respectable families, always taking into consideration equality in social standing.

The Weaver of Talpa

by Reyes N. Martínez

At Talpa, a village five miles south of the town of Taos, on a side road a few hundred feet to the east from State Highway number three, stands a three-room adobe house. A visit to this house ushers you into an atmosphere reminiscent of a past era.

In answer to your knock, the door is swung open by a stocky-built old man, grizzled and crippled by the years. Stooping as you enter the low doorway, you are invited to sit down on one of the home-made benches in the room, as he, also, sits down at another similar bench and asks the purpose of your visit. There, before you, you see the Old Weaver of Talpa, suave and quiet of manner, and uniquely interesting in his narrative of the events of his long life, for he is eighty-four years old. Two old women keep him company. One of them, he informs you, is his wife, seventy-eight years of age; and the other is the widowed mother of his son's wife, and about eighty-five years old. The bench on which you sit is hard, but you feel comfortable in the coolness of the dirt-floored room.

Curious to know, you ask how he makes his living. The question strikes his favorite topic, and he at once assumes an intensely interesting attitude. He relates to you the story of his life. Becoming an orphan at twelve years of age, he was left with an old weaver, with whom he lived for many years and learned the trade which later became his chief occupation and means of livelihood. In his younger years, the stream at Talpa was very rich in trout, and he used to make frequent trips to Taos to sell his catch and bring back, in trade, some provisions from La Baza de Don Fernando, as Taos was known at the time. Later he confined his activities to the weaving of blankets and rugs. He became very proficient at it, and his trade drew business from the whole valley of Taos, including the Indians, who became his regular customers. Getting up at four o'clock every morning, he plied his trade sometimes till dusk. He was making a very comfortable living till the depression swept his business along the downgrade with the rest of the business world, forcing him to seek aid from the government relief agencies. Notwithstanding his miserable circumstances, he tells you, no relief has been tendered him, and he still plods along at his old trade, doing a little weaving now and then for the neighbors, or selling a blanket occasionally to effect a scanty means of sustenance for himself and the two old ladies that comprise his household.

    He invites you to see his loom. Across an open space, in another house, stands his loom, a relic of the olden days, but still useful, already smooth and shiny from long years of use. A spinning-wheel stands to one side of the loom. This is an apparatus of his own invention, combining the old with the new, consisting of a discarded bicycle wheel with a handle attached to the axle for turning by hand, and a driving-band extending back toward the old-fashioned spindle. Taking a quantity of carded wool, he demonstrates to you his method of spinning the yarn, and the winding of it on a quill inserted at the end of the spindle. He then takes the quill and places it into the shuttle, a hollow boat-shaped piece of wood, pointed at each end, and about ten inches in length. Throwing the shuttle first to the left, through the opening made in the warp-threads by the heddles, then back to the right, he carries on the process of weaving, till a considerable part of a rug is made for demonstration to you. The years have not yet dimmed his eyes, nor incapacitated him in a way to prevent him from plying the trade that he has loved and carried on for a span of more than seventy years. The pity of it is that such a humble trio have to plod along in the evening of life under such miserable circumstances. Fate, sometimes, is an unkindly weaver of circumstances. Here an opportunity presents itself for charity to serve a noble purpose.

Early Life in Questa
As Told by Frank V. García

by L. Raines

I can still see grandmother sitting in her chair at the fireplace, her wrinkled face shining in its fitful light, as she told me stories of her early life. I settled myself more comfortably on my warm sheepskin bed and she proceeded.

"Questa was settled by five pioneers in 1830. The most prominent of the group was Don Benito, who at that time had thirty Indian servants. The Indian slaves seemed to enjoy the hard work under their master, performing their daily tasks as faithfully as they could and hoping someday to be highly rewarded by their master. This valley at that time was covered by a dense forest so that the clearing of land was an important occupation for the Indian slaves.

"After enough land was cleared the planting of crops was begun. The plowing was done by means of a sharp pointed piece of iron inserted in a piece of wood to which were attached rude handles. The plow was drawn by oxen.

"By the end of 1836 more than fifty settlers, besides their Indian servants, had settled in Questa. As each new settler arrived he was assigned a section of land to clear and till. Farms were started, roads built, irrigation ditches dug. Even now the community was not safe from Indian attack. A working man in the fields had his gun and powder handy, for no one knew when the bad Indians would come. Occasionally a watch was put over the field so that the *peones* could work in peace.

"In 1838 Don Benito called a meeting of all the inhabitants to discuss plans for building a church. It was agreed that Saturday of each week all men should work on the new building, which was to have a double wall. Each wall was to be eighteen inches in thickness. Between the walls was a space a foot wide, to be filled with brush and cedar posts. Consequently the completed walls would be four feet thick. They were about fourteen feet high.

"The heavy beams which you enjoy looking at so much when you should be praying are about eighteen inches through and not less than twenty-five feet long. They were lifted in place with only thick strips of hide to aid the men in their work.

"The building was, I think, completed in 1840. It was decided to dedicate it to the holy name of San Antonio, patron of all farmers. A messenger was sent to Taos to bring Father Martínez to direct the ceremony of the Mass.

"The thirteenth day of June was to be the great day for the *fiesta*. On that day all the men mounted their horses and wheeled them into two lines. The last eight men in each file carried guns in case of Indian surprise. Four women carried the image of San Antonio which had been donated by Doña María, Don Benito's wife; all the other women and the children followed. The women chanted the hymn *Misterios de San Antonio* and all the men joined in the chorus. The procession went to the four corners of the valley so that San Antonio might see the conditions of the crops.

"During the month of Mary—or May, as we call it now—all the men, women and children attended the ceremony of the *Rosario* dedicated to Mary, which took place every afternoon at four o'clock.

"On the 24th of June all water was holy, and all the people bathed in the waters of the *Río Colorado*.

"Early in July, preparations were begun for the big days of that month: the 24th and 25th. Foot races, potato races, cock fights and other events were held on these days, which were known as the Fiesta of Santiago and Santa Ana."

Grandmother burst into a laugh and continued, "How well I remember when your father danced the *Matachines*. He was a good singer, too."

I stretched and yawned, and grandmother stopped. "You are sleepy and you must be off to bed. Tomorrow night I'll tell you how we celebrated other big days like Noche Buena, the *Pastores*, and how a group of men sang carols from house to house on New Year's Day."

I started off to bed, looking back drowsily at grandmother, rolling another cigarette from Mexican *punche*.

Slavery

by L. Raines

During the early days of Spanish occupation in the Southwest, Indian slavery existed. Las Vegas and Mora had their share. Indian slaves were, in particular, found in the homes of the wealthier ranchers, or haciendados, where they engaged in the more menial indoor and outdoor work. As in the South, the system was often beneficent. Trustworthy and dependable servants often became valued family retainers, marrying, raising their own families, and frequently taking the family name.

Hilario Romero of Las Vegas had three Indian slaves, Refugia, María, and Felipa, who served the family for almost 60 years. Refugia and María were bought in Texas for $100 each. On a business trip in Mexico Don Hilario loaned $200 to an Indian friend. Meeting him again in Mexico the following year he requested payment. Unable to meet the demand the Indian arranged to give his daughter in payment. Thus Felipa came into the family. She was to serve longer than the other two. She did only housework, while the others worked outdoors. After many years María and Refugia were sent home, where they died several years later. Felipa lived to be a very old woman.

Source of Information: Mary A. Fulgenzi.

NARRATIVES

"After saturating their systems with Milligan's famous liquors, they made a race track of the plaza's only street using the rocks on the hillside as targets for their forty-fives. Finally, they rode swiftly out of town amid a swirl of dust and smoke and were gone."

From "The Mexican War at Reserve" by H. P. Collier

Canuteros and the Death of Colonel Means

by Lorin W. Brown

Shortly after the Civil War there existed in Taos, New Mexico, a clique or group of individuals called "Los Canuteros." This name was given to them because of their addiction to the game or pastime of "canute." This game, simple enough, was all the rage then, and was an excuse for many social gatherings. Everybody played it, but a certain group of the more prominent native families were given, and specifically known by, that name. These families were bound together by mutual interests—religious, political and social. Meetings at the homes of the different members were occasions given over to discussions of different topics and gossip, as much as to the game itself.

There were some Americans who were admitted to the more or less exclusive gatherings, for the most part those who had married into Spanish families. But no American was received as enthusiastically as was a certain Colonel Means. A genuine Kentucky colonel with all the traits of and vices of such gentlemen from the South, he chose to ally himself with the native population, adopting and adapting himself to all their customs. These customs seemed to harmonize with the traditions of hospitality and courtesy which he had brought with him from the South. Soon he was well known for his love of fine horses and whiskey and gambling, all traits of a gentleman from Dixie, also his quick temper and his sympathy for the Southern cause, which got him into many disputes and arguments with the rest of the Americans, most of whom had fought on the Northern side. Among these were Captain Simpson, George Ross, Joe Hearst, Scheurich and others.

The Colonel being a giant in stature and likewise a crack shot with the brace of pistols, which he always carried—nobody ever dared carry any argument with him to a definite physical conclusion. Which fact made him more hated as a direct effect of fear.

Don Pedro Joseph de Tevis, father of Antonio Joseph, later

Territorial Representative from New Mexico, had died a few years before Colonel Means appeared in Taos, leaving a not inconsiderable fortune. Colonel Means married his widow, Doña Mariana and thereby incurred the active and powerful enmity of his sons and their friends. They were very much opposed to a stranger having control of the late merchant's estate.

As I have said before, two of Colonel Means's loves were love of fine horses and of whiskey. He combined the display of both on many occasions. Many times he would take one of his magnificent saddle horses from his stables. He would ride him at a fast pace around town, stopping now and then to drink at the homes of friends or at one of the many saloons around the Taos plaza. At this time the famous "Taos Lightning" was distilled near Taos and acquired fame for its potency throughout the Territory and beyond, and, needless to say, was the Colonel's favorite drink. Entering the saloon the Colonel's pistols were aggressively displayed and his flowing moustache seemed to challenge anyone to refuse to drink with him. It was said he was very good at shooting off boot heels, if provoked by a refusal to enjoy his hospitality. These wild rides soon wore out his mount for the day and at this stage the Colonel, dismounting, would remove the saddle and strap it on his own back. Thinking he had relieved his mount of part of its burden he would again mount and return home bareback.

At other times, while drinking and in the mood to celebrate, he would drive his spirited buggy team up and down the narrow streets of the old town and around and around the square. Beside him on the front seat, would be Doña Mariana bravely trying to appear as if this were only a peaceful outing after a breath of fresh air. On the rear seat were always a pair of musicians energetically rendering every piece called for by the exuberant Colonel, who punctuated his demands with shots into the sky. Inocencio Martínez, the violin player, and Salvadore Archuleta, the guitar player, would be generously rewarded for these public appearances. Even so they skipped many a beat as the buggy took the corners on two wheels. But the Colonel was a superb horseman and handled the ribbons in such a masterful way that these expeditions never met with any accident.

The only unfortunate aspect was the treatment from which

Doña Mariana suffered at the hands of the Colonel after some of these drinking spells. This came to light after she had him brought before the local magistrate on two or three occasions. The charge was, in every case, mistreatment. However, on the first occasions she was prompt to forgive him and pay his fine. Now it was that Colonel Means gave his enemies a—to them—valid excuse for open condemnation. His enemies were very outspoken in their chivalrous resentment of the Colonel's treatment of his wife. They had never been so vocal about other of his acts which had not appealed to them. But now they had a very noble and legitimate grievance.

The Colonel's last appearance in court was the occasion for a determined move on the part of these men. The judge was induced to refuse him any fine or bail and ordered his incarceration for a certain period. The Colonel sensed something more than a disciplinary measure in all this. He asked for certain of his Spanish friends by name and further requested that they be allowed to stand watch around the jail and courthouse, or "Leave me my pistols and I will take care of myself," he said. The first request was granted in preference and six well-armed friends of his showed up for guard duty. Some of these posted themselves on the roof of the building while the others kept watch below.

Western customs of that day and age would never deprive a prisoner of his whiskey. So that evening a flask of Taos Lightning was brought to the Colonel along with his supper. The guards were as hospitably brought a quantity sufficient for six men to keep away the chill night air. Any men eligible as guards and of gun packing age were just naturally whiskey drinkers. It was an accepted fact, commonplace and everyday. So the guards gratefully returned thanks as they passed the jug for their first drink. It was their last that night for the whiskey had been drugged and they very peacefully fell into a deep slumber.

Shortly after this effect had been noted a group of white-masked men appeared at the jail door, drifting in from the deep shadows around the plaza. They possessed themselves of the keys and, entering, very quietly and efficiently hanged Colonel Means to one of the thick beams which spanned the old adobe jail building. Quietly and efficiently I say, because they had very prudently drugged the Colonel's whiskey as well. Next morning the town seethed with excitement and curious groups making for the jail. The Colonel had been found hanging there, the doors open and six shame-faced men pleading ignorance of how all this had come to pass.

There were not lacking persons who had seen this hooded band before and after the deed, but they could not or would not identify any of them. Now it was known that these men had worn white woolen stockings over their everyday foot wear. This was a necessary precaution because in that day foot wear was as varied as the individuals wearing it and could have been a means of identification.

Doña Mariana claimed the Colonel's body and gave him a grand funeral. She never ceased denouncing this cowardly act and in later years publicly accused different individuals of participation.

My grandmother, Juanita Montoya de Martínez, who told this story over and over again to my mother, Cassandra Brown-López, related, moreover, a sequel which took place two or three years afterwards.

Naturally this incident was food for conversation for a long time. Conjecture as to the identity of the mob was a subject of never-ceasing interest. No positive identification was possible, but there were many proofs advanced for the presence of this one or that one in the crowd which lynched the Colonel. "Los Americanos fueron" (It was the Americans), said the native population. Burden of proof was on their side, because of the animosity of the Americans for the deceased and because the "Canuteros" were sure of their presence at the home of one of their members on the death night. That is, with the exception of the six guards. Yet the Americans brought up the counter accusation that "Los Canuteros" were the guilty ones, citing the very fact that they so unanimously vouched for each other's presence at the Canute game.

"You may have been lynching Colonel Means instead of playing Canute," was their contention. Even the poor guards came in for their share of suspicion. So the argument went on for many years with no one being positively identified as one of the mob.

Later at a "Canute" gathering Captain Simpson was present, having been admitted to the "Canuteros" by virtue of his marriage to Josefita Valdéz. He and my grandmother Juanita were with the group whose turn it was to hide the canute. Shielded from the rest of the

"Canuteros" in the large room by a couple of blankets held up by some of their number, the question as to which canute should hold the counter was decided. This having been decided and the canute called "Mulato" chosen, this group started the chant reserved for this stage of the game. Under cover of this chanting Captain Simpson spoke to my grandmother, "Mira Juanita, voy hacer 'pojoquante' a este canute" (Look Juanita, I am going to make a charm over this canute). So saying he produced a piece of rope, about a hand's breadth, decorated with ribbon and passed it over the canute. This was a charm to keep the other side from choosing this canute first, since it held the counter and thus they would score. Continuing, Captain Simpson said that he and his other companions had possessed themselves of the rope after Colonel Means had been cut down and had divided it among themselves as a souvenir. This admission of guilt my grandmother never divulged until Captain Simpson died many years later.

At another time my grandmother, a great friend of "Chepita," Kit Carson's wife, was visiting at their home. Grandmother and Chepita were having a very heated argument regarding the question of the Colonel's death. The argument had reached the stage of direct accusation.

"The Americans hanged El Coronel Means," was grandmother's accusation.

"No, Los Canuteros were the ones," responded Chepita angrily.

Just then the door leading into the next room opened and Kit Carson looked into the room.

With a stern, "Calla, mujer" (Quiet, woman), the door was closed again as he withdrew. Completely squelched, the two women took up another time when it could be resumed without danger of such preemptory interruption.

Source of Information: Cassandra Brown López.

El Adivino Casual "A Fortune-Teller by Accident"

by Lorin W. Brown

*T*here was a very poor married couple and the wife gave birth to a son. This married couple had as neighbors a very rich family and the poor couple thought that if they invited the rich man as godfather for the newly born son, that he would give them some money and so relieve the straitened circumstances in which they found themselves.

And so they did; they invited their rich neighbor to baptize the newly born babe and he accepted the invitation with much pleasure, saying that the next Sunday after mass he and his wife would present themselves as sponsors of the babe.

The child's parents prepared a modest festal board in honor of their new "compadres"; after the feast the godparents left the table and said, "Thank you, compadres, for the honor you have conferred upon us in inviting us to be compadres of our best of neighbors and have the honor of saving a soul from mortal sin, bringing it to God's grace." Whereupon they left for their home, having given nothing to the newly christened babe nor to its parents. After a time the mother of the child began to meditate about how it was that her neighbor being so wealthy had been so stingy as to have given his godson not even one cent.

The following day she conceived a plan for getting money out of her "compadres" and getting her husband's attention said to him, "Listen, my husband, you know very well that I would not steal nor harm anyone, but it grieved me very much that our compadres did not turn loose of a single cent with which to buy even diapers for my son. I have thought of a plan by which he will give us some money, he has plenty." The husband said: "What plan is that?" "Listen, you know that our compadre has a horse which he values very highly; go to his corral, take the horse and hide it."

That night the husband went to the corral and carried out his wife's orders; he took the horse out of the corral and took it to some woods. In the morning his wife went to see her "compadre" and greeted him: "How are you, compadre?" "Not very well, comadre," he replied. "Well, what has happened to you, compadre?" "Well, that which has happened to me is that someone came last night and stole my favorite horse. I would very willingly give one hundred dollars to whoever will give me information as to the whereabouts of my horse." "Do not worry, compadre, my husband is somewhat of a diviner and it is possible that he might divine the whereabouts of your horse."

"Well, summon my compadre immediately and if he should divine the whereabouts of my horse I will give him one hundred dollars, for that is a horse which I value more than all of the horses in my stable." The comadre went home, quite pleased, yet seemingly much grieved and when she reached her home she told her husband what their compadre had said. The husband then left for his compadre's home and after greeting him extended his sympathy for the loss of his horse.

His compadre said to him: "My comadre has informed me that you are somewhat of a diviner and if you divine the whereabouts of my horse I will give you one hundred dollars."

"Very well, compadre, but I must retire to my home in order to concentrate." He went home and the following day he returned to his compadre's home with a map, a very crooked map which traced a course which crossed and doubled back on itself until it reached a woods and he said to his compadre: "If the system which I use in divining has not deceived me, following this map will reveal the whereabouts of your horse."

The rich man immediately ordered two of his servants to saddle two horses and to take the map and set out in search of his horse. The two servants followed all the turns indicated by the map and when they reached the woods they found the horse tied to the trunk of a tree. The servants untied the horse and returned rejoicing. When the owner saw them draw near he was filled with joy and told his compadre to go bring his wife, there would be a feast, at which time he would give him the one hundred dollars for having divined the whereabouts of his horse.

This event became generally known throughout the neighborhood and everyone rejoiced in having a diviner for a neighbor.

Within a few days a ring belonging to the Princess was lost and the courtiers told the King that they knew of a diviner—the King ordered him to be brought before him.

When the King's servants went to call him they explained the reason for the King's summons and he told them to leave and tell the king that he would follow soon, that he would have to change his clothes before appearing before the King.

When the King's servants had left, the diviner very sadly said to his wife: "Oh, beloved wife! What a fix you have gotten me into, how can I divine where the Princess's ring is?" He said goodbye to his wife and children and left for the King's palace. He was conducted to the King's presence and the King said to him: "It has come to my ears that you are a diviner. The Princess's ring has been lost—if you divine the whereabouts of the ring I will give you two hundred dollars, but if within three days you do not, I will have you executed."

The King ordered that he be imprisoned in a room for three days so that he might concentrate on finding the ring. On the following day the King ordered one of his servants to take the prisoner his breakfast. After the prisoner had partaken of his breakfast he exclaimed: "Thanks be to God, of the three I have seen one." The King had three servants and they were the ones who had stolen the Princess's ring so that when the prisoner exclaimed: "Thanks be to God, of the three I have seen one!" he thought that the prisoner referred to him, but the diviner exclaimed and gave thanks to God because he had lived to see one of the three days which the King had granted him.

The servant left and said to his companions: "That diviner is going to give us away, he is going to find us out because when he had finished his breakfast he exclaimed with much satisfaction, 'Thanks be to God, of the three I have seen one!'"

The following day the King sent another of the three servants with his breakfast and after the diviner had eaten he exclaimed: "Thanks be to God, of the three I have seen two."

This servant left the room and hurried to where his companions were and said to them: "There is no way out, this diviner will expose us to the King who will not only throw us out of the palace but he will have us executed for being thieves! What shall we offer the diviner so that he will not expose us?" They determined to offer him one hundred dollars.

One of them went to the diviner's room and said to him: "We are very well convinced that you are a genuine diviner and if you do not expose us we will give you one hundred dollars." The diviner replied: "If you will do as I say and if you give me the one hundred dollars, I will not expose you. Go to the granary for some corn, place the ring with the corn, then watch carefully to see which turkey eats the ring, then come and tell me."

The servant did as he was told and noted very carefully which turkey swallowed the ring: then he went to the diviner's room and told him: "The grayest turkey of the flock ate the ring." The diviner said that they should go tell the King that he had divined the whereabouts of the lost ring. They took him to the King's presence and he said to the King; "Have the grayest turkey of your flock killed." A servant very joyfully returned to the King with the Princess's ring.

The King and the Princess were overjoyed and the King paid the diviner the two hundred dollars and the servants paid him the one hundred dollars, which had been promised. He took the three hundred dollars and left for a far country where he could never be found again, very pleased at having come out so well of such a ticklish situation.

Source of Information: Florentina Baros, Taos, New Mexico; Simeon Tejada, Taos, New Mexico, Translation, 2/6/39.

El Leoncito

by Lorin W. Brown

Don Manuel Chávez, born at Cebolleta, was thus known as The Little Lion for his singular bravery and valor as an Indian fighter. When a band of Navajos swept down on the Río Grande settlements and drove off several thousand head of sheep Don Manuel with his half brother Roman followed the raiders with fourteen picked men, overtaking them at Ojo de la Monica. The hostiles were routed and the stock recovered. Charles L. Lummis in his *A New Mexico David*, gives us an account of the subsequent events.

"Next morning his camp was entirely surrounded by hostiles. Roman had stopped at Fort Craig for a frolic, promising to catch up next day, but he failed to come. From sunrise to dark the heroic fifteen fought off the swarming Navajos. Colonel Chávez had posted each man behind a tree, and at intervals walked from one to another to cheer them up. It was the deadliest struggle ever recorded in New Mexico. One by one the brave Mexicans sank transfixed by arrows. One daring Indian on a fine black horse was conspicuous all day, rallying his companions to the fight. At last in a desperate charge, he was shot dead by Colonel Chávez within twenty feet.

"At the beginning of the fight the Colonel had eighty-two bullets; at the close he had fired eight, and for every one an Indian or a horse had fallen. He never fired until dead sure of killing. His own escape was miraculous, especially as he had a red handkerchief around his neck all day, being too hard pressed to take it off."

Source of Information: Paul Horgan, *New Mexico's Own Chronicle*.

Los Comanches

by Lorin Brown

"Sí, Señor, if my daughter had not put iodine in my eye in place of the medicine given me by the doctor I would be out with my sons helping them plow."

These were the first remarks from Sr. Vicente Romero of Córdova after we had exchanged salutations and I had commented on his good health. After a lapse of several years I had found my old friend partially blinded due to his daughter's unfortunate mistake.

"And for the grace of God who has given me my good health and the company of my wife I give thanks. Fifty-seven years have gone through this life together. I was married quite old, when I had thirty years. I have lived a very active life and it is hard for me to be sitting here by the fire-place so useless." Around him were eight grand-children, just a fraction of the twenty-six he has, not counting great grand-children.

"Not always have I been so helpless. If I do say so myself I have never been afraid to work or to risk my life to acquire the necessities of life for my family. And when I was young we were surrounded by so many savage nations that any trip away from the village had to be made in force. Four times I have been on trading trips to the Comanches and three times to the plains on buffalo hunts. We used bows and arrows and the lance as weapons when hunting at first. Later we were able to trade for guns at Santa Fe. We would take venison and fish and other things to trade in Santa Fe. There were many deer then and the rivers were full of fish. But everything comes to an end in this world.

"The first two trips to the Comanches I went with my uncle Guadalupe Márquez, who was the commandante or leader. I learned enough of the language and customs so that the last two trips I went as commandante. Our first trip took us about three months. We took salt, blankets and strips of iron for arrowheads. We also took big packs of a very hard bread, which our wives baked especially for trading to the Indians. Another article of trade was dried apples and plums.

"We went by way of Peñasco and Mora. When we came close to Fort Union we would wait until night to slip by the Fort. The Americans did not want us to go into the Comanche country because it might cause trouble. After we had gotten by the Fort without being seen we would have to hunt for the Indians. These savages were always traveling, hunting or following the buffalo herds, so that we never knew where we would find them. We went here and there over the plains looking for signs of the Indians. When we finally found the trail of a large group, in which there were signs of women and children, we knew we were close. Following this trail until the sign was quite fresh, our commandante ordered us to make camp. Locating the closest water supply we started to unpack. While we were doing this our commandante made a smoke signal on a high point near camp.

"'Now boys, in the morning we should have the Indians here and we can start to trade,' he said. 'Be very careful how you act with the Indians.'

"We did not sleep very much that night. In the morning we were surrounded by a large group. They made camp next to us, the women doing all the work. The children and the dogs made lots of noise. At first the children were afraid of us but after a few days became very friendly, always begging for something. The Comanches are a very fine looking Indian, light complexioned and well built. There are many savage nations on those plains. On one trip we traded with a group of Kiowas. It is a good thing the government guards these savages because if they ever fought us all together they might kill us all off now that they can get good rifles.

"After a sort of feast with the Indians we started in to trade. This would take a long time because there would be much talk over such trade. Sometimes an Indian and one of us would fix up a horse race. They liked to bet and that way we won many articles from them. We did not stay in the same camp but traveled from spot to spot with our customers, following the buffalo trading as we went. I enjoyed this life very much. It was very new to me, we were always watchful and on our guard for some act of treachery on the part of the Indians. But they had need of the goods we had to trade so they treated a trading party with a certain regard and usually avoided any act which might cause trouble. We were more careful than they were perhaps, always thinking of our families and the goods we were to take home with us. The younger men in our "escuadra" would run foot races with the Indians and amuse ourselves in other ways, such as breaking horses and contests with the bow and arrow. We had wrestling matches in some of which I took part. I very often raced a "grullo" (dark gray, with a black stripe down his back and on each shoulder), which was a favorite hunting horse, with first one and then another of their horses. I won six out of about nine races and not being held back by thoughts of a wife and children at home, bet many blankets and other articles and so added considerably to my store of goods, because my grullo was pretty fast. Another young fellow, Anacleto Mascarenas, two years older than myself (remember I had only eighteen years), almost brought calamity on our little "escuadra" (troop or gang).

"For some time several of our group had had conversation with a young girl of the tribe, who had been taken captive from some place in Texas, San Antonio del Arbol she called the place. Where that place is I don't know. She had tried to persuade us to take her away from her captors, promising us that her father would pay us in gold and cattle, should we return her to her home. Her story was that the Comanches had seized her as she was taking some clothes to some servant women washing at a stream near the house. As she was passing a clump of wild plum bushes three of these painted savages had jumped out, took hold of her, one of them closing her mouth with his hand to keep her from crying out or screaming. They led her to where they had left their horses. One of them took her on his horse and rode off, followed by the other two. A short distance from her father's ranch they were joined by others in charge of stolen stock, also belonging to her father. She was shown the mutilated bodies of two of her father's herders and by sign showed her what to expect if she did not go quietly. One of the men who had carried her off had made her his wife. Pobrecita! She had to work very hard like the rest of the Indian women. Her pleas were very pitiful and some of us younger fellows felt like risking a rescue.

"In every important decision our commandante's word was

final because we had entrusted ourselves to his care and given him full authority. Some of us took up the girl's case with him for his decision. We could almost guess what his decision would be. There were two of us who did not care so much about the gold or reward from her father, but had dreams of taking this really "muy bonita" captive as a bride, and enjoying the surprise she would cause when our folks saw her after the Salvo to San Antonio. It was the custom for any group returning to Córdova from a hunt or trading trip, to discharge their fire-arms at the crest of the ridge circling our home village. This Salvo was in honor of our patron saint of the village and was a means of announcing our arrival. Those were very joyous times and I will never forget the first time I belonged to one of these returning parties. But let me finish telling you about this girl. I was one of two who wanted to take the girl back with us, but our commandante said, No, it can't be done. Any effort to free her or take her away might destroy our whole party, as far away as we are for the number of Indians against us. Even if we were so lucky as to get her away with little or no loss none of us could ever return to trade with these Indians. But Mascarenas insisted and threatened to carry her away against the commandante's orders. He secretly made preparations to do so. When the commandante found this out he ordered Mascarenas seized and bound until he gave up his plan and promised to obey our leader's orders in everything. This seemed very cruel, but it was very necessary for the good of our whole party. So the Pobrecita stayed there with the Indians, perhaps for life. Así le toco (That was her fate). Those were very hard times.

"I remember now something that happened on my last trading trip with the Comanches. Among our party was José Antonio Vigil and his son. This man was later known as El Capitán Vigil. He was afraid of no Indian or twenty of them even. I could tell of many deeds of valor of his against the savages, but now I will tell you of what happened on my last trip. I was in charge as commandante and our whole group was composed of men from Córdova or El Valle. This man Vigil had a very fast and enduring sorrel horse which was known as El Álazan. The Indians coveted this animal and Vigil received many offers for his horse. One Indian even offered him two captive women amongst other things. This was a good offer, for these captive slaves were very much in demand among the "ricos" and prospective bride-grooms and brought a very good price. But Vigil refused all trades because he could not bear to part with this very excellent animal.

"Early one morning Vigil and his son left camp after antelope without my permission. He was very far from camp when he and his boy were overtaken by an Indian known as Captain Corona. This Captain Corona was so called because of the peculiar way his hair grew. At one time in some fight his enemies had started to scalp him while unconscious, thinking him dead. The operation revived him before his scalp had completely parted company with his skull. Being a renowned fighter he had scattered his would-be scalpers. However, his scalp did not fit back snug to his skull like it had been before. It had grown back in a bunch on the top of his head making a crown-like growth. And that was the reason for his name, Corona meaning crown. At any rate he was a very tricky Indian and a fighter with a reputation, being a chief amongst the Comanches. This day he hailed Vigil and his son and catching up with them rode along between them. Being as eager as any of the other for Vigil's horse he started talking trade as they rode along. José Antonio being always on his guard pretended to agree to trade so as to keep Corona in good humor. The tricky savage decided to get the horse for nothing because without warning he knocked the boy off his horse with a club which he carried in his left hand. At the same time he reached over with his right hand and pulled Vigil off his horse with his right hand. All this was done very suddenly. However he was not quick enough for Vigil, who at the instant drew his knife. Catching Corona in the pit of the throat he ripped him open completely disemboweling him.

"His first thought was of the trouble he might cause the rest of his companions. Putting the body on the Indian pony they covered any marks of the fight, and buried the body quite a way from the scene of the fight. His horse was taken to the edge of a cliff where he also was killed and his body pushed over the edge. Riding back to camp late that night I was awakened and told what happened. Vigil, after telling of the fight, said, 'I have brought this trouble on us myself. My boy and I will leave tonight. The Indians missing us will think that Corona has taken us captive. If you folks make no fuss the Indians will believe as I have told you. As soon as you finish trading you had better leave because they might accidentally find the body. I leave all my goods in your care to take to my family in case I do not get home. But I will not stay and make trouble for the rest of you. This is the only way. Adiós amigos.' 'Vayan con Dios,' I answered.

"There was no doubt that everything was for the best this way. Luckily it rained very heavily that night covering their tracks and the Indians were suspicious; they finally must have believed as Vigil thought they would when Corona failed to show up also. This was another time when one or two individuals suffered in order to preserve the safety of many. I am glad to say that Vigil and his boy arrived safely home after many narrow escapes from the Indians and from hunger.

"José Antonio lived to found Cundiyo, settling it along with his sons and their families. His descendants and the descendants of his eight sons were the reason that in Cundiyo today the family name you hear is Vigil. Here, in the defense of Cundiyo from Indian raiding parties, José Antonio received the name of El Capitán Vigil. The Indians learned to leave him alone after he had killed several of them and Cundiyo was fairly safe from their raids.

"One time I remember Capitán Vigil was taken to Santa Fe to show how he fought against the Indians. With his body wrapped around with a raw-hide rope and with his shield he kept off the arrows which were shot at him. I think it was the captain of the American soldiers at Santa Fe who took him there for this exhibition. I do know that he came home with a team of mules and as he said with $300 American money. He was a very valiant man; very famous for his valiant deeds.

"After finishing with our trading we made preparations to leave the Comanche country. The Indians escorted us for three days out of their country. They did this with all trading parties when the trading was over. After again slipping by Fort Union we were very happy to be on our way home. We were still in some danger from Apaches or Navajos who liked to come through that part of the country to raid the pueblos and even on horse-stealing trips among the Comanches. The Comanches were very great enemies of the Navajos. One Comanche told me that the Navajos were all magicians or practiced witchcraft. To prove this he said that whenever they were about to overtake a bunch of horse-thieving Navajos they would turn themselves and the stolen stock into soap weeds and they would have to return empty handed. That is why they had no use for the Navajos.

"The closer we got to our homes the more we pushed our poor horses with their loads. And, thanks to God, we finally reached Truchas and now we were practically home. Soon we were firing our fire-arms in the Salvo to San Antonio. We could see the people on the roof-tops counting us as we rode down into the village to see who were missing. My poor mother cried with joy to see me back safe. The next few days were filled with feasting and the nights with dancing. Blessed be God; those were the times. This was my first trip to the Comanches and I was to make many more, but I always remember this one especially."

The Ambuscade

by Lorin W. Brown

One of the interesting ranch homes of old Taos was the home of Don David and Doña Marcelina Martínez of Taos. This rambling many roomed dwelling four miles west of the Taos Plaza is remembered, principally by the writer, as the scene of many hours spent in play and exploration of its many corners. Possibilities for amusement for myself and the grandson of "Mana" Marcelina were many. There was the ditch in which we waded, made water-wheels and tried to catch the elusive waders, that quick darting insect which can skim over the surface of the water with so much agility. The orchard, the corrals all were used in turn as the scenes of our activities.

And when tired of playing we would turn to the conversation of our grandmothers for diversion. These two, cronies and contemporaries, never tired it seemed of talking over old times and events, many of which centered about this same farm house. For shortly after the American occupation troops had been quartered here, the location of the farm made it a natural outpost for defense of Taos from the raids of Apaches and Navajos. The former Indians were the most feared for their sudden savage attacks, although the Navajos were equally ferocious but seldom ventured that far North.

We would listen with interest as they would tell of the curiosity with which the population of Taos would flock to the vicinity to examine and comment on the different activities of the cavalry troops. Sundays would always find a good portion of the townspeople there, gaily dressed and in family groups, bringing their lunch with them so they could spend the day. Here they watched the soldiers drilling, grooming their mounts and at target practice. Relations between the people of Taos and the soldiers were very friendly because there was a realization on the part of the former that these new conquerors were serving as a guard against their much feared enemies "los herejes" or the heretics as the Indians were usually called.

Then it was that many friendships were begun which resulted in the marriage of some of these soldiers with Spanish families, making for mutual appreciation.

The arrangement of the different parts of the old farm house made it a natural fort. The walls of the living quarters on the south and east were continued on the west by a high adobe wall continued on the north. An adobe wall pierced by a strong wooden gate closed the gap between the Northern end, the front of the house on the east. All doors to living quarters were fashioned of thick hand hewn lumber and the windows were guarded by thick shutters with openings for loop-holes. The North walls of the stables and "dispensas" or granaries were blank except for conveniently placed loopholes. The enclosed corral served admirably as safe quarters for the troop's mounts. In the northeastern corner of the large kitchen was a fireplace of huge proportions. I have seen only one other of its size and construction. Open on two sides, made entirely of adobe, it was large enough for myself, a ten year old boy, to enter without stooping and standing erect under its bell-shaped roof gaze up to the sky through a chimney large enough for the entrance of an exceedingly fat St. Nicholas. Here meals for a whole company were put on to boil in large iron pots and roasted on the long iron spits which we had found and used for spears.

The part of the narrative for which we always waited impatiently was the account of the disastrous rout which the Indians inflicted on these troops on one occasion. I have no recollection of any other battle being recounted, perhaps there were, but the horror with which this one filled our young minds effectively erased memories of any other account. It seems that shortly after the posting of the troops at the farmhouse, they were ordered out in pursuit of a group of raiding savages. These Apaches, ignorant of the presence of the troops or in defiance of them, had raided some ranches nearby and had escaped with stock and captives, leaving behind not a few dead settlers. Their trail was easily followed as they were all for making haste in their get-away. Now these troops, new to the west and to fighting Indians, spurred their horses into a furious charge when the trail signs showed they were close to the Indians. This charge led them into a small thickly wooded valley surrounded by outcroppings of rocks.

Here the wily Indians had dismounted and hidden after sending their stock and saddle ponies ahead under guard of a certain of their party. As the troops rushed in their horses were stampeded by a painted horde of painted savages, uttering their demoniacal war hoop and fluttering blankets to further frighten the troop's horses. Many of the troopers were thrown or impaled on the junipers or scrub piñón which were so thick there. Completely demoralized, the scattered soldiers were made easy victims by the Apaches who easily dispatched the fallen or lanced the plunging horses as they came by them and finished his rider before his dying horse had fairly fallen to the ground.

Not all of the troops were killed, some having been saved by the very headlong rush of their frightened horses. Reassembling, the survivors returned cautiously to the scene of their defeat. The Indians were gone, satisfied with their surprise attack. They left behind them the mutilated remains of nearly half of the troop and took with them some of the cavalry horses as an added insult to the crest-fallen survivors.

As ready with their sympathy and help as they were with their admiration and interest the women of Taos hastened to minister to the wounded and prepare shrouds for the dead. My grandmother, although only twelve years old, had accompanied her grandmother, María Teresa, wife of Pablo Montoya, leader of the ill-fated Taos Rebellion. So it was that she could recount from her own recollection the events above set forth.

This ready solicitude of the people of Taos strengthened the bond of sympathy between the civilian population and the new government. It was further demonstrated by the crowds which followed coffin-laden military wagons to the graveyard where one grave received all of the victims of that fatal ambuscade.

Another house which served as an outpost was the home of the Jeantettes, located on a high point on the southwest edge of the town. Here a small group of soldiers had their quarters. Here also a large hall was the scene of many bailes which the officers gave and to which the townspeople were invited.

Some artistic officer had decorated one wall of this hall with the figure of an American Eagle with outspread wings. This figure was left there for many years after the soldiers had disappeared.

It was no wonder that after hearing these tales my friend and I would be moved to get on the slow plow horses and try to make them break into the semblance of a cavalry charge firing at imaginary Indians with imitation muskets through some of the few remaining loop-holes. Tangible evidence of the troopers remained in the distorted lumps of lead which we dug out of the thick adobe walls of the stables which had served as a back-stop for their target practice.

The Mexican War at Reserve

by H. P. Collier

It happened in the spring of 1884—election year, too. Had it not been spring and election year, no doubt this story would never have been written. Don Pedro Simpson was sheriff of Socorro County and was up for re-election. Many new people had come into the county between 1882 and 1884. Don Pedro sent his young deputy, Elfego Baca, to the western part of the county in search of votes. Baca had been at Milligan's plaza (now Reserve) several days when a bunch of cowboys rode into town from the ranches. Nature had on her holiday attire—the ground carpeted with green grass mingled with wildflowers of many colors, buds swelling and bursting on the trees, birds flitting from tree to tree calling lovingly for mates. Spring, indeed, after a long ice-bound winter! These cowboys were in tune with Nature: spring affected them like old wine. After saturating their systems with Milligan's famous liquors, they made a race track of the plaza's only street, using the rocks on the hillside as targets for their forty-fives. Finally, they rode swiftly out of town amid a swirl of dust and smoke and were gone.

Later Baca, accompanied by others, rode out and arrested one of these cowboys, Charley McCarthy, who now (1936) lives near Reserve, and brought him back under heavy guard. Swift riders rode to the S U ranch, on to the W S ranch near Alma telling of McCarthy's capture. The W S boys with the Alma deputy sheriff, Bechtol, rode to the S U ranch. Joining forces they rode into the plaza, thirty heavily armed, grim and determined men. All was quiet at the plaza and it was learned that McCarthy was being guarded at the lower plaza. A messenger was sent to Baca at the lower plaza asking him to bring his prisoner to Milligan's plaza to be tried before a justice of the peace according to law. Baca, McCarthy and others came. McCarthy was taken before the justice of the peace, fined five dollars, which he paid, and was released.

Racial feeling was bitter. Baca left the courtroom, walked down the street a short distance and went into a small picket house covered with dirt. Some of the cowboys mounted and started away, others went into Milligan's for refreshments. Here this affair should have ended, but it did not. Someone proposed that Baca should be asked to leave town. Captain French, Charley McCarthy, Hern and one or two others went to the shack where Baca was and knocked, but no answer. Hern stepped up and kicked the door; the answer was a bullet fired through the door, striking Hern in the abdomen, inflicting a fatal wound. Captain French and Charlie Moore exposed themselves and were immediately shot at by Baca, putting two bullet holes through Captain French's hat. Hern was taken to Milligan's where his wound was dressed and he was made as comfortable as possible. The others from the church across the street from Baca poured volley after volley into the door and window of the picket house where Baca was hiding. Those who had started away heard the shooting and came rushing back to town. Learning what had happened they all joined forces and the battle raged. Two messages went out from the battle front, one, the hated "greaser" has fatally shot a white man, the other, the despised "gringoes" are trying to kill Baca who has taken refuge in a picket house at Milligan's plaza. Men, arms and ammunition were eagerly sought by both sides.

Late in the evening it was thought Baca was dead, for no answering shot had come from the picket house for hours. A man stood up, a bullet slapped the adobe wall a few inches from his head. Baca was still alive. Guards were posted to prevent his escape in the night. Hern died during the night. Shooting was resumed at intervals during the morning. Scouts were sent out to watch the enemy. The Mexicans were heavily armed and moving on the plaza, the scouts reported. They appeared on the hills west of the plaza. Hundreds of shots were exchanged but no damage was done, the distance being too great. It was then decided to burn the house where Baca was. Men approached the house on the side where there were no openings and built fires against the picket walls. Soon Baca would be forced to come out; then his body would be riddled by bullets. Had it not been for the timely arrival of Mr. Rose, deputy sheriff from Socorro, many persons would have met death in the next few hours. He took charge of Baca and the opposing sides dissolved and moved away toward their homes; thus ended what is known locally as "The Mexican War." It was learned from Baca that he had saved his life because he had lain on the floor close to the wall nearest the street where the ground outside was much higher than the floor inside. The principals in this affair are both alive: Charley McCarthy lives near Reserve, Elfego Baca lives at Albuquerque. The old feud has long been forgotten and the two are close friends.

Pioneer Story: Mrs. Lorencita Miranda

by Edith L. Crawford

I was born August 10, 1861, in the town of Las Placitas, New Mexico, in Socorro County, New Mexico. (Las Placitas is now the town of Lincoln, and is in Lincoln County, New Mexico.) My father Gregorio Herrera married my mother Gerelda Torres in Manzano, New Mexico, about the year 1860. They moved to Las Placitas, New Mexico, and I was born there. On August 18, 1861, about ten days after I was born, my father was killed in a drunken row in Las Placitas. Another man was killed at the same time and we never were sure who did kill my father. After Father's death my mother went back to Manzano to live with her people. My mother gave me to one of my aunts, Trinidad Herrera, (who was nicknamed Chinita) who, with my mother, moved back to Las Placitas when I was about two years old. I have lived the rest of my life in Lincoln County. I will soon be 78 years old.

In the year 1869, when I was eight years old, all of the territory lying east of the Mal Pais, was created into Lincoln County, and the county seat was established at Las Placitas and the name was changed to Lincoln.

I was married to José Dolores Miranda in January, 1877. We were married in the Catholic Church at the Torres Ranch by Father Sambrano Tafoya of Manzano, New Mexico. This church is about six miles west of Lincoln, New Mexico. I remember that we had to walk about five miles to the church to get married.

My husband had a two-roomed adobe house built for us to live in. It had a dirt floor. We had no stove and I had to cook on the fireplace. All eight of my children were born in Lincoln. Seven of them are dead and buried there. My youngest son, Emelio Miranda, is married and has twelve children. He lives in Lincoln and is the post-master there. One of my grandsons lives with me on my little farm, a half mile west of the town of Lincoln. I raise a few chickens and a small garden which helps to keep me busy.

The house where I was born in Las Placitas (now Lincoln) stood on the site of the old Laws Sanitarium. The place then belonged to Sabino Gonzales, who was one of the men that helped build the old Torreón in 1855. My father-in-law Felipe Miranda also helped to build the Torreón. This old Torreón was rebuilt and dedicated in 1935, by the Chaves County Archaeological and Historical Society.

My husband and I were living on our farm just above Lincoln, New Mexico, all during the Lincoln County War. We liked both factions so we never took any part in the war. I remember the day the McSween home was burned. We could see the flames and smoke from our house but we stayed at home for we were scared to death to stick our heads out of the house. We could also hear some of the shooting. Billy the Kid came to our house several times and drank coffee with us. We liked him for he was always nice to the Spanish people and they all liked him.

My aunt, Chinita Herrera, started to walk to Socorro, New Mexico, to see her brother. (I do not remember the year.) She was seen on the road to Socorro by Mrs. Susan McSween Barber who gave her a drink of water and some food. She was not far from a ranch house and Mrs. Barber thought she would get along all right, but my aunt was never seen or heard of again. We never did know what became of her.

My mother married a man by the name of Octaviano Salas and lived in Lincoln, New Mexico until her death in September, 1926.

My husband José Dolores Miranda died October 28, 1928, in Lincoln and was buried here.

Pioneer Story: Rumaldo Águilar Durán

by Edith L. Crawford

I came to Lincoln County, New Mexico, in 1867, from Franklin, Texas (now El Paso, Texas), and have lived in Lincoln County for fifty-one years.

My father, José Águilar, married my mother, Salomé Durán, at Old Mesilla, New Mexico (I have forgotten the date). They moved to the Upper Mimbres Valley in Grant County, New Mexico, where my father worked in the mines at San Vicente, Luna County, New Mexico, which is near what is now Silver City, New Mexico.

After my father's death my mother went to live with her father and mother, Nestor and Santos Durán, who lived in the Upper Mimbres Valley, not far from us. After a few years my grandparents and my mother moved to Franklin, Texas (now El Paso, Texas), where they lived for several years. My grandfather worked at his trade as a carpenter and mill worker. While we were living in Franklin my mother married a man by the name of Amado Montero. They had one child, a girl named Nestora.

In September 1887 we left Franklin, Texas for Lincoln, New Mexico. We traveled in a covered wagon drawn by two small ponies. In the crowd were my grandfather and grandmother Durán, my step-father Amado Montero, my mother, my step-sister Nestora, and myself.

It took us about a month to make the trip. The sand was so deep between Franklin, Texas and Tularosa, New Mexico, that we had to travel very slowly. While we were traveling through the sand we broke an axle on the wagon and had to lay over for a week while the men went up in the mountains and got a piece of timber to make a new axle for the wagon.

We came by way of Tularosa, the Mescalero Indian Agency, through Dark Canyon to the Ruidoso River and up Gavilan Canyon to Alto, New Mexico. From there we traveled almost due north, down Cedar Creek Canyon, by the "V" Ranch, and on toward Fort Stanton Army Post. Just before we reached Fort Stanton we heard shooting. We were all very much afraid of the Indians and my grandfather, who was driving the wagon, drove off to one side of the road in the brush. Leaving the rest of us hidden in the brush, my grandfather and step-father took their guns and sneaked up the side of the mountain to see what was going on. When they got to where they could see they found that it was soldiers from Fort Stanton at target practice. That was the only scare we got on our trip but the men always kept their guns where they could reach them, as the Indians had been giving a lot of trouble in this part of the country in the early eighties. From Fort Stanton we traveled southeast down the Río Bonito and arrived at Lincoln, New Mexico, about the middle of October, 1887.

We first lived in a house belonging to the Catholic Priest just south of the old Catholic Church. My grandfather worked at his trade as carpenter. Sometime later, I do not know the exact date, my grandfather bought a small farm about a mile south of Lincoln, where we raised corn and vegetables.

On July 20, 1900, I was married to Honorata Mirabal. There were seven children born to us, six boys and one girl. Aurra, Juan, Simón, Romundo, Isidor, Enrique and Manuel. All of these children died in infancy. Not a one lived to be over three months old. When our last child, Manuel, died we adopted my wife's brother's little boy who was the same age as our Manuel. We called him Teodoro Durán. We have three adopted children now. Teodoro, who is married and lives here in Carrizozo, a girl named Emma Lucero, who was fourteen months old when we adopted her and who is now eighteen and lives with us here in Carrizozo, and we adopted a baby boy named Isidoro Martínez, who was two months old when we got him. He is eleven now and lives with us here in Carrizozo.

In 1915 my wife and I moved from Lincoln, New Mexico, to Encinoso, New Mexico. A man named Sam Farmer and I put in a general merchandise store and had the post office, too. In November, 1918, I was elected sheriff of Lincoln County and served for two years. In December, 1918, I moved to Carrizozo, New Mexico, and have lived here ever since.

I served as County Commissioner for Lincoln County from 1906 to 1916. I was Assessor for two years, 1925 and 1926. I was Treasurer for two years, 1931 and 1932.

When I was a small child my step-father left my mother and my grandparents raised me and I took their name of Durán. My grandfather and grandmother both died while we were living in Lincoln, New Mexico. I do not remember the dates of their death. I do not know whatever became of my step-father. My mother is still living and lives with me here in Carrizozo. My half sister is now Mrs. Nestora Griego and lives here in Carrizozo, New Mexico.

Source of Information: Rumaldo Durán, aged 58 years, Carrizozo, New Mexico.

Padre Antonio José Martínez of Taos, New Mexico

by Luis Martínez

Antonio José Martínez was born at Abiquiu, New Mexico, on the 17th day of January, 1793, his parents being Antonio Severiano Martínez and María del Carmen Santistevan. At the age of 10 years he attended what was then known as the alphabetical school, learning in a short time to read and write correctly and the first principles of arithmetic. After attending school for two terms in his native village his family moved to the Taos valley and young Martínez was put to work at different duties on his father's extensive farm, but he utilized all his spare time in reading, writing and going over his numerical problems with an enthusiasm and an interest very rare in those by-gone days.

In the year of 1812 Antonio José married María de la Luz Martínez, also a native of the village of Abiquiu and a daughter of Manuel Martínez and María de la Luz Quintana. No relationship existed between the young couple, although bearing the same family name. Young Martínez's wife died a little over a year after their marriage, leaving a baby girl which was named Luz and who died in 1825.

Finding himself a widower when still a young man, and always fired by that interest and love for education which he had displayed since his tender years, Antonio José Martínez decided to study for the priesthood to which his parents gladly assented, furnishing him the financial means with which to undertake his lofty project, and on the 10th day of March, 1817, he left for Mexico and entered the famous Seminary of Durángo where he remained until the early part of 1823 when he completed his courses in Latin, Grammar, Rhetoric, Ontology, Metaphysics, Theology, General Physics, Mathematics and the Roman Rubrics. On the 10th day of March, 1821, he received what is known as the four minor orders; on the following day the order of sub-deacon and on the 25th of the same month the order of deacon. On the 16th day of February, 1822, he was ordained as a presbyter, and three days later he celebrated his first mass and was authorized to administer confession, preach, administer benediction and in fact to perform all the ecclesiastical duties of a Catholic priest.

Padre Antonio José Martínez became to be known as "The Presbyter," and practiced the priesthood in Durángo from the first day of June, 1822, until January of the following year when he returned to the home of his parents in New Mexico. In November, 1823, he was put in charge of the curacy of Tomé; serving there for a time, he was given charge of the church of Santo Tomás de Abiquiu, his native place, in May, 1824. But in July of the same year he was transferred to the curacy of Taos where he served interim until 1830 when an ecclesiastical synod was convoked at Durángo, Mexico, to which he was requested to attend by Archbishop Zubiría. The liberal ideas of Father Martínez brought him into conflict with some of the diehards at the synod, but he bested his opponents and, after all formalities had been observed, he was given full charge of the curacy of Taos.

The Mexican constitution forbade the tolerance of cults, except Catholicism, but Father Martínez came out for it and in 1830 he wrote a book (which was never published), in which he stated that religious freedom was really necessary for the security and stability of a prosperous and free government; that Mexico, already free from the yoke of intolerant Spain, could insure the happiness and prosperity of its people and avoid the danger of internecine strife by conceding to its inhabitants the enjoyment of religious tolerance.

In 1826, Father Martínez, having decided to make his permanent residence in Taos, and knowing that the cornerstone of the advancement of any people is education, established in his home at Taos a college to which young people of either sex were admitted. He had employed teachers at his own expense, and he supervised all the classes. Boys attending the college from distant points were furnished board and lodging free of charge in the house of the Presbyter. Twenty of his disciples became Catholic Priests, others lawyers, and others followed commerce or politics. Hon. Antonio Joseph, who eventually went to Washington as territorial delegate, and Hon. Francisco Manzanares were two of the many who owed their learning to Father Martínez. The Father himself studied during this time the Code of Rights of Spain and the part of the Mexican code dealing with international law, mastering both of these branches in 1839.

In 1829, Father Martínez, after making a survey of the lamentable condition in which the people of the territory existed due to the usurious charges that the clergy had been permitted to impose on them for religious services, protested to the Departmental Assembly against such abuses of the clergy, contending that such methods were a betrayal of the Catholic faith and also of the most sacred principles of civilized peoples. His protest was so strongly and wisely worded that the same was not only approved by the Assembly, but was passed by that body to the National Congress. The press disseminated it all over Mexico and as many of the most prominent men of the republic sided with the Taos Priest in that regard, the Mexican Congress, in 1843, put a stop to the arbitrary practice that the clergy had exercised until then of exacting exorbitant dues from the poor masses. This humanitarian and fearless attitude of the Presbyter in coming to the defense of an outraged people, and his insistency in later years to collect a thousand dollars that he loaned to Archbishop Lamy were in fact the chief motives for the hostility that Lamy and his friends displayed against him which finally culminated in Father Martínez being deprived of his priestly rank by Lamy. But the Presbyter held his ground like the real Spaniard that he was, and, being a man of ample means, built his own church and kept his flock together until death.

In 1830, 1831 and 1836 Father Martínez served as a member of what was known as the Asamblea Departamental de Nuevo Mexico (the equivalent of our State Legislature,) and that august body by unanimous vote maintained him as speaker and leader.

In 1833, when His Excellency Archbishop Don José Antonio Laureano de Zubiría visited New Mexico for the first time, he brought to Father Martínez what are known in ecclesiastical terms as Pontifical Letters, sent to him directly by His Holiness the Pope.

In the early part of 1837 a rebellion broke out at Santa Cruz in which the Indians of the Pueblos of San Juan, Cochiti, Santo Domingo and San Felipe took part. One of the first victims of the uprising was Governor Alvino Pérez. The brothers Ramón and Santiago Abreu, prominent in public life, were murdered by the rebels near Santo Domingo.

The rebellion spread out to Taos and José Gonzales and another man known as "El Coyote" Vigil joined as leaders. Padre Martínez endeavored to the limit to persuade the seditious mob to lay down their arms peacefully, but it was too late, and he had to call on General Armijo at Santa Fe, where he not only offered his services to Armijo but impressed on him the necessity of putting down the rebellion at all costs. The services of the Padre were accepted, but for some reason it took Armijo a long time to organize the militia, and he did not meet the rebels in actual battle until the 7th day of August, 1838, when the two forces clashed at the Puertecito de Pojoaque, a few miles north of Santa Fe. The rebels took to flight almost immediately, many of them being killed by the militia while running.

Armijo arrived with his forces at Santa Cruz that evening and took up quarters in the convent. José Gonzales, who had been proclaimed Governor by his followers, realizing now his defeat, came to General Armijo addressing him thus: "Cómo le va, compañero?" (How are you, partner?) Then he told Armijo that he had come to ask guarantees for his people, to which the General replied that none of his requests would be granted. Then, turning to Father Martínez, Armijo spoke these eventful words, that so many writers have endeavored to translate into English but none so far has done it correctly. Said Armijo: "Padre Martínez, confiese a este genízaro para que deb cinco balacos," which verbatim would be: "Father Martínez, confess this genizaro (of mixed blood) so he can be given five shots;" in substance: "Administer confession to this genizaro to have him shot." And the "new Governor" confessed and was shot.

Shortly the uprising was subdued and most of the other rebellious leaders were also shot. But as crops had been destroyed by the marauding bands especially in the Taos valley, the danger of famine became imminent. The noble Presbyter came to the rescue. Possessor of a big estate in which bumper crops were raised, he always kept large quantities of grain in storage on which the needy could at all times depend without any cost. This time Padre Martínez appointed a committee for the purpose of distributing grain and provisions which he bountifully supplied by throwing his bins and larders open; thus, through his magnanimity, he not only averted the impending suffering, but seed for the coming planting season was also insured.

In 1835, and while still a leading member of the Departmental Assembly, Padre Martínez directed his attention to another important undertaking and that was the establishment of a printing plant at Taos which was to blaze the trail of journalism in the soil of the west. In it he published *El Crepusculo* (*The Dawn*), which was the first periodical published west of the Missouri river. He also printed many of the text books needed in his college, such as works in orthography, grammar, rhetoric, physics, arithmetic, etc., and many religious books. Most of the books he printed were his own originals, but some were reprints, two of them being *Points in Logic* and *The Bill of Rights of Castile and the Indies*. Some of those books still exist and besides being masterpieces from an enlightening point of view, are a credit to the printing profession for their clean graphic appearance and their mechanical arrangement. Don Jesús María Baca had charge of his printing plant.

The Presbyter was always opposed to the concession of land grants to any one, predicting since those remote days that such methods of favoritism practiced first by Spain and then by Mexico would eventually retard the development of New Mexico. He also vehemently opposed the granting of permits to French and American traders to build forts in any part of the territory, contending that these foreign traders were constantly inciting the nomad Indians to commit depredations in the native settlements and furnishing them with liquor and arms. He also predicted that the said traders would in time bring about trouble enough as to cause the overthrow of the established authority in New Mexico. The Mexican government, however, treated his warnings with indifference.

But, opposed as Padre Martínez had been to the intrusion of foreign traders, he nevertheless, when the change of government became inevitable, accepted philosophically the command of destiny, and cooperated heartily with the American authorities in the establishment of a permanent government under the stars and stripes as will be noted farther on.

While talking to his disciples in the month of September, 1846, after General Kearny had taken possession of Santa Fe and established American authority over New Mexico, the Presbyter addressed them in these words: "Boys, you came to this college with the purpose of studying for the priesthood; in this connection I have endeavored as much as possible to help you attain the desired end. But, having now a change of government, a change of ideas might be necessary. The policy of the American government moves in complete harmony with the tolerance of cults and a complete separation of the church and state. From this you can easily surmise that the clergy has been crippled." "What, then, is the form of the American Government?" enquired one of the pupils. "Republican," answered the Presbyter, adding: "You may say that the American government might resemble a donkey, but on this donkey the lawyer, and not the clergy, shall ride."

The American government had not been long established in New Mexico when the loyalty of Father Martínez was put to a real test in an emergency seldom equaled in the annals of western America: I refer to the bloody Taos rebellion that broke out in the early hours of the 19th of January, 1847, when the Indians of the Taos Pueblo, led by some desperate Mexicans, and under the influence of liquor, attacked the town of Taos, murdering Hon. Charles Bent, Governor of the territory, the Sheriff Louis Lee, the Prefect Don Cornelio Vigil, Don Narciso Beaubien and many others. The Americans who were able to get to the house of the Presbyter together with a great number of natives were immediately admitted by that great humanitarian who at once organized adequate armed protection for the persecuted and sent a messenger to Santa Fe calling for American troops after the arrival of which he offered his house and his services to the American commander, cooperating with him until the rebellion was quelled. As I have already given a full detail of this horrible uprising in an article entitled "The Taos Massacre" which soon will appear in the press, I will limit my comment on this subject now to what I have already stated.

The Presbyter was elected to the first territorial legislature under the American government in 1851 and by the unanimous vote of that body was selected as speaker and the old records show that he was the leading mind in the deliberations of that legislative session and in the drafting of laws. With equal honors he served in the territorial legislature in 1852 and 1853.

Having arrived at his old age possessing considerable wealth and large farms from inheritance of his parents and the fruits of his labors,

Padre Martínez divided most of his estate and personal property amongst his brothers, leaving enough to continue his charity work amongst the needy to whom he ministered until his last days, and also to keep him in comfort while living. Conscious of the approaching end during his last illness he kept reminiscing past events with an evident clear conscience and repeating quite often, "Oh Lord, Thy will Must Be Done!" And so, on the 27th day of July, 1867, Antonio José Martínez, the great Presbyter, the first educator, the first journalist of New Mexico, and, from a Christian and human point of view, one of the worthiest sons of colonial America, answered the call of his Creator and passed to the great beyond.

Source of Information: Doña Ana María L. Salazar, maternal grandmother of Luis Martínez, Raton, New Mexico; Don Manuel Martínez; Major Pedro Sánchez, Taos, New Mexico.

The Taos Massacre—1847

by Luis Martínez

Due to the negligence of the Mexican government, General Manuel Armijo, who was Governor of the Department of New Mexico in 1846, found himself at the head of a semi-destitute and disorganized army when the tidings of the approach of General Stephen W. Kearny and his forces reached Santa Fe in the summer of 1846 and, apparently, lacking himself the qualities of a real leader and organizer, he abandoned New Mexico to the invaders and crossed into Old Mexico.

While traditionally patriotic, but well acquainted with the indifference with which the Mexican government had treated New Mexico, the natives in a majority did not look with disfavor at the probability that their Department would be annexed to the progressive and liberal republic of the north—the United States.

Also, admonished by the able Don Juan Bautista Vigil y Alarid, who had become military Governor ad interim after Armijo's flight, to submit peacefully to American authority, the majority of the New Mexicans, especially those of Santa Fe and vicinities, accepted the order of destiny and approved of the territorial government organized by General Kearny after his arrival in Santa Fe, August 18th, 1846.

But to the north and northeast of Santa Fe, there were three important towns with surrounding settlements whose inhabitants apparently had not been taken much into account in the formalities attendant to the change of government. To the northeast of Santa Fe there were Las Vegas and Mora with their proud Spanish characteristic, but with a population whose temper, even to this day, puts them in the category of the rough and ready, fire-eating element. Taos also counted with a potential Indian Pueblo just a few miles from the county seat.

As far as the inhabitants of the three places above mentioned were concerned, all that was needed for a bloody outbreak against the Americans was leadership, and that soon appeared in the person of a

"Mexican" citizen who in reality was a die-hard Spaniard, was Colonel Don Diego Archuleta, of Río Arriba county, who had been on Armijo's staff and who, aided by Don Tomás Ortiz and Don José Manuel Gallegos, of Santa Fe, organized a secret movement that had as its object the overthrow of American authority in New Mexico.

Historians have done an injustice to the three leaders just mentioned in stating that their plan was to assassinate all Americans found in New Mexico. It is hard even to imagine that men possessing the high culture and education that they possessed could harbor such a diabolical thought, and it is safe to assume that the killing of civilians did not form part of their plans.

Colonel Archuleta, having real military training and laboring under the delusion that a strong Mexican army would advance from the south to retake Santa Fe, conceived the idea of organizing the masses still loyal to Mexico to harass the Americans from the north with guerrilla warfare and then close in on them when the expected Mexican army contacted them from the south. If his plan had materialized as intended, perhaps the tragedy of the Alamo, in a bigger scale, would have been repeated at Santa Fe. But the plan was destined to fail for two reasons: one was that the strong Mexican army that the Colonel had imagined did not come from the south nor from any other direction; the other reason was that having enlisted the Indians from the Taos Pueblo in his guerrilla project, Archuleta committed the grave mistake of allowing them to partake plentifully of liquor which turned them into real savages and they ran out of control, that being the real cause of the butchery at Taos and the Río Hondo. As stated repeatedly by Colonel Archuleta in post bellum verbal narratives of the bloody Taos uprising, his intention was to make prisoners of war of the Americans in Taos and to furnish his forces with the necessary provisions from the stores owned by some of the Americans. But the Indians, already intoxicated as before stated, when Taos was attacked, disobeyed all orders and the massacre ensued.

The Governor of the Territory, Mr. Charles Bent, had heard rumors of a contemplated conspiracy for an uprising and had taken what he thought to be the necessary measures to nip the said conspiracy in the bud. Thinking that all danger of a rebellious outbreak had been removed, he had come to Taos to visit his family on the 14th of January, 1847, and the eventful night of the 19th of the same month found him on the very same spot of the barbaric assault and he was one of the victims. The Indians first killed the Sheriff, whom historians call Stephen Lee, but who was known to the old timers in Taos as Louis Lee; then they killed the Prefect, Cornelio Vigil; then Governor Bent, Pablo Jaramillo and Narciso Beaubien.

The attack was as rapid as it was bloody, and the first inkling the community had of the killings was when a frightened crowd started yelling at the door of the house of Father Antonio José Martínez, calling in Spanish: "For God's sake open the door! Open it!! The Indians are murdering Don Carlos Bent, Don Luis Lee and others!!!" The Presbyter, as Father Martínez was known, immediately admitted in his house the alarmed crowd which included the families of the murdered Americans, a brother of the Sheriff whom the natives called "General" Lee, and a large number of Mexicans, men, women and children.

Father Martínez, seeing the rebellious mob approaching, ordered every door in his house locked securely and, possessing a good supply of firearms and ammunition as the epoch demanded due to the repeated incursions of nomadic Indians, armed all of his male servants and directed them to build breastworks on the top of the building and other points of vantage and to repel any assault at all cost. The Presbyter also sent at once a courier to Colonel Price at Santa Fe acquainting him of the Taos rebellion; then the magnanimous priest continued to direct the defense of his house personally and held the rebels at bay until the arrival of Colonel Price and his troops in the month of February, 1849, thus saving the lives of the only Americans that escaped the fury of that terrible carnage which is known as the Taos massacre. Perhaps it won't be amiss to state here that Father Martínez has received a posthumous reward for protecting the lives of the persecuted Americans in time of real danger, the libel of false accusations of pseudo writers and ignoramuses who at different times have endeavored to write the history of New Mexico turned upside down, some of them having gone so far as to accuse the great Presbyter of having been the instigator of the sanguinary drama which I am now describing.

Early the next day after the night of blood in Taos, a party of Indians and a few Mexicans attacked the distillery owned by a certain

Mr. Simon Turley, on the shores of the Río Hondo river about two miles west of the present village of Valdéz, formerly San Antonio, and about ten miles northwest of the town of Taos. Mr. Turley and five other Americans were at the distillery at the time of the assault; they fought for about two days and managed to kill some of the Indians, but finally, being vastly outnumbered, Turley and four of his companions were killed in the distillery and one that got away wounded was overtaken in the nearby hills and was also killed.

Historians have committed the error of placing the scene of the murders of Turley and his friends at Arroyo Seco, and also of stating that the man who escaped, wounded, was not killed. As the narrator is guided by reliable information obtained from old timers who were "on the ground" and knew the facts, I feel in a position to say that I am stating them as they actually occurred.

It was known at the time of Mr. Turley's tragic death that he had a big sum of money in his distillery, estimated at not less than $40,000.00. The supposition is that he buried said treasure during the fight, but all the digging and searching that has been done at the old distillery and its premises by different parties at different times since the death of Turley to the present day have failed to disclose the coveted cache. The ruins of the old distillery still stand as a memento of the romantic and bloody days that have passed into history.

As I have mentioned before that Colonel Archuleta had enlisted the cooperation of Don Tomás Ortiz and Don José Manuel Gallegos in his anti-American undertaking, I have to deviate a little from my Taos narrative to state that from information that the writer has gathered it appears that the two lieutenants of Archuleta struck for victuals and prisoners in the towns of Mora and Las Vegas at the same time that Taos was assaulted. But although some Americans were killed in both of the above mentioned places, the attacks never developed to the magnitude of the Taos outbreak. What became of Ortiz and Gallegos after the uprising was quelled is unknown to the writer.

It took Colonel Price and his forces longer to reach the scene of action in Taos than could be reasonably expected considering the emergency. And again I have to disagree with the historians in regard to the date of Colonel Price's arrival in Taos. Most historians set the 3rd day of February, 1847, as the date when the American forces arrived in Taos. But the writer, trusting once more the details given to him by reliable old timers, especially those close to Father Martínez, will say that, according to that information, Colonel Price and his soldiers did not reach Taos until the 15th of February, 1847. Of course, we must not forget that the American soldiers had to fight two minor battles with rebel forces during their march to Taos, one at Santa Cruz and the other at Embudo. But those were only little engagements from which the Americans easily came out victorious and could not have detained them for such a long time.

Colonel Price established his headquarters in the house of Father Martínez, and then went and sized up the situation at the Taos Indian Pueblo from a distance. Next day the real attack on the Pueblo began. The Indians fortified themselves in the church and fought for about three days with everything they had, but a terrific artillery fire concentrated on the church soon began to show its effects and the Indians had to surrender after suffering heavy casualties in killed and wounded. The Americans suffered a heavier loss than most historians have reported, according to eyewitnesses of the fight.

The rebellion quelled, a court-martial was held in the house of Father Martínez, and Pablo Montoya, one of the Mexican leaders of the rebellion, was sentenced to die. The other leaders were tried by the district court and most of them got a death sentence.

As concerns Colonel Archuleta, he had been traveling southward since right after the abortive Taos uprising. First he came towards his home situated in the settlement known as Los Luceros, about ten miles north of Española, on the East side of the Río Grande, but upon learning that a detachment of American soldiers were already searching his house and the neighborhood for him, he remained in the hills for a few days until one night he sneaked into the house of a relative from which he emerged the next day disguised as a female Indian servant and, going right past the soldiers who were so eager to meet him, he just kept on going south until he joined the main body of the Mexican army which by that time was battling the Americans far to the south of the border. He was given the command of a unit and served all through the war, returning to his family in New Mexico after the treaty of peace was signed. After his return to this country, Colonel Archuleta became an American citizen and followed his profession as a lawyer, serving also in the territorial legislature. He died in Santa Fe during a session of the legislature. A daughter of the Colonel, Miss Carlota Archuleta, and a granddaughter, Miss Adela Lucero, still live in the neighborhood of the San Juan Pueblo in Río Arriba county; and another granddaughter, Mrs. Mercedes L. Ulibarrí, lives in Tierra Amarilla, county seat of Río Arriba county.

Source of Information: Traditional knowledge of family.

Hallucinations and a Wildcat Venture

by Reyes Martínez

*I*t was in the early spring of the year 1880 that representatives of a mining company came to the village of Arroyo Hondo and contracted with the residents for the right to conduct placer mining operations throughout the little valley, on the lands not used for farming and, also, along the bed of the river. The contract specified that only local labor was to be employed in all operations, wherever practicable; also, that only surplus water was to be used for the purpose.

The first work done was the widening of the Atalalla ditch, which served to irrigate that north half of the little valley, to increase its flow of water. This job was in the charge of one of the engineers of the company, who acted as foreman. The widening of this ditch was finished within thirty days and the workmen were then employed in laying the pipe and the flumes along the arroyos and the hillsides, also along the river. The washing of dirt started soon thereafter. Mining operations continued for two years, or till the close of 1881, which created a boom for the little village.

It was at this time that Don Julian (Julian A. Martínez) started his little store and saloon and established the first post office in the village (all in a small, 12 x 22 ft. room). Two other men had ventured in the merchandise business previous to Don Julian, but had failed and closed doors within a short time. Don Julian, it seems, started just at the right time and his business increased by leaps and bounds, many a time requiring the assistance of his young wife, Doña Marina, to attend to the customers. The men worked diligently all week and celebrated on Saturday nights at the little store and saloon, gambling and drinking.

Among the workmen employed was Pascual Padilla (name fictitious), a handsome, well-built man in his late thirties, who was married to one of the fairest young matrons of the village. Through some strange turn of fate, the foreman, himself a handsome man, became intimately familiar with Padilla's wife, till an infatuation for each other developed between them. The husband seemingly sensed their intimacy. Suspicion and worry seemed to take a hold of his being, and his formerly jovial disposition changed to one of melancholy and despondency. As time passed, the woman and her paramour became more bold in their illicit relations, being often seen together in public. The situation finally reached the breaking point and Padilla and his wife parted company. Padilla left his job with the mining company and went to work in the state of Colorado, leaving his young wife and little daughter to shift for themselves.

After two years of intensive work, the company closed down, having found no gold in paying quantities. It had been, more or less, a wildcat venture from the start, and in the early spring of 1882 they removed their machinery and left the country, the foreman going along, too, thereby ending an illicit romance that broke up a once happy home. Pascual Padilla remained away for several months thereafter, then returned to his native village. Relatives of the estranged couple managed to effect a reconciliation between them; but Padilla never was his former genial self again. As time passed, he became sullen and morose. His despondency increased. Strange hallucinations seemed to creep into his mind. He became taciturn and avoided company, and he passed many a while wandering up and down the river, muttering incoherently. At times reminiscences of his former connection with the mining company filled his thoughts. At the beginning of the mining operations, Padilla and the foreman had become friendly, attached to each other (a friendship which was soon after to cool off), referring to each other as "partner." Now the mere mention of the word "partner" or the word "company," for some strange reason aroused in him an ill-feeling toward the person who inadvertently mentioned the word, a feeling which he always expressed by some sarcastic remark, indirectly said, but obvious in its meaning. Padilla, before ill luck struck him, was a man brilliant and quick of mind and had a remarkable ability, although uneducated, for composing poetry, which even his domestic troubles had failed to diminish, and when the occasion presented itself (at the mention of the words, "partner" or "company"), he composed a verse almost in the twinkling of an eye. Such a verse usually referred to some fault or incident unfavorably connected with the life of the person for whom intended, the person using either of the "baneful" words. There was always fear of a more violent outburst from him, and he usually was not molested further.

Pascual Padilla and his wife finally separated for good. He took their daughter, now a young maiden, and lived with her till his death, about the year 1900. He died ever sensitive to the last to the mention of the words "compañero" and "compañía."

There is only one case mentioned where serious consequences were narrowly averted as a result of the mention of the word "partner." This was an occasion when Antonio Herrera, a neighbor, went to Padilla's house and asked him for a saw to cut some boards, saying to him: "Compañero (partner), will you let me have your saw for a few minutes?" Herrera had a habit of addressing mostly everybody as "compañero," on account of which he was called "Pane" (pania), an abbreviated form of the word compañero by most of the men of the village. Padilla immediately became indignant at the unintentional insult on the part of Herrera, and being a bigger and stronger man, caught and overpowered Herrera, and, placing one foot on him to hold him down while he held his (Herrera's) head with one hand, he took the saw, which was close by, and was about to saw off Herrera's head when his wife, hearing his loud appeals for help, entered the room just in time to save his neck, hitting Padilla a blow on the head and felling him with a club that she had picked up on the way over from her house. Pane, thereafter, was more cautious in the use of the word compañero (partner). His narrow escape at the hands of Padilla almost cured him of the habit.

Source of Information: Julian A. Martínez, Santa Fe, New Mexico.

Wamsley's Crossing

by Reyes N. Martínez

A column of smoke arising above the horizon at a point one hundred yards above the junction of the Hondo river with the Río Grande indicated to Julian Arellano, a resident of the lower town in the village of Arroyo Hondo, pilot and keeper of the boats, that some person wished to be ferried across the river. He would hurry down immediately, untie one of his boats, and paddle across the river to bring over sometimes a lonely passenger, on other occasions several persons and one or more wagons that had previously been taken apart at the top of the hill and brought down the steep path, together with their cargo of goods, on the shoulders of the men. Charging twenty-five cents per single passenger, and from fifty cents to one dollar for each wagon and its load of goods, the business was considerably remunerative to the intelligent pilot.

This was during the period previous to the year 1892; then no road existed between the Taos Valley and the west side of the Río Grande. However, the building of the Río Grande railroad from Colorado into Taos county and down south to Santa Fe, together with the mining boom at Amizette on the upper Hondo river, made the construction of a road and bridge over the Río Grande river an imperative necessity for the transportation of mining machinery, merchandise and passengers.

Thus it was that in the year 1892 the people of Arroyo Hondo, under the supervision of a Mr. Wamsley, an old pioneer that had come to Taos in the late eighties, built a road starting at a point one and a half miles west of the village and leading down the lower canyon of the Hondo river to a point about one hundred yards above the junction of the Hondo with the Río Grande. There a bridge was built across and a road up the steep west slope. The location became known as Wamsley's Crossing. This is an interesting scenic attraction, and is, also, historically connected with the mining developments on the upper Hondo river. This was originally a toll road, but was taken over by the state highway department several years ago, and an excellent highway is now being constructed, replacing the old, steep Wamsley road.

Standing at a point directly opposite the mouth of the Hondo river and facing the east, about one hundred feet down the descent on the west side, a magnificent view spreads out before the observer; the gully of the Hondo river joining the black chasm of the Río Grande ravine in striking formation; the slumbering valley of the village of Arroyo Hondo beyond to the east; and the grandeur of the mountain range in the distance furnishing an impressive background to the picture.

Wamsley's Crossing may be reached by taking a road branching off westward from state highway three at the corner of the J. I. Rael store, in the village of Arroyo Hondo, the distance being about two and one-half miles. Besides interesting scenery, good fishing and bathing at a nearby hot spring are available.

The Masons

by L. Raines

Jesús and Epitacio Mason were the most important rancheros (small farmers) of Tinaja. They were very poor when they came from Sonora riding their burros and driving a pack animal with the image of the Virgin strapped on his back. They settled near the spring where Pablo Candalarias had a choza (hut) and used an ox and a burro as a team to break the soil to plant the field of frijoles (beans). Their small herd prospered, and soon they married girls from the nearby villages over the mountains and built homes. They operated a cantinita (small saloon, bar room) and an inn, since they had fortunately chosen a location for their ranch on the freight trail from San Rafael and Camp Apache by way of El Morro to Xuni and other western villages.

Cristóbal Romero was a captive Navajo slave. He had been reared in the home of Epitacio's mother-in-law, but when his mistress, la señorita Romero, had married and gone over the mountain to live, he had gone too and had become very devoted to his new master, Epitacio, whom he called Hermano (brother).

For several years the brothers were partners in business, but trouble arose over the division of profits. Jesús decided to end the contention and seize for himself and his family the business. He hired Cristóbal Romero to kill Epitacio.

On the night set by Jesús for the murder, Cristóbal was stationed near the cantinita. He was to shoot the first man who stepped out of the door. Jesús, Epitacio, and the freighters played cards. Soon the angry voices of the quarreling brothers were heard above the conversation in the room. Epitacio calmly remained seated, because Cristóbal had revealed the plot to his beloved hermano, Epitacio. Jesús, in his anger, flung the door open and stepped outside. He dropped dead with the bullet from Cristóbal's gun in his heart. Cristóbal was surrounded and killed before Epitacio could utter a word in his defense. Vengeance was quick where there was no law.

Source of Information: Elizabeth Morgan, "Brief Sketches of Regional Tales of Western New Mexico," A. M. Thesis, New Mexico Normal University, 1935. Translated from Spanish as told by Estabans Baca.

Old Days in Socorro, New Mexico

by N. Howard Thorp

The Citizens of Socorro New Mexico, mostly Americans, during Christmas week held a church festival; this was in 1881.

Mr. A. M. Conklin, who was at that time editor of the Socorro Sun, conducted the services. This was the Mr. Conklin who in 1879 arrived on the stage to Las Vegas, and with his wife saw the four outlaws, "Dutch" Henry, John Dorsey, Jim West, and Bill Randall hanging by their necks to the windmill tower in front of the Ilfeld store on the Plaza of old Las Vegas.

Leaving Las Vegas, the Conklins moved to Albuquerque. During the services in the Socorro church already alluded to, two Mexicans, Abran and Onofre Baca, pretty drunk, entered the church. Mr. Conklin— as these two were noisy—told them to keep quiet or leave the church. Mad and drunk the two wanted to fight but eventually they left. After the services were over Conklin with his wife left the church. As they were going down the steps Abran Baca caught Mrs. Conklin by the arm, and pulled her away from her husband's side, as Onofre Baca shot and killed Mr. Conklin on the church steps.

Posses were sent in all directions after the murderers, but the Bacas eluded them, and got into Old Mexico. The Governor of the State of New Mexico offered a reward of five hundred dollars for their capture, and the Citizens of Socorro also offered five hundred dollars for their capture dead or alive. This offer of a reward and description of the two men was broadcast over the west, and a copy eventually was received by the Texas Rangers stationed at Isleta below El Paso, Texas on the Río Grande.

The Bacas at that time happened to have an uncle José Baca, who was county Judge of El Paso county Texas, who also owned a large store at Isleta, which was at that time the County Seat.

On receiving the description of the two men, and the offer of the reward, young Sergeant Gillett—of Captain Baylor's company of rangers—watched the home and store of Judge Baca for several weeks, but with no luck.

In the month of March in 1882, a man came to Gillett, and told that he had seen two well-dressed Mexican "Strangers" sitting on the porch of Judge Baca's home.

Taking some rangers with him, Gillett captured the two men, believing them to be the Baca brothers, and started for New Mexico with his prisoners. Before he reached El Paso, he was overtaken by Judge Baca, who offered one thousand dollars for their release—just let them slide out into the Bosque, said the Judge, and I will give you the cash. Gillett told him he couldn't buy him at any price; the Honorable Judge thereupon returned to Isleta, and Gillett continued on towards New Mexico.

On arriving in Socorro, Gillett found he had one of the murderers, Abran Baca, but the other man was Masias Baca, a cousin of the murderer, who having no connection with the case was turned loose.

The Officers in Socorro paid their part of the reward, and Colonel Eaton, deputy Sheriff of the County, gave him a receipt for the delivery of Abran Baca, and the Governor of the Territory sent him a check for the remaining two hundred and fifty dollars, enclosed with a letter of thanks.

About a month after the capture of Abran Baca, a friend told him he had seen a man in Saragosa, Mexico whom he believed to be Onofre Baca, and that he was clerking in one of the largest stores in town; Onofre Baca was of very light complexion and had dark red hair. Gillett knew that if he arrested Onofre Baca in Mexico and turned him over to the Authorities of Saragosa, owing to the influence of his wealthy relatives, he would be turned loose.

Gillett could not tell his Captain what he intended to do as Baylor would follow the law.

Saragosa was a little Mexican town of five hundred people about four miles west of Isleta in Old Mexico, but in a straight line not over a mile across the Río Grande.

It has always been considered a great sport, among the old Mexicans, to get behind an adobe wall, or on some roof and shoot at any Gringo who was caught on the Mexican side of the River, most especially a Texas Ranger. Gillett knew from former experiences that he could not go to Saragosa, arrest Baca, stay over five minutes and live to tell the tale. Gillett told another ranger, George Lloyd, of his plan and Lloyd agreed to help him. They planned to try and capture Baca the following morning, as he was told Baca was still clerking in the same store.

As soon as the two rangers crossed the Río Grande, to avoid being seen, rode through the bosque to Saragosa, where before the store in which Baca was working they dismounted, Lloyd holding the horses, while Gillett entered. Gillett saw Baca waiting on an old Mexican woman, and stepping up to him shoved his gun to Baca's head and ordered him to come on, the old woman in the meantime proceeding to fall to the floor in a faint, while two others ran out of the door screaming at the top of their voices.

When the pair reached the horses, Baca was mounted behind Lloyd and they left Saragosa on the dead run. As they galloped along, the church bells began to ring, and soon the whole population of Saragosa was saddled and in pursuit. As they got about halfway to the river, a bend in the road showed a bunch of the foremost pursuers a few hundred yards behind, who immediately began shooting.

As Lloyd's horse was tiring, Baca was changed to Gillett's horse. They at last reached the Río Grande, which at this point was about a hundred yards wide, and as the ford was shallow they hit the water running. They lost no time in reaching camp with their prisoner and two run-down horses, and everyone turning out to meet them.

Captain Baylor asked who the prisoner was, Gillett replying it was Onofre Baca, the man who had killed Mr. Conklin. "Where did you get him, Sergeant?" he asked. And Gillett had to tell him he had kidnapped Baca out of Mexico.

As Gillett tells it Captain Baylor gave him the devil about it, saying it is a wonder the Mexicans did not shoot you and Lloyd . . . .

Gillett reminded the captain of the fate of Morgan and Brown, and how the authorities at Guadalupe had turned loose their murderers, Esquibel and Molino.

"Sergeant!" Baylor replied, "it is against my best judgment; I ought to take the prisoner back across the line and turn him loose, but as you have risked your life in getting him, you may go."

Gillett with his prisoner took the stage to El Paso and reached Mesilla on the train after dark. He was afraid to put Baca in jail there, as he had no warrant or extradition papers to hold him, and he was afraid the Jailor might not return the prisoner to him in the morning. So he handcuffed Baca to himself and, securing a room, they slept together until morning.

Gillett wired the Sheriff at Socorro: he had captured Baca and would soon be there.

Baca's friends had also heard of his arrest, and asked the Governor to have the prisoner taken to Santa Fe. At San Marcial Gillett was handed a telegram instructing him to bring Baca to the capitol and not to stop at Socorro. The train got to Socorro about midnight, and as soon as it stopped was boarded by many armed men, headed by Deputy Sheriff Eaton, to whom Gillett showed the Governor's telegram, but Eaton replied Baca was wanted in Socorro and that was where he was going. Gillett told him he was going to take Baca to Santa Fe, but he was surrounded by too many armed men to make a fight of it.

Gillett and Baca were then put in a bus that was waiting. The jailor entered the bus first, Baca next, while Gillett sat near the door with his Winchester in his hand, the driver being ordered to drive to the jail.

Gillett says they had not driven far, when in the moonlight he could see at least a hundred armed and mounted men following. They swarmed around the bus and several grabbed the horses by their bridles, while others tried to force the bus doors open. Gillett asked the jailor if he could depend upon him to help stand the mob off, but he replied it would do no good; all right said Gillett, I am going to stand them off myself. He poked his gun out as the door was forced open, and told the mob to stand back, but they paid no attention to him, and someone quickly jerked his gun out of his hand. Another grabbed him by the collar and pulled him out on the ground, while someone else kicked him. Gillett told the crowd, the hanging of the prisoner would place him in an awkward spot, as the reward by the Territory was for the delivery of the murderer inside the jail doors of Socorro County. The leaders considered, and decided Gillett was right. As soon as Baca was delivered inside the jail, Colonel Eaton wrote a receipt for the delivery of Baca, and handed it to Gillett. The mob then took Baca, and hung him to a big beam over the top of a gate. This gate was reported to be on property just west of the Park Hotel, in an alley known as death alley, on account of so many hard characters having been hung there.

Source of Information: These are facts known to all the old timers living in Socorro, New Mexico. The dates have been verified by the book *Six Years with the Texas Rangers*, by J. B. Gillett.

Mexican Boy Captured by Apache Indians

by Clay W. Vaden

Today there lives up a picturesque canyon six miles southeast of Quemado one of our most reliable pioneer Mexican citizens, Sr. Felipe Padilla, who was born May 22, 1866, and who lived for many years at the original site of Quemado, now Swenzem's ranch, five miles east of the present location of the town. At that time the place was called El Rito Quemado. The town was established in 1870, and Mr. Padilla has lived in Catron county for 65 years.

In a personal interview, he says:

"In 1880, sometime in May, some Apache Indians under Chief Victorio captured me, a muchacho, about 14 years of age, while I was herding sheep on the hills in the Rito lake canyon.

"When the Indians surrounded and captured me, they took me on horseback around the mountains several miles north of Swenzemville. On the mesa they saw a large herd of wild horses and were so anxious to capture some of the caballos that they left me in care of a squaw.

"When the Indians returned from running the horses they told me to go on in front of them. After traveling 200 or 300 yards, one of the braves struck me across the face with a quirt; then the Indians, thinking perhaps they had killed me, ran their horses at full speed westward.

"In 1881 a band of Apaches killed three Mexicans near Tres Legunas and stole several teams of oxen, burned two wagons loaded with wool which belonged to my grandfather, Jesús Padilla. Then they passed through Quemado and killed three men, August 7 of that year: Crescencio, from Old Mexico, Juan Salis, and José Ortis. These men were buried in the old cemetery at Swenzem's ranch, now called "Boothill Cemetery." The same day they captured two young muchachos, about ten years of age, Militón Madrid and Telesfor Sánchez, and kept them with their tribe for three years. After capturing these two boys, they made their way to Las Cebollas (Onions) rancho, owned by Tibursio García, north of Quemado. There the Indians murdered two more men and captured a young woman, Plasida, August 10, 1881."

WITCHCRAFT & GHOST STORIES

"After riding a little further the trunk began to rattle again. This time the noise was louder and sounds began to issue from the inside. They attempted to tie it up again but the trunk would not stay tied. All of a sudden the trunk worked itself completely loose and fell off the back of the mule and began to roll away. The men turned their horses and began chasing the trunk."

From "The Trunk" by Manuel Berg

New Mexico Folklore: Goblins of Truchas

by Manuel Berg

Mrs. Emilia A. Pacheco of 1610 North 7th, Albuquerque, has lived her entire life in New Mexico. For many years she taught school in the mountain districts. She was raised in the Truchas section of Río Arriba County. The following is a story of "duendes" (goblins) which her mother told her:

"As a child my family lived in Truchas. It seems that there was a family near us who were being made very uncomfortable. It was not only that they heard noises during the night, but each morning when they got up they would find all kinds of dirt and rubbish spread over the floor and table. This bothered them very much and one day when they searched to see if they could find any trace of who was making their house dirty, they found tiny tracks of what looked like tiny footprints. This discovery upset them still further. They did not know what to do. Finally they decided to move away from Truchas to get away from the trouble. There was a sick girl in the family. The father of the family went to Chimayó to find a house at that place and then came back to help pack the household goods and take the family away.

"Now at one particular place along the road to Chimayó there was a very steep hill. This hill was so steep that it was almost impossible for the horses to pull the wagon up. Just as they reached the bottom of the hill the older girl suddenly said, 'Oh! We forgot something.'

"'What did we forget?' her mother wanted to know.

"'We left our broom behind.'

"The father had stopped the wagon, but said that it would not be possible to go back for the broom. While they were talking the matter over they heard strange voices calling from behind them.

"'Here it is! Here it is!'

"But when they turned around they could see nothing.

"The mother said, 'My, my, this is such a steep hill, I don't think those "duendes" (goblins) can follow us. They have been calling us to try and get us to go back to Truchas.'

"When they arrived at Chimayó they drove over to the new house and began moving their things inside. While this was going on one of the children happened to look behind the door and there was the very same broom they had left at Truchas. Who had brought the broom? Everyone knew that it was the 'duendes' that had done this, and the mother said, 'Now you will see. Something is going to happen.'

"They quickly prepared supper and later all went to sleep. In the morning the house was again full of dirt and so was the fireplace. They cleaned up the place and then, as it was lunchtime, they sat down at the table. While they were eating there were funny noises, and bits of dirt kept falling from the ceiling into their plates, making it impossible to eat. The ones who were well could go outside and sat under the sky, but the girl who was sick couldn't do this. She went hungry and in a few days she was suffering so much that they finally went and put a cover over the ceiling but this only held the room clean for three days. By then the goblins had come through again and were dropping dirt on the sick girl's plate. She was never able to eat again for they spoiled her every meal so that she starved and died."

New Mexico Witchcraft: A Magical Cure

by Manuel Berg

Mrs. Emilia A. Pacheco, of 1610 North Seventh Street, Albuquerque, relates the ensuing account of a "witch doctor's" cure:

"In the little town of Santa Cruz there used to live a man by the name of Juan Luján. He was known as a healer; that is, a man who could break the spell of a bruja. At the time I speak of I was teaching school in Chimayó. There was a boy, one of my school-children, who was very sick. The sickness of this boy had caused lumps to come out all over his legs and these lumps were as big as a fist.

"The boy was getting worse, so one day his parents sent for Juan Luján to come and see if he could help. Juan Luján came and looked over the boy and then he said that he could cure him, but he could not start the cure until after dark and then only in a dark room. That night Señor Luján went into the dark room with the sick boy and rubbed some strange stuff on the boy's legs. We did not see what it was that he used. Then he said that the boy was to be wrapped up in many blankets so as to bring on a good sweat.

"The next morning Juan Luján came again to see the boy. This time he did not need darkness to do his work. He undressed the boy and began rubbing each of the bumps on the legs of the boy. After rubbing each bump awhile he would slowly begin to squeeze it. And as he squeezed harder and harder he would bring out a cricket. Juan Luján squeezed out a cricket from each bump on that boy's legs! Not long after that the boy was well and began coming to school once more."

New Mexico Witchcraft: The Dancing Light

by Manuel Berg

Mrs. Emilia A. Pacheco of 1610 North 7th Street, Albuquerque, relates the following story:

"My brother-in-law was working a piece of land about five miles from Chimayó. He was raising chili. He was quite a young fellow and liked to go to dances. If he heard there was to be a dance anywhere in the countryside he would saddle his horses and away he would go. Well, one night after he was finished with his work he saddled his horse to go into Chimayó to a dance. After he had been riding for a while, and the night was very dark, he noticed a light dancing along the road in front of him. First it would be on one side and then on the other. He did not pay much attention only tried to make his horse go faster and run away from the light. In a little while he passed the light and then he turned around to see where the light was and there was the light right in back of him, sitting on the horse. He spurred the horse to make it go faster and didn't turn around anymore. After he had passed 'El Potrero' the Sanctuary and reached the first house beyond, he jumped off his horse and started running to the door of the house. But the light had also jumped off and got in front of him. He let out a horrible cry and fainted on the doorstep. The people of the house took him in and the lady later told me that my brother-in-law was unconscious for four hours from the fright that this strange dancing light had given him. She had to give him yerbas to make him well again."

New Mexico Witchcraft: The Flying Brujas

by Manuel Berg

From an interview with Mrs Emilia Pacheco, 1610 North Seventh St., Albuquerque:

"When I was a young girl I went to school at Peñasco, in Taos County. Among my girlfriends at school there was one named Vicenta Chacón, who was about fifteen years old. Vicenta would tell me that her grandmother, whose name was Luz Chacón, was a bruja. Then Vicenta told me that one afternoon there was a meeting of old women at her grandmother's home and all of the old ladies there were brujas. Each of the brujas came to this meeting with a black cat and a pumpkin. Grandmother Luz put Vicenta to bed, but Vicenta lifted the blanket and watched what was going on. First they brought out a lot of wine and food, which they ate and drank. Then they sang and danced for many hours. After this each of the ladies got the cat they had brought. Then they began singing to the cats and while they were singing they took out the eyes of each cat and exchanged them for their own, putting their own eyes into the cats.

"The next thing they did was bring out all the pumpkins. They chose the largest one and took out the seeds and the other insides of the pumpkin until they had it the way they wanted. Then making themselves as small as possible, about the size of a duenda (dwarf), they took a stick and all climbed into this one pumpkin. When they were all inside of the pumpkin one of the brujas said, "Con Dios y sin Santa María" (with God and without Saint Mary).

"The pumpkin then lighted up, sparks began to spread out all around and it began to fly in the air. Vicenta got out of bed and went to the door and saw the lighted pumpkin flying in the air.

"About four or five o'clock in the morning the pumpkin and the brujas came back. The brujas got out of the pumpkin and then brought out the cats again and changed back to their own eyes.

"Vicenta was peeking from under the blanket and her grandmother saw her watching. Because the girl was watching her, old Luz could not change back her eyes with the cat; so she began cursing the girl.

"Afterward the old grandmother could no longer see very good even in the daytime. In fact she was almost blind and she would curse Vicenta all the time. I don't know what kind of curse the old lady put on Vicenta, but the poor girl became as thin as a skeleton and nothing could be done for her. Vicenta then became so weak and thin that she finally died because of the things she had seen."

New Mexico Witchcraft: The Hanging Tongue

by Manuel Berg

*T*he following story was related by Mrs. Amalia Selva, 415 West Santa Fe Avenue, Albuquerque, New Mexico, during an interview.

"When I was a little girl my family lived in a small town in the northern part of Valencia County. The land around the town was hard and dry. No single family was wealthy enough to have a well for water in their own yard. The well would have to be sunk very deep and was an expensive thing to do. The result was that everybody paid whatever they could and a community well was sunk in the center of the town. To get a child to go to the well for a bucket of water was about the easiest thing to get done because the well had become the meeting place for the town. You could not always be sure how soon the water would be brought home as there was bound to be a number of children there, always ready to waste some time playing.

"One day a group of children were at the well waiting to fill their buckets. They were pushing each other around, spilling water on each other and making a lot of noise. In the midst of this play a very old lady came up to the well and wanted to fill her bucket with water. The children wanted to have some fun with her so they surrounded the well and would not let her get near. The woman begged them to let her get some water. The children just laughed and when the old lady came near they would push her back. The old lady became very angry and began yelling and cursing the children. They only laughed the harder and kept her from getting near the well. Finally the old woman slapped one of the little girls who got in her way. The little girl backed away from the old lady but backing away from her she called the woman a bad name and stuck out her tongue. The old woman turned on her in a rage and yelled at her that she wouldn't be able to put her tongue back in her mouth. We all watched this little girl but she couldn't put her tongue in. The little girl began to cry, making funny noises because her tongue was sticking out. Then the rest of us became frightened and some even began to cry. We all hurried away from the well and the old woman. The old bruja went and got her water and went home.

"The child went home with her tongue hanging out and we all followed her. The girl's mother tried all kinds of ways to push the tongue back into the child's mouth but couldn't make it stay in. That evening the girl's mother and father and a lot of other grownups went to the bruja's house. They begged the mean old woman to take away the curse she had put on the little girl. The old woman would not do it. At last the people became very angry and said they would chase the old lady out of town and maybe do her harm if she wouldn't do what they asked her. The bruja then said that the best she would do was to stop the curse after twenty-four hours. She said the children had been very bad and she was going to punish them. The parents then said that if the curse was not off in twenty-four hours it would be too bad for the bruja.

"The next day, at the same time as it began, the little girl was able to put her tongue back. All of us children were very scared of this old woman for many years and I never heard of anyone ever trying to have any fun with that bruja again."

New Mexico Witchcraft: The Magic Ointment

by Manuel Berg

Mrs. Rufujio Ávilla, of 417 Anderson Avenue, Albuquerque, is eighty-seven years old. When I arrived to interview her she was ill in bed. I suggested that she remain in bed and not rise but Mrs. Ávilla refused, insisting on getting up even though it was necessary for her to lean on the arm of her son during the entire interview. She has lived in and around Albuquerque for the past sixty years, having come from old Mexico. She still recalls the occasion of the French invasion of Mexico. When I asked her about folk stories and legends or for instances of witchcraft, about which she knew or had heard, she related the following account. The story was attested to by her son and several friends who were in the house at the time:

"The first time that I ever came into contact with any example of what witch doctors could do was several years after I came to Albuquerque. At that time there was a man living in Isleta who everybody called a Bruja (Broo-ha—a witch). One day I went to visit a friend of mine who was pretty sick. When I got there this man from Isleta was there. The woman's husband had brought him to the house. The bruja asked a lot of questions about people who had come to visit her and about how she felt. Finally he pulled out a little cup from his pocket in which he had some ointment. He put a little of this ointment on the arm of the sick woman and started to rub the arm. It wasn't long before he pulled a stone out of her arm—a stone almost as big as a pear! And it wasn't long after that that the woman got well again. I was there and I saw this man do this. And if you do not believe it I will tell you something in which I myself took part.

"About 1905 there lived a man by the name of Juan Bautista in Atrisco. He was a good bruja if there ever was one. A lady was very sick and she was a cousin of mine and I was asked to come and nurse her. This Juan Bautista was called in to see her and he rubbed some ointment on this woman's chest and pulled out an apple which he said was making her sick. And that was true because she got well at once. Now the man took some of this ointment stuff and put it on a piece of paper which he gave to me.

"After my cousin was well I went home and took his magic stuff along with me. But by the time I got home everybody knew I had some of this wonderful medicine. Now there was a family by the name of Archuleta who lived on the north side of Albuquerque, and they came to me and begged me to go and see a woman called Tomacita who was their good friend and who was very sick. I said I would go, and took the magic ointment with me. When I got there the lady was in great pain and I rubbed some ointment on her just the same as the Bruja did, and then I rubbed her for quite awhile. Pretty soon I pulled out a thing that looked like a porcupine quill. I rubbed some more and pulled out some more and when I was through at last I had pulled out fourteen of these porcupine quills and she became well right away. All of this I did myself.

"Another case that I helped with this stuff was a young girl who also lived at San José where I lived. She had had a little baby and was very sick and they sent for me. I still had some of the ointment left and I used it on her and pulled out a little, teeny chick. That was why she wasn't getting better until I came and helped her get better."

New Mexico Witchcraft: Victims of a Bruja

by Manuel Berg

*I*n an interview with Mrs. Ajapita Montoya, 400 East Mountain Road, Albuquerque, she related the following story:

"Can you tell whether I have been very sick? I guess you wouldn't know because you did not know me at the time. Only during the last year I have recovered and now feel as well as I ever did. But for ten years I was sick. I went to doctors—they seemed to do nothing. I went to *arborlarios* (witch doctors)—and they didn't help. I could eat very little, and became very thin. I found it hard to get out of bed and was unable to cook, clean my house or take care of my family. Not one person knew what was wrong with me.

"But now I am going to tell you just what took place and how I was cured. I know that it will sound impossible but I have a dozen people who will be witness to the truth of what I say.

"My daughter, Natividad, is married to Joe Cassado, they live in Bernalillo and have a small daughter. Joe has lived in Bernalillo all his life and he has a good friend there, a young man who has worked with him for many years. The father of this friend of Joe's was an *arbolario* who lived in Mountainair. When Joe told him about how sick I was, the friend said that he would tell his father to stop in and see me the next time he came to Albuquerque.

"Several weeks later this *arbolario* came to my house. My husband, Cresencio, was very angry and wanted him to leave the house right away. Cresencio said that all the doctors did was rob him. The *arbolario* quieted him down and said that he wanted no money. If we would give him room and board for nine days he would try and cure me. To this my husband and I agreed.

"This man asked my husband to get him a certain kind of oil which is sold in drugstores, some coral powder and *camino* seeds. These things he mixed together and made into a drink. He had my husband and me drink a glass of this stuff every day for nine days.

"On the morning of the third day I got up out of bed. I felt fine. I swept and cleaned my house, cooked and did whatever work was necessary. This was the first time in ten years I had been able to do that. I was sure this man was a magician—Cresencio felt the same way. We kept on taking the strange drink daily.

"At the end of the eighth day the *arbolario* went around our house and counted all the doors and windows. There were eighteen doors and windows. He next asked my husband to get him eighteen needles and some black thread. When Cresencio brought him these things he said that he needed a statue of the Sacred Heart. Cresencio went to Old Town and bought such a statue from the priest there. The *arbolario* then buried the Sacred Heart statue under the front doorstep. Next he stuck one needle threaded with the black thread into each door and window frame in the house. My husband was then asked to bring some coarse salt, which he did. Then the witch doctor sent Cresencio to Bernalillo to bring back my grandchild.

"On the ninth day, at eleven o' clock in the evening, we all were gathered into one room and everyone began to pray. We prayed for over half an hour. Then the *arbolario* dampened the salt and mixed it with something. From this stuff he made an image which he covered with paper. This he gave to the child to throw into the fire. I became scared and didn't want to allow this because I was sure someone would die because of this. The witch doctor said that he would be the only one to die. The little girl threw the image into the fire and a great crackling and sparkling began, and pretty soon we all saw stars rise out of the fire.

"The next day he said that in about six months a lady would come to the house and apologize. She couldn't come right away because she was suffering from serious burns and would be in the hospital for quite some time. When this woman did come he himself would either lose his eyesight or become very sick.

"Six months later almost to the day, a woman neighbor of ours came to see me. She had been away in California. This woman began to cry and pray and begged me to forgive her for having been mean to me. I couldn't understand what it was all about and asked her what she meant.

She told me that many years ago, before I became sick, she lived near my house. At that time I used to keep a lot of clothes on my back porch. She said she stole some things from my porch. A girl had seen her take them and she thought this girl had told me about it. She said that I asked her to help me search for them, but she thought I did this just to humiliate her. She was sure I believed she was the guilty person. Then she admitted that she was a *bruja* and had brought down a curse on me and that was why I had been sick. I could hardly believe this and said so. Then this *bruja* said that I had had an *arbolario* cure me. Being afraid, I denied this and so did my husband. The *bruja* only laughed and called us both liars and said she would prove it. She lifted up her skirts and showed us her legs which were covered with burns that had hardly healed over, and said that this was how she knew that we were lying. Still she again forgave me and once more apologized and went away.

"Several days after this my son-in-law from Bernalillo came to Albuquerque and told us that the *arbolario* was very sick and was going to be brought from Mountainair to Albuquerque. The poor man came to Albuquerque but couldn't seem to get well. Four days after coming here he was dead. I was very sorry for the poor man, but there was nothing I could do. Now as for me, since the third day of that *arbolario's* treatment I have been perfectly well and happy."

The Trunk

by Manuel Berg

*T*he following story was told by Mr. Pat Tafoya, 108 West McKinley Avenue, Albuquerque, during an interview at his home:

"When I knew Pedro Martínez he was already an old man. He owned a little farm about ten miles east of Truchas, in Río Arriba County. Many times, when several of us boys came to see him, he would tell us marvelous tales about things he had seen and done and heard. One time he told us of a trip he made into Old Mexico with three other men. They were going to do some prospecting in the State of Chihuahua.

"Pedro and his partners spent almost a year mining in the hills of Chihuahua. They had pretty good luck and arrived at Juárez with a good deal of money. They planned to stay in Juárez for several weeks, having a good time and then return to the mountains for another long spell.

"A week after their arrival in Juárez one of the partners received word that his mother was very sick and wanted him to return home. His partner's name was Gil Barreras. Now Gil had become good friends with a very beautiful woman in Juárez and did not want to go home but since his mother was so ill and quite an old woman, he felt that he must return to his home in New Mexico.

"The other partners decided to return with Gil. They didn't feel that it would make a great deal of difference since they had all done so well on this trip and could always return some other time. The next day the four men went to the marketplace and bought a great many things to take back as presents to their families and friends. Gil bought himself a big leather trunk made of rawhide. This trunk he filled with the shawls, clothes and jewelry he had bought for his mother and many of the things purchased by his partners.

"They all wore beards as a result of living in the hills. The day before leaving, Gil told his friends that he was going to the barbershop but instead he went to see this woman-friend. She was very sorry to hear that he was leaving so suddenly and wanted him to give her something as a remembrance. He asked her what she would like to have, but she would not tell him just then. They sat and talked for some time. Then Gil said that he must leave because he had told the other men that he was going to get a shave and that he had better get it before they started looking for him. The lady told him that there was a razor in the house and that he could shave there. He very politely refused to do this. Then the woman said that if he did get a shave at the barber's, would he save the hair and give them to her for a remembrance. This he promised to do for her.

"Near the barbershop he met his partners and told them about the strange request of his lady friend. One of the men told him not to do this and the other two agreed. They felt that there was something very queer about this woman. Gil wanted to know what he should do, for he had promised that he would return to the woman's house with the hair. One of the partners said that they should go back to their lodgings and shave some of the hair from the rawhide trunk and give it to the woman, pretending that it was real human hair. They all thought this was a good idea. The men returned to their rooms and Gil decided to shave himself while one of the others scraped some hair off the side of the trunk. When Gil was through, the man who had warned him in the first place burned Gil's own hair. Gil then took the false hair and gave them to the woman who said she would keep them as sacred as 'the balls of my eyes.'

"The next day the four men left Juárez for New Mexico. All of their belongings, including the rawhide trunk, were tied on the backs of several pack mules. The first day of travel went by without any trouble. The men were all on horseback but could not go very fast on account of the pack mules.

"During the afternoon of the second day the trunk began to work itself loose on the back of the mule and it began to rattle. The mule became frightened and began to run. They caught the mule and tied up the trunk with a reata very tightly. The partner who had been suspicious from the very first said, 'I told you that the woman meant you no good. She does not want you to get home and I bet she is a bruja.' The other men laughed at him and told him he was crazy.

"After riding a little further the trunk began to rattle again. This time the noise was louder and sounds began to issue from the inside. They attempted to tie it up again but the trunk would not stay tied. All of a sudden the trunk worked itself completely loose and fell off the back of the mule and began to roll away. The men turned their horses and began chasing the trunk. The faster the horses went the faster the trunk seemed to go. It was impossible to catch up with it. And the trunk kept on rolling back toward Juárez. After following it for several miles they decided to leave the trunk go by itself, because they felt that it was heading straight back to Juárez and the woman. Also if they once got back to where the woman was they might never get away for she might bewitch them.

"They turned and caught up with their pack mules and returned to Truchas, but Gil had lost his trunk with all his things. Gil's mother had gotten much better by the time they all reached home. But very soon after their return Gil became sick and within a week he died. The partners were certain that this was because the bruja at Juárez had not wanted him to return to New Mexico and leave her."

A Witch Story

by Lorin W. Brown

The trader had stopped for the night at his friend's home in Truchas, as was his custom on his frequent trading trips to that up-land mountain village. After sitting up most of the night before the fireplace trading gossip and news with his loquacious host, Don Melitón Vigil, the trader, went to his canvas-covered wagon for his bed roll. He took his bed roll into his host's front room and unrolling it lay down to sleep.

He had been asleep a short while, it seemed, when he was awakened by a most ungodly noise. It seemed to come from just outside the door. In his half awakened state the trader did not at first identify the sound, but after a while, his mind clearing, he knew the sound to be the hooting of an owl, not just one owl—one owl could not make all that noise.

Opening the door, he looked out and saw two owls sitting on the cross pole of the gate which opened into his host's patio. There was a full moon and the huge birds seemed much larger as the moonlight etched their horned figures against the sky. It is very strange to see two owls together, and at best they are fearsome beasts, but that could not explain the trader's evident fear, as crossing himself, he hastily slammed the door to.

Crossing the room he bowed his head as he entered the low door which led into the room where his friend slept. He found his host awake; he, too, had heard the owls, and was sitting up in his bed, rolling a corn husk cigarette. The trader asked him if he had a gun, saying that he was going to shoot the owls, and added that they had been following him from village to village, and that now he was going to put a stop to it.

The old man pointed to the corner where his rifle stood and said, "If you think that those two owls are some evil ones, who mean to harm you, you had better cut a cross in the bullets, otherwise you will not touch them."

The trader complied with his host's suggestion by levering all of the cartridges out of the rifle and making a cross on two of them with his pocket knife, and loaded the gun with them as he crossed the outer room. Reaching the door he threw it open and, raising the gun to his shoulder, fired two shots in rapid succession.

One of the owls fell to the ground with a dull thud, but the other flew away with one leg trailing, showing that it had been wounded.

The trader crossed the moon-drenched patio and gingerly picking the dead bird by one leg, hurled it across the road and down the hillside.

On his next trip to Truchas the trader recounted the sequel to the killing of the owls. It seemed that he had had some difficulty with two Indians of the Tesuque pueblo over a horse trade, and they had sworn to get even with him. These two Indians had the reputation of being witches, and the trader was certain that these two owls, which had followed him so persistently on his way from town to town, were his two Indian enemies seeking to harm him in some manner. On his return to his home from the trading trip on which he had killed the owls, he was met with strange news concerning his Indian enemies.

They had gone hunting at the time the trader had started out on his trading trip. And one morning they rode back into the pueblo, but one of them was slung across his pony. He had shot himself accidentally—so said the survivor—and he himself had a broken leg. His horse had fallen with him on the way in—that was the story the surviving Indian told. The trader, however, was certain that he and his friend, Don Melitón, alone knew the truth of how the Indians had met their fate. The Indian with the broken leg recovered. He must have ceased practicing witchcraft for he never bothered the trader again after the death of his companion.

Source of Information: Sr. Melitón Trujillo, 70 years old, of Truchas, NM.

Flight to Mexico

by Lorin W. Brown

"Which way and how far is Old Mexico from here?" asked Tía Lupe.

I had stopped in to see her and found her seemingly absorbed in profound reverie and at first indifferent to my entrance. This opening remark gave me a clue as to where her mind had been wandering. It was difficult for me to give her an idea as to the distance between Old Mexico and Córdova, but I tried to explain in terms of the number of days it would take to reach Mexico on horseback.

"Oh, then it is beyond Río Abajo?"

"Oh, sí Señora, much farther," was my answer to her next query. Río Abajo was the local designation of the lower stretches of the Río Grande including in the term all settlements from Belen to Soccoro.

"Yes, it must be, because my foster-father, José María Martínez, used to start out with his trading caravan in Chimayó for Mexico and be gone for six months from the month of María (May) to the month of the Muertos (November). He always tried to get back before the month of Noche Buena (December). He liked to be here for the feasting, and besides, there was more time for trading then. Everybody was enjoying themselves then; there were many bailes and the Matachines amused the people every afternoon until the New Year. Blessed be God, what wonderful times those were. The people really enjoyed themselves then, 'tho they endured more dangers and hardships than now. I was quite small but I remember all this well. And all the beautiful and curious things that my foster-father brought back. Ay, what silks, shawls and rebozos for the women. Also oranges and lemons, dried pomegranates for medicinal use, anil and brazil for the weavers. And many other curious things to trade. Oh yes, piloncillo and melcocha (brown sugar and a kind of taffy), and the wines for the feasts. All kinds of good things which we lacked here.

"My foster-father was very rich and we lived very well in a big house near the Potrero. With the gold he brought back from his trading trips he had bought many Indian slaves so that Doña Pabula, his wife, had only to give orders. And he needed all this help because there was always a big feast when he arrived from a trip and before he left, the house was always full of people trading with him and making arrangements for going with him on his next trip. Always much noise and excitement while he was home. I must have been very curious because I was always around all the time and that is why I remember all this so well. Myself and the other children they raised were treated as their own if they had had any.

"And the gifts they would give me from my grandfather who lived in Chihuaha! What handsome things for me alone! What do you think? A grandfather whom I never saw. I was told he was very rich, a merchant in Chihuaha with whom my father stayed in Mexico."

"How did it happen that your grandfather was in Mexico and you here?" I asked.

"That is a long story," she answered, "but I am going to tell you, so listen well. My grandmother died when my mother was a little child and soon afterwards he married a widow. This widow, Salomé Baca, had two sons who weren't much account and were of no help to my grandfather. But we will leave that. My grandfather was very unlucky in his second wife because he found out she was a "bruja," or witch. And I will tell you how this happened. These brujas are very sly people and are not always known as such. That any one should sell themselves to the Devil like they do I can't understand. But there are people for everything in this world. And this Salomé was one all right. It seems that she would cast a spell on my grandfather on the nights when she wished to get to a witches' gathering or on some wicked errand for the devil, her master."

Here Tía Lupe made the sign of the cross and murmured an "Ave María Purissima." Any evil spirits having been thus dispelled, she continued.

"These spells which Salomé would cast over my grandfather would keep him asleep until she returned from these trips. One morning he got up rather late and could not hear his wife getting breakfast. Thinking she had gone for water he went into the kitchen. Now he knew something was wrong because there had been no fire built. Looking around, what was his surprise to see his wife lying by the fireplace, apparently dead. On closer examination he found that she had a bad wound in one shoulder and had apparently fainted from loss of blood. Calling in two neighbor women to take care of his wife he then went for his "padrino" or godfather. Returning, they found the woman revived, but could get no information from her. She seemed to be very angry and cursed them while they were questioning her.

"'Let's see what we can find out for ourselves,' said the padrino. 'How did this woman get hurt?'

"'I do not know,' answered my grandfather, 'but see here, there is blood inside the fireplace and in the chimney. Look, the ashes look like they have been brushed by some bird's wings. Let us go up on the roof and see what we can find.'

"You will not believe but they found blood on the edge of the adobe chimney and near it some bloody wing feathers. These were owl feathers. There was no doubt then that this woman was a witch and was returning home in the shape of an owl. Somewhere she had been shot and was just able to get home before the first rooster crowed. You know, witches can be out at night only until the first rooster crows and no matter what shape they take for their deviltry they return to their own body at that time. Even after his wife confessed my grandfather did not believe her promise to quit. More so since she seemed to hate him for having found her out. So really he was afraid of her and what she might do to him.

"One day he came home to find the door locked and nobody home. Breaking the lock he went in, looking for his wife, but from the looks of the house he guessed she had gone for good. Very much relieved he started to get himself a meal. Near the fireplace was an earthen pot covered with a cloth and in which dough was kept. Hoping to find dough ready for tortillas he lifted the cloth. He found dough, yes, but lying on top of the dough he found a large toad. He was very much frightened because he didn't know in what way his wife might try to bewitch him with the things left in the house. Leaving the house without touching anything more in it he never returned. Finding my mother at his sister's home, where Salomé had left her, he made preparations to go to Mexico.

Arranging for my mother's care he left and never came back. Fear of this "maldita bruja" made him get as far away from her as possible.

"But, as I say, he always remembered us by sending presents, first to my mother and later to me. On my foster-father's last trip my grandfather gave him directions for finding a buried treasure over there between Cundiyo and Nambé, on or near the Cerro de la Patada. He described this place as being on the west slope of this Cerro down near a little plain. As I remember the best marks to be looked for were two peach trees, between which the treasure had been buried. These fruit trees must have been planted there by some member of some caravan, as that vicinity was a favorite camping place and on the regular route through here and on to Truchas and Peñasco.

"It seems that this treasure had been buried by a party who had been attacked by Indians. Having killed most of the party the Indians stole their pack and saddle animals. It must have been all the Indians wanted or maybe the three survivors were too much for them. At any rate these three buried their goods there and made their escape. My grandfather was told this tale in Mexico and he passed it on to my foster-father. He made one effort to find it with no success, and, being old, never went again. That treasure has never been found, at least nothing has been known of its recovery. Those fruit trees would be hard to find now. I suppose their trunks are completely rotted away by now. That's the way it goes. Years ago I tried to get my nephews to go and look for it but they have always been lazy and disinterested even if they are my nephews.

"This treasure was supposed to have been of gold and silver, coin and bars, a golden image for one of the churches and other goods such as silks, shawls, fajas, besides all the equipment of the party.

"Bendito sea Dios, that which is not supposed to belong to one will not be. So many beautiful things from Mexico have I seen displayed in the bailes and fiestas by beautiful women. Of all that, only the gold and silver ornaments remain, I guess. Even the pretty women that wore them are gone. That must be the way it is in that hole where that treasure is buried. All the pretty shawls, fajas and silks have rotted away long time ago, no doubt. Only the gold will be there until found or until the world is no more."

With this bit of philosophy Tía Lupe wound up her tale which had me in imagination on the trail to Mexico beset by witches. On hearing the part about the treasure I made a firm resolve not to be bitten by the treasure-hunting bug again, but piñón season found me on the sides of Cerro de la Patada searching more for the ghosts of departed peach trees than for piñón.

Tales of the Moccasin Maker of Córdova: Witchcraft

by Lorin W. Brown

Manuel Trujillo was busy making a pair of "Teguas," or cow-skin moccasins, and had only ceased plying his awl while he gave me a "good-day." Seating myself in his doorway, we talked first of this and then that as I watched him at his work. He was acknowledged as one of the best moccasin makers in the village. I could well believe this as I noticed the efficiency with which he worked and the neatness of the escalloped edges where the sole was stitched to the uppers. The soles were made of well-softened cowhide used hairy side out and when new gave the wearer the same effect as walking on a deep-napped rug. Deer hunters keep a pair of these new moccasins in reserve because they render their footsteps noiseless in the woods. Before factory-made shoes and boots were introduced into this country moccasins were commonly used for every day. Any shoes or boots acquired through trade with Mexico were very carefully saved for feast days or other great occasions. In those early days a good moccasin maker never lacked for work and food for his household; he was paid in produce, money being almost unknown.

Suddenly the tolling of the bell broke in on our conversation.

"Must be that José Dolores has died," said Manuel, "He has been quite sick. But let's see." Stepping outside he lifted his old eyes to the bell tower. All the patios of the village were full of people after the same information and the bell toller was straining his voice trying to make himself heard above the reverberations of the bell. Since everybody was asking the same question he kept repeating, "Commend to God the soul of Teodorita Garduño."

"They are tolling for Teodorita, who died in Taos; may God have mercy on her soul," was Manuel's comment.

"Oh yes, I remember her," I said, "she seemed to be a very good woman. I remember she was the one who always rang the bell for the vesper services during the month of May, and she was so old it must have been a real sacrifice to climb that long ladder every evening of the whole month."

"Yes, she kept that up until her granddaughter took her to live with her in Taos," answered Manuel. "But I happen to know how she took on that duty. That and other seeming pious acts of hers were just to make us believe she was a good Christian and were done through fear. I happen to know she was a witch, and that she was made to beg for forgiveness in public twice, and even for her life. Maybe she really repented before she died. God only knows. But I will tell you. The first time was when José de la Luz Chávez's wife swore before the alcalde that Teodorita was trying to bewitch her or her baby and swore that she had proved her a witch. She testified that she had tested Teodorita once when she had called her at home. After Teodorita was inside she had secretly placed two needles in the shape of a cross over the door frame. Teodorita tried to leave the house several times but would get as far as the door and return. She tried this several times and became desperate at her inability to go through that door. Finally Luz's wife, taking pity on her, removed the needles and showed them to her.

"'Now I know you are a witch and I want you to promise never to harm me or my family,' she told her. But Teodorita rushed out the door and in her anger cursed Luz's wife and threatened her baby and herself with unmentionable evils. This was the testimony sworn to before the alcalde. Whereupon the alcalde named two men to accompany Luz to punish Teodorita. They were empowered to whip her if she did not confess and promise to refrain from harming Luz or his family.

"In those days the alcalde was the law and what he ordered was carried out. One of these men was Salvador Martínez who helped kill that witch in Chimayó. Because of some harm done him by witches when he was younger he had a very great hatred for them and would gladly kill one. And this time he had authority given him by the alcalde. When they reached Teodorita's house and read the accusation she at first denied everything but when Salvador approached with a lariat with which to tie her she knew she could expect no mercy. His reputation was too well known to her. Throwing herself on her knees she begged for mercy, confessed herself a witch and promised to repent and to not harm Luz or his family. She did not get off so easy because she was made to pray the Rosary with her bare knees resting on gravel from ant hills. That is very painful, I know very well. I doubt if she ever did quit even if she did appear to be so saintly. Many times have we noticed those balls of fire, bounding down the hillside as if from Truchas. Reaching Teodorita's house they would disappear as if down the chimney. And the owls used to hoot always in the trees near her house. I doubt if she ever reformed. At any rate everybody in the village was afraid of the old woman and would cross themselves on meeting her. Very few people ever ate anything she prepared and she never had any visitors except those which came through the air.

"At another time a group of our brethren were going on a visit to Chimayó. As we were going along singing we noticed a ball of fire rolling along the top of the ride just to the right of us. Juan Mondragón was with us. You know a Juan can catch a witch no matter in what shape she is. So Juan stepped over in front of this ball of fire and making the sign of the cross drew a circle in the air with his finger, that is, more or less around, or in the path, of the ball of fire. And look you, there was Teodorita with her little eyes glaring at us in the lights from our lanterns. She was very mad and implored Juan to let her go. We would not let him until we had made her pray with us, then we made her accompany us, barefoot, to Chimayó and back again to Córdova. Then it was that she promised again to behave and perform good deeds in penance for her years of being a witch.

"I have seen many strange things on those night visits to other Moradas made in company with other of my brethren. When we had a visit to make to Alcalde we did not go by way of the road. But we would cut across through the hills by way of the Sentinela. Twice after leaving here and getting to the Cañada Ancha we were joined by departed brethren. Amiguito, the flesh of our bodies would crawl and creep when these ghosts joined us, even though we knew they meant us no harm. They were, no doubt, the spirits of those who had neglected some sworn vows while on earth and had been sent back to fulfill them in this way. Before we knew it they would be with us and they would accompany us until we started down towards the first houses in Ranchitos. The lights from our lanterns seemed to shine through them and we could see their ribs and the bones of their arms as they walked along with us. They were all hooded, some were flagellating and others dragged crosses. How strange to see those 'disciplinas' fall on those ghostly, scarred backs and to see those heavy crosses being dragged along without a sound. And when we stopped to pray our brethren from the other world stopped with us crossing themselves at the proper times, but never making a sound. You may be sure we were very glad when they would leave us and we waited until daylight to make the return trip.

"These were undoubtedly brethren who had made vows while on earth, to make some penance or pilgrimage and had neglected to do so while alive and had been sent back to fulfill them before being able to enter heaven. Pobrecitos, may God have given their souls rest before this."

Ghostly Revenge

by Genevieve Chapin

Summer in the beautiful San Miguel country. A summer twilight, deepening into night, brought cooling shades and refreshing breezes to the little Spanish home, nestled under the trees, and the most recent bride and groom of the little village lingered in the shadowy dooryard, enjoying the soft velvety air of the evening after a too-warm day.

Neither spoke for awhile—humming abstractedly the tune that was being thrummed out by skillful fingers from a soft-voiced guitar farther down the street.

Finally, stirring uneasily in the arms that encircled her, the little bride spoke apprehensively:—"Think you it will come again tonight?—that figure—those sobs and moans—ugh!"—and she hid her face on his shoulder.

"There—there, littlest;—it is nothing to fear—four nights now it has come—and we are still unharmed—."

"But I cannot bear it—I cannot, I tell you!" she cried, hysterically. "If it comes again, I go to my mother's home!—why should she come, and wail and moan at your bedside?—What was she to you—that dead girl—?"

"There, there, little one—tomorrow we go to our own little home, even though it is unfinished; we will stay no more here. This was my home—the only one I ever knew—and this—this dead girl was my sister. But we will leave her to make her ghostly plaints to her parents."

"But why can she not rest? Why must she have died, in her youth—and on the night after our wedding?—Why—?"

"Hush, dear one—the saints above only can tell!—You must not distress yourself so. See—I will bring out the big chair, and hold you in my arms while you sleep—nothing shall harm you."

So, through the long night sat the young man, holding his dear one in his arms. Spent and exhausted, she slept till morning, and never knew that at midnight the same ghostly form floated before the agonized gaze of her husband, moaning and crying.

Next morning, with white, set face, he made a pretext to leave her long enough to go, by roundabout way, to the home of the parish priest.

Here he unburdened his heart. The good Padre listened gravely, then said—"This is a strange thing, my son; only this morning, the herder who lives in the cabin under the bluff told of passing the church last midnight and seeing the same figure, moaning bitterly inside the church. Tell me true, son—did you wrong to your foster sister in any way?—Or why troubles she your rest?"

"No—Padre—no; I loved her from a little child—but only as a sister—I swear it—" and the young man buried his face in his arms, his form shaking with sobs.

Well it was that he did so, that the Padre might not see the look of the lie that stamped itself upon his weak, handsome face.

"Peace, my son—peace!" admonished the priest, laying his hand upon the heaving shoulders. "Go to your home—and about your usual business. I will try to see the maid when next she comes, and find, if may be, a means of rest for you—and her." So the young man departed.

But that night, near the midnight hour, a message from the priest summoned him to the church.

His little bride clung sobbing to him, but when he fain would have made excuse to stay and comfort her, she pushed him from her and bade him—"Go—see what the Padre has to say—you must go—!"—and, perforce, he went.

But he did not know that his little bride followed with silent steps behind him and slid, unnoticed, into the darkness of the church door, where she hid from sight and watched.

All was utterly dark, save for an evanescent glow that surrounded the ghostly white figure of a beautiful girl, scarce older than the terrified and shivering little girl-bride who crouched in the dark corner.

All was utterly silent, save for the choking sobs and heartbroken moans that seemed to shake the beautiful, unearthly figure.

As the young man advanced falteringly up the aisle, a wild shriek burst from her. "Peace—peace—daughter; this is holy ground where-on you stand!—Tell us now your grief," spoke the priest, "that we may make amends, if possible."

Seemingly with great effort, the figure regained self-control, and began to speak. The voice was sweet—low and sad—beyond mortal sadness.

"You know me," she spoke to the man cowering before her. "I am the little sister—child of your foster-parents who gave you the only home you ever knew. I am the companion and playmate of your childhood—the sweetheart of your youth—the promised bride-to-be of your early manhood. Had you kept your promise to me, I should have been the mother of three children born to you—a son, who would have been trained for the priesthood, another who would have been a doctor, and a girl, who would have become one of the blessed sisters. I loved you, and was true to you through long years—but you—you forgot your promises to me when a fairer face dawned on your vision. You broke your promises, and I—I died, when my heart broke of its grief."

Silence—except the sobs of the speaker, and of the wretched young man who had sunk to his knees and clutched the hem of the Padre's robe.

After a time, she spoke again:—"I am sorry for your girl-wife; she did no wrong—she did not know. After tonight, she will see me no more. I want her to be happy. As for you—come close, that I may look one last time on the face of one I loved too well."

Shiveringly, coweringly, the wretched man arose and approached the figure, as though moved by some power outside himself.

Long she gazed at the weak, handsome face upturned to hers. Then, commandingly—compellingly—she spoke. "Put out your tongue!"—and, as he hesitated—"Put out your tongue!" she exclaimed, more compellingly than before.

Then, as he obeyed—before the startled priest could intervene she grasped the tongue, exclaiming—"You will never deceive again!"—and, putting forth superhuman effort, she wrung it—round and around—until he lay choking—gasping—dying, at her feet.

As he breathed his last, she disappeared. Nor was she ever seen again.

Source of Information: This story was told for me in Spanish by Mrs. Trujillo, of Clayton, and translated by Mrs. Felix Mares, of Clayton. Mrs. Trujillo says it was told her by her mother, Mrs. Arguello, of Clayton, who says it happened near her home something like fifty-five or sixty years ago, in San Miguel county.

The Witch of Arroyo Hondo

by Reyes Martínez

*E*ven at the beginning of the 20th century, superstition was rampant among the inhabitants of the smaller New Mexican villages.

A ball of fire seen arising out of the chimney of the house of Toña Trujillo (Tonia Trooheo), in the village Arroyo Hondo, at about the hour of midnight, indicated to observers that it was the meeting night of the witches of the neighborhood. Tía Toña, as she was familiarly known, was supposed to be a witch. Certainly, her appearance (as witches are supposed to look) would indicate that she really was one. She was a small, slender woman of some sixty years of age, quite lively for her years, her small, wasp-like eyes half-hidden by her abnormally wrinkled face and a complexion that indicated a scanty acquaintance with soap and water. Her head was crowned by a matty mass of disheveled hair. Children were afraid of her and older folks held a feeling of awe for her, although her kindly disposition belied any evil tendencies that her outward appearance might indicate.

Floating high into the sky, the ball of fire would travel eastward till it was lost to view. This occurrence took place with exact regularity, once a month, on a certain fixed date. On such occasions, Tía Toña was never found at home. No one ever knew where, if at all, the ball of fire alighted. Presumably she transformed herself into a ball of fire on such occasions and flew away to the witches' meeting place. Many a time, in conversation at home, she would allude to some happening that conveyed the idea that she did attend meetings of witches.

Outside of the particular nights when she joined the other "balls of fire," Toña Trujillo's house was the nightly meeting place of the gamblers of the village.

Her house was situated at the southern end of the long row of houses that lined the callejón de arriba (upper valley), the extra-wide street of the village. On this street were several goat corrals, built in the front yards of the houses, and the disagreeable odor arising from them at times permeated the air of the whole neighborhood, especially so after a rainfall or at night when the goats were brought down from the hills south of the village and shut within for the night. Every evening when the young herders drove the goats (which were all herded in one flock during the day) towards their homes, as the herd crossed the river and neared each corral, the goats belonging to each individual owner would separate automatically from the rest and enter their respective corrals to be milked and to join their kids that had been left shut in the corrals all day.

After nightfall the devotees of the games would wend their way toward the house to Tía Toña and soon a good-sized crowd would gather and the games get into full sway. This was during the depression (1893) of the second Cleveland administration (1892-1896) and money was very scarce. Such games as Monte, Poker and Coon Can were the favorite games played. (Coon Can is a sort of Mexican Poker played with a special deck of forty cards. Instead of the usual symbols of hearts, diamonds, clubs, and spades, they have swords, clubs, cups and golden discs. The clubs are gnarled-shaped representations of cudgels. Number ten card is a gaily dressed prince with a large club in his hand. Eleven is the same prince on horseback and on twelve he has become a king. On the number one card the symbol is always drawn larger. The colors are a brilliant red, green and yellow with sometimes blue. It is possible to play Coon Can with the usual cards after the eight and nine have been eliminated.) The stakes were buttons, matches, sacks of grain, goats, cows, horses, and cash. Old man Ramón Archuleta, who still had a considerable amount of money he had saved from the mining boom days of the '80's, did a flourishing business loaning it out to the players at ten percent interest, payable that same night if the player was lucky at the games, otherwise not later than the following Saturday night, principal plus the ten percent interest.

Tall, lean and grizzled, his bushy eyebrows overhanging a pair of alert, cat-like eyes, old Ramón would sit behind or walk about the circles of players squatted on the dirt floor, watching his chance to collect as his debtors made substantial gains at the game; and it seemed that his money sometimes had a lucky charm which made his business all the more lucrative. Jollity reigned throughout the night. Jokes, stories, songs and sayings were the order intermingled with the playing. The room was lighted by two kitchen lamps hung on opposite walls, and by the glow of the fire in the earthen fireplace at one corner of the room, beside which sat the old witch woman attending to her cooking of chile-con-carne (peppers with meat), atole (a kind of gruel), tortillas (pancakes), goat milk and coffee, which constituted the night lunch she furnished the players; they in turn enabling her to make a comfortable living. Marcos Valdéz, a big, husky young fellow, called her "Mí Vieja" (my old woman) and always asked her to cook for him a "gorda" (a rather thick tortilla) on the embers of the fireplace to go with the bowl of chile-con-carne and the cup of coffee that she served him.

In an adjoining room a strange guest made his abode. Tía Toña hauled her own firewood from the hillsides north of the village and kept a burro for the purpose, lodging him every night in the room adjoining the gambling room. A door opened between the two rooms. Sometimes, though not often, some strange notion would get into the donkey's head and he would break into a loud intonation of asinine melody at a late hour of the night, causing a momentary hush among the players while the ludicrous braying continued, then an outburst of uncontrollable laughter. This occurrence would serve to intensify the jocularity of the gathering throughout the remainder of the night. At the approach of dawn most of the players would leave for their homes; a few of them remained till daylight, so irresistible was the fascination of the game.

It was a moonless November night in the year 1895 and an unusually large number of players had gathered at Tía Toña's place. Marcos Valdéz was to drive his team and wagon the following day to the railroad station at Tres Piedras twenty miles west of the Río Grande, for a load of freight (merchandise) for the local store. That night he left the joint earlier than was his usual custom, close to the hour of midnight.

As he went out someone jokingly advised him to watch himself on the way, as his vieja (old woman) might take a notion to accompany him in some form or another. He never did believe in the unnatural anyway, so he climbed upon the saddle (he had come down earlier that night on horseback) and started his horse at a slow trot. Past the store on the south side of the river and along the Cordillera road that led from the lower plaza eastward toward the upper plaza where he lived, he sped, urging his horse to a more rapid pace till he reached the last house along the Cordillera and entered a stretch of road void of houses, about one half mile in length. Here his horse began to slacken its pace. He applied the quirt vigorously to its flank but the horse began to rear and balk and finally advanced as if in fear of something, swerving from one side of the road to the other. A strange presentiment came over Marcos Valdéz. This was not a vain premonition, for soon he began to discern, some yards distant, what seemed to him to be a long, white veil that flew back and forth across the road close to the ground. It approached him—passing under his horse, swishing about its legs in rapid motion, then rising in front and continuing its motion in the shape of a vertical elongated figure eight. Swish! Swish!

The strange apparition took many different shapes about the horse and its rider until it finally wound itself about the upper part of the man's body, tightening itself around his neck, choking him. In consternation he pulled the thing and found it gave way easily. Tearing it apart into several lengths, he flung the pieces away from him. To his amazement the thing again assumed its original shape and flew ahead of him close to the ground, outdistancing him, till it reached the upper town where it disappeared at the door of the house of Pedro Barela, the man with whom he had had several altercations in the past. Now he remembered a threat Barela had made against him over a bet at poker one night at Tía Toña's gambling joint. He had said: "You fleeced me this time, but I will fleece you later when you least expect it." The implication was obvious to him now. Pedro Barela also was supposed to practice witchcraft. Many strange things were told about him. It was said that when he stripped for the purpose of bathing or to change his undergarments, that a flame could be distinctly seen inside of his chest, and that on some dark nights the glow would penetrate through his clothing like a visible aura. As Valdéz approached Barela's house, he saw through a window what he believed to be the flicker of a lighted candle being moved about the room. Curious, he approached closer to the window. There, inside of the room, he saw what a few minutes before he had thought was a long white veil but in reality was the white fleece of a sheep, twisted and disheveled, upon the covers of a bed, a strange, flickering radiance emanating from it that illuminated the whole room. As he watched, it slowly began to assume human form and presently transformed itself into the likeness of Pedro Barela. Unnerved by his harassing experiences of the night, Marcos Valdéz went home and retired to his bed, mystified but still unconvinced regarding unnatural phenomena.

For several nights after his encounter with the fleece, Marcos Valdéz absented himself from Tía Toña's place. During all this time he had been delving into the mysteries of witchcraft and had already figured out a plan whereby he believed he could unravel the mystery. He decided to try his investigation on Tía Toña on the night she was accustomed to leave home. Accordingly he invited a companion, Erineo Martínez, three or four years his junior, and both rode over on horseback after nightfall and stationed themselves on the Cuchillo, the ridge south of the Hondo River, one mile east of the upper plaza. That high point commands an unobstructed view of the village below and of the range of mountains to the east for several miles. At about the hour of midnight they saw the mysterious ball of fire arise from the chimney of Tía Toña's house. Higher and higher it arose, in increased momentum as it floated eastward, passing high over the heads of the two observers who immediately followed it at breakneck speed on their horses over the road along the edge of the hill. It reached Valdéz, the "Witch Town," ahead of the two men and circled over the village. As it circled a second time, another strange phenomenon took place. A multitude of balls of fire arose from the houses of the village and trailed after the first one as it headed northward in the direction of Cañada Escondida (Hidden Canyon), at the foot of the mountains, about one half mile distant from the village, where they all alighted a few minutes later. The two riders followed, passing through the village and reaching the place shortly after the fireballs.

There a strange celebration was in progress. From a vantage point the two observers could see a merry dancing party in an open space in the canyon. The fantastic figures of the dancers were gaily dressed, strangely semi-transparent and the group illuminated by a diffused light from some unseen source. Not a sound or a noise of any sort could be heard, but the varying expressions on the dancers' faces and their rhythmic movements of body clearly indicated that jollity, laughter and music was the order. The whole scene seemed to the two young men more of a chimera than a reality. Opposite the dancers, on what appeared to be a throne, sat Tía Toña, as queen and master of ceremonies. But not the old disheveled hag usually seen at the gambling joint, for now she was a woman of refined appearance, attired in elegant, flowing gown and sparkling jewels.

The approach of dawn made the figures gradually less and less discernible till the illusion finally disappeared, fading away as fantastically as it had come on the scene.

"Por Dios! Mi Vieja! (God! My Old Woman!) I do believe in witches now," ejaculated Marcos Valdéz. And revenge upon Pedro Barela and his sheep fleece was hastily forgotten as the two spectators turned rein and rode back to the safety of home.

Source of Information: Related to the writer by Marcos Valdéz, now deceased.

Chile and corn drying outside home, Santa Cruz, New Mexico, ca. 1910–15, unattributed, NMHM/DCA, #008088

Burros loaded with firewood, Agua Fria, New Mexico, ca. 1925–45, T. Harmon Parkhurst, NMHM/DCA, #005517

House and oven, Agua Fria, New Mexico, ca. 1900, unattributed, NMHM/DCA, #056647

Chicken pull in Agua Fria, New Mexico, ca. 1900, unattributed, NMHM/DCA, #057659

Two Mexican Boys at Agua Fria near Santa Fe, New Mexico, ca. 1911, Jesse Nusbaum, NMHM/DCA, #139519

Church bell at Santa Cruz, New Mexico, ca. 1911, Jesse Nusbaum, NMHM/DCA, #013935

"Valley and town of Mesilla, New Mexico," 1856, Middleton, Wallace, & Co., NMHM/DCA, #133628

Unidentified wedding group at Santa Fe, New Mexico, 1912, Jesse Nusbaum, NMHM/DCA, #061817

Interior, de la Peña House, Santa Fe, New Mexico, 1912, Jesse Nusbaum, NMHM/DCA, #015335

Rear of church, Córdova, New Mexico, ca. 1900, unattributed, NMHM/DCA), #058847

Relatives of artists Eliseo and Paula Rodríquez husking corn, Santa Fe, New Mexico, ca. 1970?, Ed Andrews, NMHM/DCA, #071218

"New Mexican Threshing Machine," northern New Mexico, undated, Philip E. Harroun, NMHM/DCA, #015374

Plastering adobe, Abiquiu, New Mexico, ca. 1897, Philip E. Harroun, NMHM/DCA, #012535

"Mexican Woman Baking, Santa Fe," ca. 1898-1900, Christian G. Kaadt, NMHM/DCA, #069106

Chimayó weaver, Chimayó, New Mexico, undated, unattributed, NMHM/DCA, #013770

Birds eye view of Chimayó, New Mexico, ca. 1911, Jesse Nusbaum, NMHM/DCA, #014450

Procession at Santuario de Chimayó, Chimayó, New Mexico, 1910, Jesse Nusbaum, NMHM/DCA, #014379

Street scene, Truchas, New Mexico, ca. 1925–45, T. Harmon Parkhurst, NMHM/DCA, #011594

Cart (New Mexico History Museum Artifact No. 9500/45), undated, unattributed, NMHM/DCA), #011838

Acequia Madre, Albuquerque, New Mexico, 1881, Ben Wittick, NMHM/DCA, #015754

Interior of McSween Store, Lincoln, New Mexico, undated, Lincoln County Collection, NMHM/DCA, #089733

Main Street of Lincoln, New Mexico showing Watson house, site of burned McSween house and Tunstall Store, undated, Frasher, NMHM/DCA, #105473

Group in front of Lincoln Hotel, Lincoln, New Mexico, ca. 1890–1900, unattributed, NMHM/DCA, #110991

Church at Trampas, New Mexico, ca. 1912, Jesse Nusbaum, NMHM/DCA, #014164

Funeral procession, Mora, New Mexico, ca. 1895, Tom Waltom, NMHM/DCA, #014757

Home, Manzano, New Mexico, ca. 1900, unattributed, NMHM/DCA, #037438

Church, San Miguel, New Mexico, November 14, 1882, Adolph F. Bandelier, NMHM/DCA, #009673

BILLY THE KID

"José García y Trujillo doesn't believe that Billy the Kid was ever shot. He feels sure he got away to South America. He wouldn't be surprised if he is alive somewhere today, an old man with many memories and a quick mind, like himself."

From "Interview with José García y Trujillo" by Janet Smith

Billy the Kid

by Edith L. Crawford

(As told by Francisco Trujillo, 85 years old, of San Patricio, Lincoln County, New Mexico.)

I arrived at San Patricio in the year 1877. During the first days of October, Sheriff Brady appointed a committee to pursue some bandits whom we found at Harry Baker's ranch at Siete Ríos. There we arrested them and brought them to the jail at Lincoln.

In November the people of Peñasco went to take the bandits out from jail. Among the people coming from Peñasco, was Billy the Kid. At about the same time Francisco Trujillo, my brother, Juan Trujillo and I went to Pajarito to hunt deer. We were at the mouth of the Pajarito Canyon skinning a deer, when we saw two persons passing. One was Frank Baker, the other was Billy Mote. One was a bandit and the other a bodyguard whom Marfe kept at the ranch. The last one was a thief also. When they passed, my brother said, "Let us get away quickly, these are bad people." So, we got our horses, saddled them and left in the direction of San Patricio. On the way we met the bandits and the people who were coming from the jail at Lincoln.

The bandits surrounded Juan, my brother. I started to get away but Billy the Kid followed me, telling me to stop. I then turned around and saw that he was pointing a rifle at me so I jumped from my horse and aimed my gun at him. He then went back to where my people were and aimed his gun at Juan saying, "If Francisco does not surrender I am going to kill you." Lucas Gallegos then shouted, "Surrender, friend, otherwise they will kill my compadre Juan." Billy then took my gun from where I had laid it and we returned to the place where the people were. Billy then said to me, "We have exchanged guns, now let us exchange saddles." I said that suited me, picking up the gun when another Texan said, "Hand it over, you don't need it." At this point Lucas Gallegos interposed saying to my brother, "Let me have the pistol, compadre." Then my brother gave Lucas the pistol in its holster. Then and there we parted and left for San Patricio to recount our experiences. . . .

From Aleman we left for Berendo where we found a fandango in progress. We were enjoying ourselves very thoroughly when Don Miguel came up to us and said, "Better be on your way boys, because presently there will arrive about fifty Marfes who are probably coming here to get you." Esteco, our leader, agreeing with Don Miguel, commanded us to saddle our horses. We had not been gone half a mile when we heard shouts and gun-shots so we decided to wait for the gang and have it out. Our efforts were of no avail, however, as the gang failed to show up. We then pursued our course toward the Capitán mountains and arrived at Agua Negra at daybreak and there we had our lunch. At this point the party broke up, the Anglos going to Lincoln, the Mexicans to San Patricio whence they arrived on Sunday afternoon. Billy the Kid then said to José Chaves, "Let us draw to see who has to wait for Macky Swin tomorrow at Lincoln." The lots fell to Charley Barber, John Milton and Jim French White, whereupon the leader decided that all nine Anglos should go. Bill thought that it was best for none of the Mexican boys to go and when Chaves protested saying that the Anglos were no braver than he, Bill explained that it was a matter of policy, all Mexicans being sentimental about their own. Chaves being appeased urged the rest to go on promising to render assistance should a call come for help. A Texan named Doke said that since his family was Mexican too, he would remain with the others. Stock then gave orders to proceed. The horses were saddled and they left for Lincoln. Doke, Fernando Herrera, Jesús Sais and Candelario Hildalgo left for Ruidoso. The next morning Don Pedro Sanches left for Lincoln to make some purchases at the store. Being in the store about eleven, the mail arrived and with it Macky Swin. There also arrived Brady and a Texan named George Hamilton. At this juncture Brady also arrived where he found Billy the Kid, Jim French, Charley Barber and John Melton. They were in the corral from whence two of the gang shot at one, and two others at the other, where they fell.

Billy the Kid then jumped to snatch Brady's rifle and as he was leaning over someone shot at him from a house they used to call "El

Chorro." Macky Swin then reached the house where the nine Macky Swins were congregated—the four who were in the coral and five who had been at the river. There they remained all day until nightfall and then proceeded to San Patricio. The next morning they proposed going to the hills should there be a war and so that it could be waged at the edge of town and in order not to endanger the lives of the families living there. The same day, toward evening, six Mexicans came to arrest Macky Swin. They did not arrive at the Plaza but camped a little further down between the acequia and the river at a place where there were thick brambles. Shortly after the Mexicans arrived Macky Swin came with his people to eat supper at the house of Juan Trujillo—that being their headquarters, that also being their mess hall, having hired a negro to prepare the meals. After supper they scattered among the different houses, two or three in each house. In one of these at the edge of town Macky Swin and an American boy whose name was Tome locked themselves in. Next day early in the morning the six Mexicans who had been looking for Macky Swin showed up. When they arrived at the house where Macky Swin was Tome came out and shot at the bunch of Mexicans and hit Julian López in the arm. They then fled to the top of a near-by hill. An hour having passed from the time that Tome shot Julian, about forty Marfes came down to San Patricio killing horses and chickens. At this point there arrived two Marfes, an American and a Mexican. The American's name was Ale Cu, and the Mexican's Lucio Montoya. When the Macky Swin became aware of them, they began to fire and killed all the horses. The two Marfes ran away to San Patricio where the rest of the Marfes were tearing down a house and taking out of the store everything that they could get hold of. From there all the Marfes went to Lincoln and for about a month nothing of interest occurred. . . .

In October the Governor accompanied by seven soldiers and other persons came to San Patricio camping. Having heard about the exploits of Billy the Governor expressed a desire to meet him and sent a messenger to fetch him. The interview was in the nature of a heart to heart talk wherein the Governor advised Billy to give up his perilous career. At this point occurred the General Election and George Kimbrell was elected sheriff of the county. Obeying the Governor's orders he called out the militia having commissioned Sr. Patrón as captain and Billy the Kid as First Lieutenant.

During that year—that of '79—things were comparatively quiet and Billy led a very uneventful life.

About the last part of October of the same year, the Governor issued an order that the militia should make an effort to round all bandits in Chaves county, a task which the militia was not able to accomplish, hence it disbanded. Billy the Kid received an honorable discharge and would probably have gone straight from then on had it not been that at this juncture the District Court met and the Marfes swore a complaint against him and ordered sheriff Kimbrell to arrest him. Billy stubbornly refused to accompany the sheriff and threatened to take away his life rather than to be apprehended. Again nothing was heard for a time and then Pat Garrett offered to bring in the desperado for a reward. The Governor having been made aware of the situation himself offered a reward of $500. Immediately Pat Garrett accompanied by four other men got ready to go after Billy and found him and three other boys, whom they surrounded. One morning, during the siege, one of Billy's companions went out to fetch a pail of water whereupon Pat Garrett shot at him, as well as the others, hitting him in the neck and thereby causing him to drop the pail and to run into the house. With a piece of cloth, Billy was able to dress the wound of the injured man and at least stop the hemorrhage. He then advised the wounded man to go out and pretend to give himself up, hiding his fire-arm but using it at the first opportune moment to kill Pat. Charley did as he was told but when he went to take aim, dropped dead. Bill and the other three companions were kept prisoners for three days but finally hunger and thirst drove them out and caused them to venture forth and to give themselves up. Billy was arrested, there being no warrant for the others. Then followed the trial which resulted in a sentence to hang within thirty days. News of the execution having spread about, people began to come in from miles around to be present on the fatal day, but Billy was not to afford them that much pleasure, having escaped three days before the hanging. A deputy and jailer had been commissioned to stand guard over him. On the day of the escape at noon the jailer told the deputy to go and eat his dinner and that he would then go himself and fetch the prisoners. It was while the jailer and Billy remained alone that the prisoner stepped to the window to fetch a paper. He had somehow gotten rid of his hand-cuffs and only his shackles remained. With the paper in his hand he approached the officer and before the latter knew what his charge was up to, yanked his revolver away from him and the next instant the jailer was dead. Billy lost no time in removing his keeper's cartridge belt as well as a rifle and a "44 W. C. F." which were in the room.

When the deputy heard the shots he thought that the jailer must have shot Billy who was trying to escape and ran from the hotel to the jail on the steps of which he met Billy who said "hello" as he brushed past him, firing at him as he dashed by. Billy's next move was to rush to the hotel and to have Ben Else remove his shackles. He also provided for him a horse and saddled it for Billy upon the promise that he was to leave it at San Patricio. True to his word, Billy secured another horse at San Patricio from his friend Juan Trujillo, promising in turn to return the same as soon as he could locate his own.

Billy now left San Patricio and headed for John Chisum's cattle ranch. Among the cow-boys there there was a friend of Billy Mote who had sworn to kill the Kid wherever he found him in order to avenge his friend. But Billy did not give him time to carry out his plan, killing him on the spot. From there Billy left for Berendo where he remained a few days. Here he found his own horse and immediately sent back Juan Trujillo's. From Berendo Billy left for Puerto de Luna where he visited Juan Patrón, his former capitán. Patrón did everything to make his and his companion's stay there as pleasant as possible. On the third evening of their stay there was to have been a dance and Billy sent his companion to make a report of what he saw and heard. While on his way there, and while he was passing in front of some abandoned shacks, Tome was fired upon by one of Pat Garrett's men and killed. No sooner had Billy heard the distressing news than he set out for the house of his friend Pedro Macky at Bosque Grande where he remained in hiding until a Texan named Charley Wilson, and who was supposed to be after Billy, arrived. The two exchanged greetings in a friendly fashion and then the stranger asked Billy to accompany him to the saloon, which invitation Billy accepted. There were six or seven persons in the saloon when the two entered. Drinks were imbibed and a general spirit of conviviality prevailed when someone suggested that the first one to commit a murder that day was to set the others up. "In that case the drinks are on me" said Charley, who commanded all to drink to their heart's content. Billy then ordered another round of drinks and by this time Charley, who was feeling quite reckless, began to shoot at the glasses not missing a single one until he came to Billy's. This he pretended to miss, aiming his shot at Billy instead. This gave Billy time to draw out his own revolver and before Charley could take aim again, Billy had shot the other in the breast twice. When he was breathing his last Billy said, "Do not whimper, you were too eager to buy those drinks." It was Billy's turn now to treat the company.

Quiet again reigned for a few days. In the meantime Pat Garrett was negotiating with Pedro Macky for the deliverance of Billy. When all details were arranged for, Pat left for Bosque Grande secretly. At the ranch house, Pedro hid Pat in a room close beside the one Billy was occupying. Becoming hungry during the night Billy got up and started to prepare a lunch. First he built a fire, then he took his hunting knife and was starting to cut off a hunk of meat from a large piece that hung from one of the vigas when he heard voices in the adjoining room. Stepping to the door he partially opened it and thrusting his head in asked Pedro who was with him. Pedro replied that it was only his wife and asked him to come in. Seeing no harm in this Billy decided to accept the invitation only to be shot in the pit of the stomach as he stood in the door. Staggering back to his own room it was not definitely known that the shot had been fatal until a cleaning woman stumbled over the dead body upon entering the room the following morning.

Translation by A. L. White.

Billy the Kid Story: Donicino Molina

by Edith L. Crawford

Narrator: Donicino Molina, Tularosa, New Mexico
Age: 84

I was born in Belen, New Mexico, but have spent most of my life in Lincoln County.

I was living with my brother José Molina at Hondo, New Mexico about two miles below the Fritz Ranch at the time of the Lincoln County War.

I happened to be near the Fritz spring when several of the Murphy men rode up to the spring—there were several of the McSween men there and both sides started shooting. A fellow by the name of Frank McNab was killed, and they shot Frank Coe's horse from under him as he was running toward the river.

I often wonder how he escaped without a scratch as there was so many shots fired at him. He was captured and taken to Lincoln.

I knew Billy the Kid well as he stopped at my brother's house many times.

Billy the Kid Story: Francisco Gómez

by Edith L. Crawford

Narrator: Francisco Gómez, Lincoln, New Mexico
Age: 82

I was fourteen years old at the time of the Lincoln County War. I was irrigating a piece of land just back of the McSween home across the Bonita River. I remember seeing several men coming up the river from the east side of town—then I saw the Fort Stanton soldiers marching up the road towards the home of my compadre, Liso Salas—then I noticed that they were coming down the road and they stopped in front of the McSween home.

The officer was talking to someone in front of the house; at the same time the men I saw coming up the river had gone up to the wall back of the house. The next thing I saw, the house was on fire; and I ran from the place I was working and hid—because there was a lot of shooting going on.

I remember well seeing someone carrying a person across the river after the shooting stopped. Later on I learned that it was Igenio Salazar, who was wounded that day as he ran from the McSween home.

I was so scared I couldn't tell just what all was taking place.

I knew Billy the Kid well.

Reminiscences of Billy the Kid

by Edith L. Crawford

Narrator: José Montoya, Jicarilla, New Mexico

I knew Billy the Kid during the Lincoln County War. I was 11 years old at that time. Billy the Kid, Anastacio Martínez, a man by the name of Meletón, (I never knew his last name) and a negro by the name of George Washington, stole some horses from the Indians and drove them over to my brother-in-law's ranch on the southeast side of the Capitán mountains. The place was called Raton. Billy would let me ride his horse and also any of the Indian ponies that was gentle enough for me to ride. They stayed three or four days with us and I slept with Billy the Kid.

The Government sent a bunch of soldiers from Fort Stanton to Lincoln to keep peace between the two factions there. Billy was in Lincoln at the time the soldiers came and he got a long stick and put a white handkerchief on the end of it and held it up and waved it and rode out of town accompanied by Anastacio Martínez, Meletón and the negro man.

Billy was a small man with a small sharp nose, his two front teeth were large and stuck out in front. He was a nice fellow and well liked by the natives. He was awful good to the Mexican people and stayed with them most of the time and talked good Spanish. I saw Billy the Kid while he was in jail waiting to be hanged for the murder of Sheriff Brady.

I never heard of him having a sweetheart around this part of the country. I was living in Lincoln at the time Billy the Kid killed Bell and Ollinger and got away but I did not see him as everyone was afraid to come out of their houses until he had left town.

I don't know what became of the rest of the men that were with Billy the Kid, except George Washington, the negro. He was married to a Mexican woman but he ran away with one of Captain Baca's daughters. This Captain Baca was well thought of in the community. The people of Lincoln caught this negro and killed him and then hanged his body up to a post in the yard of his wife.

I never heard Billy the Kid speak of his mother.

Reminiscences of Billy the Kid

As Told by Sam Farmer, Hijinio Salazar, Apolonio Sedillo, Gregorio Ventura

by Edith L. Crawford

I remember very well when Billy the Kid killed Bell and Ollinger. I was about 10 or 11 years old, I was irrigating wheat with my father and older brother, it was about one o'clock I guess.

I saw a man coming riding a black horse and he rode down by the ditch where we were working and stopped. He hollered to my father, "Hello Henry!" My father said "What you doing here, Bill?"

He said, "I am going, I don't think you'll see me anymore." My father said "Why, Bill?" and he said, "I killed two men at the courthouse and I'm trying to get away, good bye."

(Answers to questions I asked him)
When he came by the ditch he was riding straddle.

He was straight and slender and walked very quick. He had light brown hair and green eyes and he wore a cowboy hat with the brim straight in front and turned up in the back. It was always on the side of his head. I never saw him with a cap or a black hat on, always it was a light hat. He was about 20, I guess.

I never saw him with a girl in Lincoln and never heard of his having one there, but I heard that he had a Spanish girl at Bosque Grande named Carolina.

I remember the Lincoln county war, not much, but the shooting and the soldiers. I remember Billy well. I liked him. I was around 11, I guess. His mother was living then. He spoke of her to my father and to Hijinio Salazar, for both of them told me so. He talked to Hijinio about her during the Lincoln County War.

I used to go with my father often when he freighted with a team of oxen. We used to stop at a camp which was on the road between Las

Vegas and Lincoln near the Gallinas mountains. We used to see Billy there. I remember once I saw him and he was eating his dinner. He used to sit with his legs straight out with his plate on his lap and his hat on his boots. I remember I asked him, "What you set that way for?" and he said, "That's a quick way to get up if I have to."

One of Billy's compadres was a man named Apolonio Sedillo. Once I was at a house of María de la Antilles and I started to go in a room. She stopped me quick and said, "Get away from that room, Coyote." The bed had a sheet put up all around it so nobody could see who was in the bed. Apolonio was in there sitting against the wall, Billy was in the bed. That was when Billy was on the dodge after the war.

(Told me by Hijinio Salazar)

A story about Billy that Hijinio told me was about a man named Mike. I don't remember his other name. Mike talked too much about Billy. He said he was going to kill Billy the first time that he saw him. One day Billy came to the saloon in Lincoln. Mike was there. Billy said, "Hello, Mike. Come on and have a drink, maybe that will be the last drink we'll have together." When they got their drinks Billy had his in his left hand. He said, "Pull your gun, Mike, you'll need it for I'm going to kill you or you me." He shot Mike right there. Billy didn't bother anybody unless they were out to get him. If he was your friend he was your friend but he was hard on anybody who talked about getting him if he knew it.

(Told me by Apolonio Sedillo)

Once Billy and Sedillo stole all the horses, mules and burros that the Indians had. The Indians were about three miles above Fort Stanton then. They could not get them all at once but they did not have very much trouble except for one old horse mule. The Indians tied a rope on the mule's neck and took the rope inside the teepee. The Indians had a little pup that barked every time that they would get close. One night Billy took a half a sack of sopapillas with him and every time the dog barked he'd throw a sopapilla to him and he went up to the mule and cut the rope with his knife. Every time the dog barked he'd throw another sopapilla to him. He finally got the mule and rode him away. Billy and Sedillo drove all the horses and mules and burros to the Chisum Ranch below Roswell.

(Told me by Gregorio Ventura)

One time Billy went across the border into Chihuahua. He went to a gambling house and held up a monte game and put all the money in a sack and came across the border. He had a lot of money and he did not kill anybody.

These stories were told to me by Sam Farmer who lived in Lincoln during and after the Lincoln County War and knew Billy the Kid. Narrator—Sam Farmer, Carrizozo, New Mexico; age 67.

Story of Billy the Kid

by Edith L. Crawford

I was born at Manzano, New Mexico. My people moved to Lincoln County when I was one year old.

In the year of 1878 we lived on the north side of the Bonito River, about one and one-half miles west of the town of Lincoln, close to the old graveyard.

I was about ten years old at that time, and remember well when my compadre, Teodoro Farmer and myself were playing near the graveyard and the first thing we knew someone was pointing a gun at us; and believe me, we started running, very much scared.

We saw the man was laughing and at the same time he told us to stop, that he was not going to hurt us, and we asked him who he was; he replied, "I am Billy the Kid." I know it was the Kid for I saw him several times later on as he visited the home of Jim Farmer, who lived near us.

At that time I remember well the day the McSween house burned. I was close to the road when the Fort Stanton Soldiers went marching by toward Lincoln; and later in that day we could see the smoke from the burning building. Later on we were told that the Murphy gang had burnt the McSween house, killed Mr. McSween and wounded Iginio Salazar — and that Billy the Kid had escaped from the building unhurt.

Source of Information: Manuel Águilar, Capitán, New Mexico, 69 years old.

What I Know About Billy the Kid

As Told by Francisco Gómez

by E. L. Crawford

In 1877 I worked in the home of Mr. McSween in whose house Billy the Kid took up abode at that time. There we both stayed, I as a worker and he as a boarder. We stayed some 6 or 7 months and I knew this young man to be kind and gentlemanlike with me and with all the inhabitants of Lincoln. During the time he was there I left this home but he remained: a little while later I saw him leave here with some other people from here on a search for some Texan assailants who were molesting the people by shooting in the streets. The sheriff gathered some people together with Billy the Kid for the search. The assailants were above the Ruidoso River at a place called "La Cuesta." There they fought and one was killed and two taken prisoner. From then on I did not see him again until in 1881 when I saw him in jail. I do not know where he was arrested. He remained there up to the time that he killed the two guards.

I have heard from several people who were around close at the time that he killed the guards, that they took him from the jail to a room above the Court Room and this is where he killed the first guard, and he killed the other outside the house on the side of the Calle Carmen; this I know through information from neighbors who saw the killings. I did not see him at the time. This if all I know relative to Billy the Kid.

Narrator: Francisco Gómez, Age 85, Lincoln, New Mexico.

The Biography of Guadalupe Lupita Gallegos (II)

by Bright Lynn

The family of Guadalupe Lupita's parents had many Indian servants and this is the way they got them, as related by María Antonia, an Indian servant of the family. The Navajo men would all leave their camps on hunting expeditions in the fall and early winter, taking with them the strongest women and leaving behind them the old women and men with the children. Often while they were away the Chimayós, a tribe of Indians living in the area, would come and steal the women and children and sell them to the rich Spaniards. The Spaniards were very kind to the Indians, Lupita says, and the Indians loved their masters. Even after the Civil War ended slavery the Indians refused to leave, preferring slavery with their Spanish masters to freedom.

Before she had grown to a marriageable age, several men had asked for the lovely Lupita's hand. But Lupita was not allowed to know the identity of these aspiring young gentlemen. Her parents were very strict with her. Once in a great while she was taken to a dance and there she must keep her eyes downcast until she was asked to dance a number.

The boys were always awaiting an opportunity to "make eyes" at the girls, but the latter were not even allowed to look around the room. Mrs. Gallegos says that the only chance a boy had of seeing a girl was at a dance or at Mass.

If a young man wished to marry a certain girl he informed his parents who in turn would have a talk with the parents of the girl and thus the marriage would be arranged.

More often, however, among the upper class wealthy parents would visit other wealthy parents who lived far off and arrange marriages for financial reasons. In many instances the bride and groom to be did not even know one another and were not even informed of the impending marriage until all arrangements had been made by their parents.

Often times a boy would fall in love with a girl he had seen at

Mass or at a dance and his parents would have a talk with her parents. The girl's parents would take a few days to think it over and then send a refusal to the parents of the boys. "Les daban calabasas." (They gave them pumpkins.) This expression meant that the girl's parents did not consent to the marriage.

A young Spaniard by the name of J. M. Gallegos lived in Los Alamos and he often came to Las Vegas to the dances. It was at one of these dances that he happened to meet Lupita, who was then only twelve years old, and he fell madly in love with her.

Mrs. Gallegos smiles when she says that she doesn't know yet whether he fell in love with her or her money. He was an excellent dancer and they danced much together. One day her father told her that two men had asked for her hand in marriage, a Jew named Rosenwall, and a J. M. Gallegos. Lupita did not wish to marry a Jew so she chose Gallegos.

Lupita, only a girl of twelve, was married in Our Lady of Sorrows church at eight o'clock in the evening. In the church was a beautiful statue of Our Lady of Sorrows. It was customary to dress the statue for every church occasion and for Lupita's wedding it wore a halo of gold, and a necklace of gold which had been given to Lupita by her grandmother's aunt Louisianita.

Lupita was dressed in a white dress of heavy silk called "espuma" (foamy) and wore a short white veil. When the groom's parents came to receive her she went to the boy's father, as was the custom, and said, "Recognize me as your daughter."

The father replied, "I shall always be at your service." Then Lupita went to the boy's mother and to each of his relatives. After all the customary preliminaries were done with, the ceremony was performed by Father Cuder, a French priest.

After the wedding feast everyone went to the wedding ball which was held just in back of where the Charles Ilfeld Company is located today.

Doubtless little Lupita was flushed with a new kind of happiness as she glided across the dance floor in the arms of her handsome husband. She was surprised when he suddenly stopped dancing and asked her to go outside with him for he had a little story to tell her. This is the story he told to Lupita as he held her in his arms, their faces turned upward to the stars:—

When Lupita's mother, María Ignacia, and father, Severo Baca, were about to be married J. M. Gallegos was a dirty little urchin playing about in the streets. He and several other little street boys saw a wedding procession going by and they knew that Severo Baca and María Ignacia were going to be married. The boys ran after the coach shouting, "Long live Severo Baca! Long live Severo Baca!" When all the guests were having dinner after the wedding, J. M. Gallegos and his friends crept up to a window to stare at the bride. Little did the young Gallegos dream that he was staring at the mother of his future bride.

For many years Mr. and Mrs. Gallegos ran a small store at San Ilario. Their store stood close to the main road and almost every traveler who passed stopped in to buy something and to pass the time of day. One day Mrs. Gallegos returned to the store from a visit with one of her neighbors. Her husband was in the front of the store talking to an American cowboy in Spanish. When her husband saw her come in he called to her and said, "Lupita, I want you to meet a friend of mine. This is Billy the Kid."

Mrs. Gallegos says that she had always been a brave woman but when she found herself actually face to face with Billy the Kid she almost fainted. The Kid seemed to be in a talkative mood for he started telling Mrs. Gallegos about his adventures and for emphasis he drew his gun and shot a couple of holes in the ceiling. The neighbors all came running to find out what all the shooting was about, but upon finding it was Billy the Kid they all started running the other way.

The next time Mrs. Gallegos saw Billy the Kid she was in the store by herself. He came in, bought some things, and left. Mrs. Gallegos says that he was always very courteous and that he was, in her opinion, a real gentleman.

Mrs. Gallegos knew Sostenes, a member of Billy's gang, very well. His parents were good people and lived in Los Alamos. As far as she knew, Sostenes was always a good boy and it was hard for her to believe that he would turn outlaw. When he did turn, however, he turned with a vengeance. Mrs. Gallegos was acquainted with an old man who was half blind and he told her the following incident:—

One day while he was traveling on his burro, Billy the Kid and Sostenes rode up. Sostenes said, "Billy, let's kill this old blind man just to see how old blind men die."

"Let him alone," commanded Billy. "He's doing us no harm." The old man thought his day had come, and when Billy prevented Sostenes from killing him the Kid became the old man's hero.

Mrs. Gallegos knew Silva, the notorious bandit, very well indeed, for he worked for her husband one year carrying trading stuff from Las Vegas to Santa Fe. She says that he was considered a respectable citizen then. She describes him as tall and handsome, rather fair of complexion and light of hair. Years later when Mrs. Gallegos was living at Los Alamos she and the neighbors used to see a mysterious person dressed in a black cap and cape with a black cloth over his face walking by the side of the river. Everyone suspected it was Silva and afterwards they discovered it was he.

Silva had his headquarters at the home of a woman named Cruz, a respectable lady on the surface, who used to come often to Mrs. Gallegos's house to visit. Of course no one knew at the time that her home was being used as the headquarters of such a notorious band of outlaws as the Silva gang.

Source of Information: Mrs. Guadalupe Gallegos.

About Billy the Kid

As Told by Ismael Valdéz

by L. Raines

Grandmother was reared by Mr. Rodolph, an uncle, one of the characters often mentioned in history in connection with Billy the Kid. She lived in Fort Sumner in Lincoln County, where most of the events of Billy's life took place.

Grandmother says, "Billy at a very early age was one of the toughest hombres of the West. He had long curly hair; he was polite to women; he could play the piano well. The greatest delights Billy had were fighting, horseback riding, dancing, and playing the piano."

Billy often came to Fort Sumner and stopped at Mr. Rodolph's home for a night's lodging. He and his companions on entering handed their guns to Mr. Rodolph for safe keeping. Grandmother tells how Billy and his associates used to go to dances "packed with precious jewels" — their guns.

One of the bloodiest occurrences in Billy's career was the blowing out of a store belonging to a Fort Sumner resident. Billy's crowd stopped at this big store for whiskey. The storekeeper refused to open his door to the unruly gang. The affront angering them, the crowd retreated to a safe distance and began shooting at barrels of powder which they spied through the store window. The powder exploded, the store went up in a rush of flame, the storekeeper lost his life, and one of Billy's crowd was mortally injured.

Source of Information: Ismael Valdéz.

Interview with José García y Trujillo

by Janet Smith

José García y Trujillo doesn't believe that Billy the Kid was ever shot. He feels sure he got away to South America. He wouldn't be surprised if he is alive somewhere today, an old man with many memories and a quick mind, like himself. When I showed him a book by the man who killed Billy the Kid, he was unconvinced.

"No, Señora," and he shook his forefinger back and forth before his face. "You think Billy the Keed let himself be shot in the dark like that? No, Señora, Billy the Keed—never. I see Billy the Keed with these eyes. Many times, with these eyes. That Billy, tenía un' agilesa in su mente—in su mente aquí." He pointed to his forehead.

Mr. García could speak but little English, and I knew almost no Spanish, but I understood that he meant that Billy the Kid had an extraordinary quickness of mind.

Again he pointed to his forehead and then with a quick motion to the sky. "Un function electrica," he said. Something that worked like lightning.

When I stopped to see Mr. García he was sitting on the ground under the cottonwood tree that shades the cracked adobe walls of his long narrow house. His hat was pulled down over his eyes and he seemed to be sleeping. As I stopped the motor of my car, however, he raised his head and pushed back his hat with one motion. He squinted at me a minute, and then pulled himself to his feet.

"Cómo se va, Señora?" Mr. García placed the one chair in the shade for me. He found a box behind a heap of wagon wheels and car fenders and sat down beside me. He squinted his long blue eyes and asked in Spanish, "What's new?"

I patted the black kitten stretched on a bench at my elbow. Beside it perched a cock and two hens. Two little brown dogs nosed at my shoes, and a big shaggy fellow laid his head against my arm. The flies buzzed.

A thin dark old woman stepped over the little goat sleeping just inside the doorway of the house, its head resting on the doorstep. She gathered up some green chili from a table in the yard, giving me an intent look as she stood there, and went back into the house without saying a word.

Mr. García asked me again, "What's new? You bring me those history books of Billy the Keed?"

I showed him the picture of Pat Garrett who shot Billy the Kid. "I don't want to dispute against you, Señora, but in my mind, which is the picture of my soul, I know it is not true. Maybe Pat Garrett, he give Billy the Keed money to go to South America and write that story for the books. Maybe he killed somebody else in Billy's place. Everybody like Billy the Keed—su vista penetrava al Corazon de toda le gente"—his face went to everybody's heart.

Mrs. García came out again and sat on a bench beside her husband. Her skin looked dark and deeply wrinkled under the white towel she had wrapped about her head. She rolled a brown paper cigarette from some loose tobacco in a tin box. As her husband talked she listened intently, puffing on her cigarette. From time to time she would nod her head at me, her eyes dark and somber.

"What did Billy the Kid look like?" I asked.

"Chopito—a short man, but wide in shoulders and strong. His forehead was big. His eyes were blue. He wore Indian shoes with beads on his feet. His clothes—muy desorallado"

"Desorallado?" I asked.

"Like yours," he said, pointing to my blue denim skirt and shirt. "Any old way."

"Muy generoso hombre, Billy the Keed—a very generous man. All the Mexican people, they like him. He give money, horses, drinks—what he have. To whom was good to Billy the Keed, he was good to them. Siempre muy caballo, muy señor—always very polite, very much of a gentleman.

"Once lots of men, they go together after Billy the Keed to shoot him. They pay us—we go—sure. But we don't want to shoot Billy. We always be glad he too smart for us."

In broken English, mixed with Spanish phrases, Mr. García told me how he went in a posse of thirty-five or more men to capture Billy the Kid. He didn't know the Sheriff's name, but the description sounded like Pat Garrett himself. "Muy, muy alto"—very very tall, and Pat Garrett was six feet four and a half. José García was working at the time as sheepherder on the ranch of Jacobo Yrissari, about ninety miles southeast of Albuquerque. The tall sheriff came by one day with a band of men, and offered him five dollars a day and food for himself and his horse to join the posse in search of Billy the Kid. He said he didn't think there was any danger of their getting Billy, and five dollars was a lot of money. The plan was to surround the Maxwell Ranch on the Pecos River, where Billy the Kid was known to spend much time.

This ranch belonged to Lucien Maxwell. "Un muy grande hombre, un millonairio," said José García. Lucien Maxwell was indeed one of the most striking figures of the early mountain frontier. Every trader and plainsman in the Rocky Mountain region knew him. He came to New Mexico from Illinois when the country was still a part of Old Mexico. There he married Luz Beaubien, daughter of a French Canadian, Charles Hipolyte Trotier, Sieur de Beaubien, and a Spanish woman. With Guadalupe Miranda, Beaubien had received from the Mexican government during the administration of Governor Manuel Armijo, a huge grant of land as a reward for pioneer services. Beaubien bought Miranda's share, and at Beaubien's death Lucien Maxwell, his son-in-law, purchased all the land from the heirs and became sole owner of more than a million acres. He made huge sums of money selling sheep, cattle and grain to the government, and built a great house at Cimarron. There he lived in as much magnificence as the times and the country could afford. His guests included cattle kings, governors, army officers, and later when he moved to the ranch near Ft. Sumner, Billy the Kid. Nearly every day his table was set for more than two dozen, and it is reputed that they ate on plates of silver and drank from goblets of gold. José García said he didn't know anything about that for he had never been inside of the house, but he thought it quite likely. He had been by the place at Cimarron several times when he was working for some people by the name of Martínez who had a ranch north of Las Vegas. The Maxwell house was "una grande mancion." But it was to the Maxwell house on the Pecos near Fort Sumner that he went in search of Billy the Kid. Maxwell retired to his place at Fort Sumner after losing much of his wealth. His son Pete later became the richest sheep man in that part of the country. It was Pete who was a friend of Billy. José García said he and other men surrounded the house for two weeks but they never got so much as a glimpse of Billy the Kid.

Mr. García said he knew a good friend of Billy the Kid, José Chávez y Chávez. When he was herding sheep on the Yrissari ranch, which was not far from Santa Rosa on the Pecos river, José Chávez y Chávez was sheepherder on a nearby ranch. One day the two of them were sitting under a tree smoking when a pack train on the way to Arizona came along on the other side of the Pecos. Just opposite the tree where the two sheepherders were sitting they tried to ford the stream. But the water was swift and the horses floundered. José García and José Chávez pulled off their clothes, jumped in and guided the horses to the bank. After the pack train went on, José Chávez showed Mr. García the twenty-one bullet scars on his body. "He had an innocent face—didn't look as though he could break a dish, but he was bad with a gun. Qué hombre!"

"Did they try to get José Chávez to go with the posse after Billy?" I asked.

"José Chávez y Chávez," he corrected me. "No, Señora, he had left the country at that time."

According to Walter Noble Burns, it was this José Chávez y Chávez who was responsible for the friendship between Billy the Kid and the wealthy Maxwells. Billy the Kid had ridden over to Fort Sumner from Lincoln with several of his men, among whom was José Chávez y Chávez. The fiancé of one of the Maxwell girls was drunk and met José Chávez y Chávez on the street back of the Maxwell house. The two men quarreled and José Chávez pulled his gun. Mrs. Maxwell ran out of the house and tried to pull her future son-in-law away, begging Chávez not to shoot him as he was drunk and didn't know what he was doing. Chávez replied that drunk or sober he was going to kill him, and he was going to do it immediately. Just then a young man walked rapidly across the road, touched his sombrero to Mrs. Maxwell, said something in Spanish to Chávez and led him away. It was the Kid. From that time until his death, he made Fort Sumner his headquarters, and was a frequent visitor at the Maxwell home. It was in Pete Maxwell's room that Pat Garrett shot him.

Mr. García asked me if there were any books in Spanish about Billy the Kid. "My wife," he said, "she taught me to read. I didn't know the letters when I married with her. She didn't know the words but she knew the letters and she taught me. I taught myself how the words went, but I never could teach her to read, no con carinioes ni estimos—neither by coaxing nor praising—she never could learn anything more than the letters."

Mrs. García shook her head. "Nunca, nunca, nunca," she said. Never had she been able to learn more than the letters.

I promised to look for a Spanish book about Billy the Kid. I sat for a minute longer watching some pigeons perched on a water barrel. They pecked at the water. The ripples reflected on their green and lavender breasts. The little goat came out of the house and sniffed the dirt around my chair.

As I rose to go, Mr. García stood up and took off his hat. "Muchas felicidades y buena salud, Señora," he said, with a little bow. Much happiness and good health to you.

Mrs. García put out her hand. Her dark eyes were always somber. "Adiós," she said, "no sé más que-decir Dios se ira con Usted." Goodbye, I can only say God be with you.

"Vuelva," they called after me as I drove away. "Come back."

Early Days in Lincoln County

As Told by Josh Brent

by Frances E. Totty

My grandfather Sotorona Baca and his wife were born in Barcelona, Spain and was considered quite wealthy for those days. They came to America and settled at El Paso, Texas where they lived for some time but the old Spanish Legend was going the rounds at the time that they settled at El Paso and it wasn't long until he decided that there was something to the story, and invested $10,000.00 in the swindling scheme, which was all lost as the people that he gave the money to were imposters of the early days and the old story of the lost bullion has gone on down the years.

Grandfather, after he lost so much money, moved to Lincoln and bought a ranch or two as he figured that he was nearly broke and he had to recover some of his losses. He started raising cattle, horses and mules and hogs. He had been a captain in the army and was hired by the government to take supplies to the Fort Stanton Reservation. He never did have any trouble getting the supplies to the Indians as Murphy was hired by the government to furnish the supplies.

My mother Carolatta Baca Brent was born in Lincoln on Jan. 17, 1865. She has a sister that still lives in Lincoln. Mother was in the middle of the Lincoln War and carried messages for both parties. The message was delivered in a bucket of beans. Mother saw Billie the Kid kill Sheriff Brady from the window in the tower. The Spanish and Mexican class of people were friends to Billie the Kid. They often hid him under the floor of their houses and in every way possible warned him of his dangers.

My father was an under-sheriff of Pat Garrett's and was with him when he captured Billie the Kid at Stinking Springs.

Pat Garrett told father after he killed Billie the Kid that a fellow from the east wrote to him and said that he would pay $5000.00 for the trigger finger of the boy. I have read many books on the boy, but this is one fact that I have never seen published. Billie the Kid was not a killer but was fighting for a cause and father told us that he was an unusually nice boy. He took the part of McSween and fought for McSween right to the finish. Mr. McSween was a very refined gentleman and never could believe that the guns should rule as they did, and could never be convinced that he should carry a gun. He died in the war carrying his Bible. Mrs. McSween was a beautiful lady, and understood the ways of the world much better than her husband who was an idealist.

Emerson Huff was living in Lincoln in the early days. He worked around the town at anything that he could get to do. He wanted to save enough money to get to Kansas City. Father was going to take some prisoners to Fort Leavenworth and told Mr. Huff that they would take him that far as a guard. He left father at Leavenworth and drifted into Louisiana and there wrote Mississippi Bubble which brought him a small fortune.

I have at home a spool made into a toy by Pat Garrett that he gave to me when I was a youngster. Pat Garrett after killing Billie the Kid always said that he sure hated to kill the boy, but he knew that it was either his life or the boy's life, and as he was sent out to bring him back he did the only thing he could do, for he realized that Billie would never be taken alive again.

Source of Information: Josh Brent.

TALES OF LAS PLACITAS

"In those old days all the houses faced the east. That was the custom. The sun shone in at the open door, and throughout the morning hours the time could be told by the position of the sunlight upon the adobe floor."

From "Dos Hombres Sabios de Las Placitas (Two Wise Men of Las Placitas)" by Lou Sage Batchen

Dos Hombres Sabios de Las Placitas "Two Wise Men of Las Placitas"

by Lou Sage Batchen

In the days of long ago every well regulated village had its wise man who spoke knowingly of sun, moon, and stars and advised the people upon the most vital of all their problems—the sowing and reaping of the sustaining substance called crops. Each spring he called the farmers together and told them when, what and where to plant. He was indeed the dictator in this all important matter, and none there were who lifted a voice against his decisions. He knew about such matters. He was the wise man. The responsibility of feeding the people became his.

And where did he acquire all this wisdom? No one knew then. In those old days wisdom indeed was power and no one possessing it disseminated it—until the proper time, and then it was given to but one he deemed the proper person, or such was the belief of the people.

It was only fitting that the wise man of the community should be chosen alcalde. As the alcalde he kept such records as were accumulated in the village. He kept the calendar and proclaimed the feast days. The wise man of the village was in truth a busy man. And above all, the wise man must be a good weather forecaster. Therein was his wisdom, and therein lay his success or failure in the pursuit of his high calling.

Within the memory of the oldest now living in Las Placitas, one of the wisest of the long ago alcaldes, if not really the wisest, was Francisco Trujillo. He was born in Old Las Huertas. He fought the Texans in the battle of Valverde, and before that and afterward made trips over the Santa Fe Trail to Los Estados.

In those old days all the houses faced the east. That was the custom. The sun shone in at the open door, and throughout the morning hours the time could be told by the position of the sunlight upon the adobe floor. That is one of the reasons why it is still recalled that all the houses faced the east. Another reason for remembering the fact was that, regardless of weather, the wise man mounted his roof each morning and faced the east at the moment of sunrise. He stood there like a statue observing the heavens, making deductions, adding them to the results of his observations of the sky, the wind, the moon on the night before. Soon he would descend from his high place, summon the men, and in the manner of an oracle utter the weather forecast. Thereafter the plans of the day's activities could be made.

The wise man was especially busy in the pre-planting weeks. Much depended upon his reckoning. The moon, the rain-band, the scurrying clouds; all had their part in causing a wet or dry season. When all the signs were favorable to a more than ordinary degree, then the wise man bade the farmers to plant fields plentifully with seeds, whether such fields were under irrigation ditches or not. There would be a copious rainfall throughout the season and the harvests would be abundant. Should all signs point to dry weather, he told them to plant seeds only on land under a ditch. Thus forewarned, the people made few mistakes in their sowing. Anxiously, Francisco awaited each "new moon" to see whether it foretold rain or drouth. Should the crescent ride flat in the sky, that clearly indicated dry weather, as no water could spill from it. Should the crescent dip, clearly there would be rain; for water could easily spill from the crescent. Early and late, the wise man studied the heavens and the heavenly bodies that his weather forecasts might be accurate, or wise ones.

Francisco kept a day by day calendar. He never proclaimed the fiesta days publicly but he told this one and that one of the coming event and asked that the word be noised among the people. Had he not kept a day by day calendar, he still could have called the fiesta days. He knew how the wise men of long ago reckoned them. Those men were students of the heavenly bodies. They foretold the days by the position of the sun, moon, and stars. Once, generations ago, the people lost track of the days. There were no priests nor wise men near their remote village who kept a calendar. But one old man remembered a date from which they could reckon. They must wait for the harvest (October), watch for the new moon, then count fifteen days forward. That day would be the feast of Las Cabañas (Cabins), or the Jewish feast of The Tabernacle, when they spent seven days in the cabins. That feast day would be the fifteenth day of October, and thus they could find their calendar again.

In the old days they made weather forecasts in August for the following year. They spoke of Las Cabañuelas pointing the right or the wrong way, but no one in Las Placitas now can explain what was meant. Nor do they know how their people of so very long ago knew of the feast of Las Cabañas or how to reckon it, and thus set their calendars aright.

In the long ago days their calendars were inscribed on properly prepared animal hides. Down through the years those calendars were preserved. It would be strange should none be among the old records at Las Placitas, yet no one speaks of the existence of such relics. Alcalde Francisco did leave some records. If his descendants yet have them they are hidden away and not brought forth for exhibition.

There was one Fiesta day Francisco favored, and himself saw to it that the whole village was up early to usher the day in with the proper ceremony. That was June 24, the feast of San Juan Day, the jolliest, carefree day of the year for the villagers of long ago.

In the dewey freshness of the morning of San Juan Day, every man, woman, and child of permissible age was astir, making ready for the event which would properly launch the festivities of the day. When all was ready they went forth from the village in a body, following the trail which led to the nearest arroyo of deep, running water. Now with one accord they walked into the water and went down on their knees and completely immersed themselves in the water. This was to commemorate the baptism of Jesus by John the Baptist. When all had been immersed, they made their way back to the village, and the day's merrymaking was on. This old custom of repeating the baptism of San Juan morning has long since been abandoned. Likewise has the old custom of choosing the wise men to direct and advise them. The advent of politics and the influence of money has set a new standard.

While Francisco was yet in his prime and a wise and honored alcalde of Las Placitas, there was another wise man in their midst. He was old Rafael, a dreamer of dreams and a see-er of visions. El adivino (The prophet) he was called. In those days of long ago, el adivino was born, not made. He announced his divine calling even before he was born. Only those destined to become prophets or soothsayers sent out a cry while yet they were in the mother's womb. So it was that the parents of the unborn baby, who was to be baptized Rafael, knew that their child was to be a prophet. He cried while in his mother's womb.

From infancy Rafael heard sounds and saw things that the other children neither heard nor saw. He grew up, not wise in practical affairs, nor caring for them. He wanted only to be left alone and to be permitted to go his solitary way in peace that he might see visions of the things to be. Talk of things to be someday was of vital importance to him. So fanciful were the word pictures he painted of the visions that came to him, that the villagers gathered about him to hear him tell of them.

None of the very old people who yet recall anything of what he foretold doubt the sincerity of his stories. He did see visions. Of that they feel certain.

The old man spent much of his time in meditation. He withdrew from his friends and family and would sit for hours on the brow of a lonely hill, just gazing into the heavens. Or he would sit by an arroyo and watch the tumbling waters and not move even a finger for hours at a time. He would take his staff and climb the mountain trails to sit beneath some lofty pine, there to "see" and think.

Always after such sessions he was ready to tell them of some vision that was revealed to him. He made two predictions which have caused the descendants of the people of his day to believe that he was in truth a prophet and that he foretold his coming by crying in his mother's womb, after the manner of all true prophets.

Once after a period of meditation in the mountains, he told the people that some day those who were living would see strange things come to pass in Bernalillo. He said the babies of his day might witness them. Then he painted for them in word pictures the vision he had beheld. In Bernalillo many men were tearing down the houses and corrals which stood in the middle of the town from North to South. They cleaned all the rock, adobes, and dirt and poles from the place and made it clean. The people who had lived in the houses had to go to other parts of the village to build new homes. Then strange men came and they brought strange-looking things to work with and they built a great highway. The highway was not like any road he had ever seen. It looked bright in the sun and the rain could not wash it to pieces.

In those old days El Camino Real was the main highway through Bernalillo and the only main road connecting it with the outer world. It was an ancient highway which was narrow, rough, and winding. It lay to the east of Bernalillo. Such were the roads Rafael knew.

A few of those who were infants at the time old Rafael told of his vision of things to come to Bernalillo did live to see the modern highway put through the town. Houses and corrals were torn down to make way for it and all happened just as the wise man foretold, so many, many years ago.

Once he told the people that the time would come when great birds would carry passengers through the sky.

There may have been other adivinos in Old Las Placitas, but only Rafael is yet remembered. And all because nearly eighty years ago he foretold the present great highway through the village of Bernalillo, and the aeroplane.

Sources of Information: José Gurulé, age 90, Las Placitas, New Mexico, whose father, Nicolás Gurulé was a friend of the Francisco of this story. José also was a friend of Francisco, and of Rafael, who was old at the time. Rumaldita Gurulé, age 69, Las Placitas, New Mexico who knew the Francisco of this story. Fermina Durán, age 75, who knew the Francisco of this story. Onofre Gonzales, age 58, of Las Placitas, New Mexico; she is a descendant of the Rafael of this story. José Trujillo, age 57, Las Placitas, New Mexico, a descendant of the Francisco of this story.

El Platero "The Silversmith"

by Lou Sage Batchen

*I*n the long ago days of Las Placitas when the barest necessities were obtained only through hard work, many long hours of it, the women somehow managed to work a little harder to raise surplus commodities in order to barter for prendería (jewelry). Those precious treasures of personal adornment which were made of silver, of copper, of iron were all hand wrought.

In those days old Narvez, none living today remember his family name, gladdened the hearts of the feminine members of the village with his handiwork. Whether his rings and bracelets were of silver (few could afford the silver), or copper, or of iron, they were all works of art; crude though they were, and they all bore designs, and never were two ornaments carved alike. To keep a piece of stolen jewelry made by old Narvez was almost impossible. By the design on it, the owner was certain to know it.

Old Narvez lived at Algodones, but much of his time was spent at or near Las Placitas, for there he found his materials: metals, a whole mine of them at the fabled old Montezuma mine, and there he found coal which he could reduce to coque (coke), and there he found barro (clay) of just the right kind, and there he found plenty of piñón wood abounding in resina (pitch) needed to raise the heat units of his fire, which he must have in his fundidor (smelter).

In making his fundidor, Narvez dug a very shallow place in the ground as large as he wished the base to be. He lined it with rock and clay, then built it up to the desired height, making it with thick walls and using plenty of adobe mud to hold the rocks together. He molded a bowl shaped crisol (crucible) of the clay and when it was finished it was as hard as rock and no degree of heat could damage it, that is, the highest degree of heat he needed for his smelting. The crisol became the top of the fundidor. Two small holes were made at the base of the fundidor. They were directly opposite each other and permitted a free circulation of air which fanned the fire to greater heat. Old Narvez did not have a bellows.

When his fundidor was ready and his ore piled near it for fusion or smelting, Narvez piled up his fuel. He had cut down an abundance of piñón wood and cut it into proper lengths with his hacheta (small stone axe). That wood was full of resina (pitch) which would raise the heat units of his fire. A mound of coque (coke) which he had made by burning the coal until combustion was greatly reduced, was ready and some dirt and clay. Narvez laid brush and dry leaves in the bottom of his smelter, on that he piled the pieces of piñon and covered them with coke. He knew how to sprinkle adobe dirt over the top to compact the fuel space, and how to set the crisol and pack the clay about it to hold it firm. He struck his flints together, ignited the dry brush at the bottom of the smelter and his fire was built. Into the crisol went the intended ore and the melting process was on.

Old Narvez made most of the jewelry of iron because there was much the greater demand for it, even for rings. But into that iron went pyrites, both of iron and copper. Those pyrites glitter like gold; in fact they are known as fool's gold. When they were smelted into the iron, rings and bracelets made of it dazzled in the sunlight and the candlelight. Then Narvez dropped pieces of copper ore and little chunks of silver ore into the crisol with the iron and got gaily flecked molten stuff from which to hammer and cut out rings and bracelets. As different metals required different heats to melt them, they were in different states of molten mass. But when in an adorning piece of jewelry, that roughness, knobby appearance, and general mixed-upness but added to its worth and beauty.

When his molten mass was ready, Narvez poured it out on a flat smooth stone as he needed it and rolled it and cut it with stone tools. He carved figures of animals, birds, reptiles, flowers and geometric symbols upon the rings and bracelets. The plain pieces made from iron alone were carved with the same skill and artistic touch as those rings and bracelets which would bring him more beans, chili, peas (both black-eyed and Spanish) and wheat or blue corn. The silver rings were beyond all but a few, unless they were to be bought at great sacrifice. But there were those who made the sacrifices and adorned themselves with silver rings, silver bracelets, and even silver earrings which were all highly polished and carved.

Narvez used pumice for polishing as well as smoothing down his melted metals. After he had labored with sand or pumice, even the roughest rings and bracelets took on a finished appearance.

In those old days there was a demand for rings of iron and the iron made to glitter by the addition of pyrites; for it was the custom of the day for engaged couples to exchange rings in a dance called la prendería given at the home of the bride, or some place chosen by her family, on the night preceding the wedding. A tragedy it was for a girl's family not to provide her with a ring to give her husband-to-be on that great night amid festivities and the eyes of friends. Then the young man would be a poor lover if he did not bring a ring to slip on the finger of his wife-to-be as they both moved to the center of the floor in the dance and came very close together to exchange rings. That ceremony meant much to all concerned and rings must be had for it. That old custom brought happiness to brides and developed the art of making jewelry in the village of long ago.

Narvez has long since passed away but his memory still lives among those who are left who wore his precious jewelry, or those who saw some of it bought by barter by their ancestors. Sad it is that the artistic work of el platero viejo (the old silversmith) can no longer be found in Las Placitas. Like other things from the hands of the artists and craftsmen of old Las Placitas, his creations, crude but beautiful, have disappeared and newer, modern, machine-made ornaments of personal adornment have taken their place.

Sources of Information: José Gurulé, age 92, Las Placitas, New Mexico, who remembers the old Narvez of this story. José was a small child when old Narvez made jewelry for the people of Las Placitas. He knew how the old man made it and what it looked like. Patricio Gallegos, age 66, Las Placitas, New Mexico, who recalled seeing the ruins of the little smelter near the old Montezuma mine and remembered how it was built. Dave Trujillo, age 50, Las Placitas, whose people lived at old Las Huertas in the old days and knew from his parents that silver and other ore was taken from the old Montezuma mine and smelted nearby and made into jewelry, though he could not remember the name of the silversmith.

How the Civil War Reached Las Placitas

by Lou Sage Batchen

*I*t was April, 1862. To be exact, it was the thirteenth day of the month. The day was bright and clear with not a cloud in the blue sky. Nowhere could a sign of rain be seen. There had been no rain in many weeks, and the dust lay deep in the roads and trails.

Men worked with oxen in the fields trying to turn up the dry, hard adobe soil with stout oak forked sticks in case a rain might come. The weather gave little hope of crops to harvest, so dry was everything—but there was always a hope that rain might come. It was well to have the fields ready.

The small community flock of sheep and goats were now pastured around Ojo del Oso (Spring of the Bear), where there was still water for them to drink. The great herd was at Cerro Pelón where some water still trickled down arroyo de Las Huertas. Already the men were discussing just where they could take their herds when these water supplies were dried up.

So that morning of April 13 seemed about like any other morning at Las Placitas. Housewives went about their work in the same old routine. Lucas, who was El Capitán of the home guards was, as always, on the alert for any signs of the notorious Navajo raiders. But the day was destined to be different. That is why all the details of that long ago day, especially the heavy dust in the road, have lived in the memories of those who lived that day in Las Placitas and can be recalled by their children as an exciting story told to them; but even those are few now.

Young José Gurulé was with the shepherds who tended the flock around Ojo del Oso. From where they watched their charges, they had a view of the whole countryside. It was while enjoying this familiar view that José's eyes fell upon a cloud of dust in the distance. That meant that someone was on the road from Bernalillo. That was nothing unusual, but the cloud of dust told the lad that something more than a few travelers were on the way to Las Placitas. Puzzled, he kept his eyes fixed on the ever increasing cloud which drew nearer and nearer. He decided that huge dust cloud had to be made by many men. They might be Indians! He knew that as yet none of the men, even if they were on watch, could see that dust from the village below. Las Placitas lay in a sort of bowl. It was his duty to warn them.

He called the other shepherds, told them to look at what was coming and get the flocks to cover. Then with as many sheep as he could round up in a hurry, he started down the mountainside with them. He must warn everybody in the village. Yelling at the top of his voice he raced the sheep through the village and to the corrals. Men aided him. Lucas made his way to a high point and surveyed the scene. His heart was filled with fear for them all. That was an army coming. Nothing less could raise such a cloud of dust.

Terror-stricken mothers gathered their broods into their houses. There was a grim haste about all their movements. In almost a twinkling of an eye the heavy doors were set in their places and stout wooden bolts shot into place. Nothing less than fire or battering rams could dislodge those heavy wooden doors when they were barred. The shutters of heavy timber were set in the windows and barred. To barricade themselves in their houses was all that they could do. They would be fools to face an army. Within their small thick-walled fortresses, with plenty of arrows, they might have a chance. Anxiously, fearfully, men and women watched through the tiny cracks they found in the shutters.

But where was the hero of the moment? The boy whose sharp eyes had seen the enemy's approach from afar and warned them? Unnoticed in the wild confusion which followed his appearance in the village, he had escaped, raced back to the mountainside and hid himself behind a rock, from which vantage point he could see all that happened and be where he could race for Cerro Peñón if the men needed to be warned. And from that point overlooking the village, José Gurulé watched the spectacular event, which has not dimmed in his memory to this day.

The invaders were rapidly nearing the village. They were Indians. But very unlike any Indians the villagers had ever seen. And they were armed with guns! There were at least two hundred of them. They entered the town. There was not a soul to be seen, nor a voice to be heard.

They came to a halt and inspected the silent, barricaded dwellings. Then together they moved on, gathered around the great cottonwood tree, which spreads its shade over the house where José Gurulé now lives. In those old days there was a wide clearing about the tree. There the Indians squatted, rested their guns, and proceeded to hold a powwow. They talked together in loud voices, a tongue no villager understood. They gesticulated wildly, pointed out a house here, a house there, as if planning action against it. Inside those houses, panic-stricken inmates kept their eyes glued to the tiny cracks in their shutters, that they might lose none of what was going on in their midst.

All at once the powwow ended. The Indians sprang to their feet and there was an energetic milling about. A fire was started. As the smoke arose, Indians danced about it, their blood curdling war cries ringing into every ear in that terror-stricken village. They danced until they seemed weary. Some Indians rebuilt the fire, others circulated about the village.

Behind the barred doors, men waited with drawn bows. At least they could pierce the hearts of a few redskins before they were captured. What an awful moment. Behind that sheltering rock the youth watched, his heart in his mouth.

Then for the time, the villagers relaxed. Some Indians had rounded up three cows and were driving them to slaughter. They were going to feast. Feast themselves upon the cow belonging to Juan Mora and two belonging to Juan Armijo in the big house upon the hill.

While the meat cooked, the Indians squatted about and talked. But to show the barricaded village that they still remembered them, they raised their voices now and then in argument, and waved their hands in varying directions, just as if they were laying out their campaign. Suspense in that invaded village mounted as they considered their chances against an army of some two hundred Indians, armed with guns.

At length the feast was ready. The Indians crowded about and tore off their portions with their hands. And while they ate, the boy concealed behind the rock suddenly spied another dust cloud along the road from Bernalillo. It moved fast. José knew that dust was kicked up by horses or mules, not by men on foot. But whoever it was coming at neckbreak speed over that winding dust-covered road, could do little to save the village.

Soon they were in plain sight. Two men on horses! They were men of his own race, gentlemen finely mounted. They rode right up to the Indians, who had about finished their own feast. For a time they spoke together. Then one of the men sent his horse galloping about the place, calling to the people, telling them that they had nothing to fear. The Indians were friendly.

That was hard to believe, yet the sight of the man encouraged them to unbar their doors and peep outside; some even ventured outside their doors. Down from his hiding place charged the lone little sentinel, but he could learn nothing of the strange invaders.

In short order the Indians had formed lines and with no sound save that of marching feet, they left the village behind. But not to Bernalillo from whence they came, did they go. But they marched on, toward the East. Eager to learn more about the strange Indians, José Gurulé stole along, careful to keep himself hidden from their view. He followed them along the narrow road leading to Cañón de Las Huertas, the new settlement which was later to be renamed Ojo de la Casa. The two men riding ahead gave the settlers there a friendly wave of their hands as the long column of Indians approached their houses. But in spite of the friendly gesture, the people fled into their houses, though they did not barricade them.

Passing the settlement, the cavalcade made its way along the foothills of the Sandías until they reached Ceja del Camino de San Pedro, at the junction of Perdizo Cañón and Cañón de Las Huertas, which was the main highway through the Sandía Mountains from Bernalillo to Tijeras. José kept his eyes upon the vanishing column until the last Indian was lost from his sight in the mountain pass. Then, believing them well out of his part of the world, he hastened back to his home to spread the good news.

He found the people gathered about the place where the Indians had held their feast. They were still excited and were talking loudly together. They all wanted to know all about the "friendly Indians" and why they should come to their village, frighten them half to death and slaughter their cattle. They wanted to know where they came from and where they were going.

These were just the things that the ever curious Nicolás Gurulé, father of the equally curious José wished to know. He announced that he was going to Bernalillo first thing the next morning to find out all about it. Juan of Tecolote said that he would go along.

The people of the village eagerly awaited their return, and when the two men arrived they were surrounded and bombarded with questions. But what they had been able to learn was all too brief and unsatisfying. They did learn the name of the Indians and now in Las Placitas, all that they remember is that it was something like Kiwanis. They learned that the Indians came to Las Placitas from Galisteo (an old pueblo on the trail from Bernalillo and Las Placitas to Santa Fe, which was later a Mexican village) and that they were on their way to Tijeras.

Both Coan and Twitchell, New Mexican historians, have this to say in effect: After the Confederates abandoned Santa Fe, the main army of the Union marched Southward under command of Colonel Paul, U.S.A. They reached Galisteo on the 10th of April, and were met there by a staff officer of the army of General Canby, April 13th. General Canby joined his forces with the main army under Colonel Paul at Tijeras Cañón.

There was nothing strange in the fact that there were Indians with the Union forces. Since our American history began, Indians have been the allies of one side or the other in times of war. The mystifying thing was that they should be under no command and choosing their own route from Galisteo to Tijeras.

After the people heard all that Nicolás and Juan of Tecolote had to say they talked it over and repeated among themselves, "Friendly Indians," and shook their heads. The way that band of redskins had whooped and danced around their fire certainly had not looked very friendly. For days they could talk of nothing else but their invasion by an army of armed Indians. Then the whole incident suddenly seemed funny. The Indians had played a joke on them! When they entered the village and saw nothing but barred doors and windows, the Indians must have thought it queer. Then when they had their powwow, they must have been talking it over and planning the way to show them what an invasion of enemy Indians, such an army of them, could be, and make good their terror. All the time those Indians were laughing and enjoying themselves. But how were the panic-stricken villagers to know that? But it was plain to them all that the Indians had staged the powwow and war dance and given those blood curdling war whoops just to torment them. "Then," said José Gurulé, "everybody felt proud. The older and wiser men in the community told them that they had seen the first public Indian show in New Mexico, right here in Las Placitas."

Source of Information: José Gurulé, age 90, Las Placitas, New Mexico, the boy in this story who warned the people of Las Placitas of the approach of the army of Indians.

Las Huertas

by Lou Sage Batchen

There is no town outside the territory adjacent to the Río Grande with a more colorful history than the old town of Las Huertas. The place is about a mile north of the Loop Drive where it cuts through Placitas in Sandoval County. There, a gate on the Drive admits to the road which joins Las Huertas with Placitas.

Las Huertas is situated in the historic Las Huertas Cañon at the foot of the north end of the Sandías, its length bordered on both sides by ridges of the mountains. The north side slopes to a mesa which stretches to Algodones, on the south side the mountains rise wall-like and their crests command a sweeping view of the Río Grande and the villages and pueblos in the broad area from the Jemez Mountains to Bernalillo. Lookout mountains they are, commanding a scope in every direction, advantageous point in the hazardous days of hostile Indian invasions. This tillable cañon watered abundantly by six springs, where surrounding mountains offered water and pasturage for livestock, was but five miles up the Las Huertas Cañon from Río Grande del Norte (Río Grande) and Camino Real (Royal Highway) along which life in the Kingdom of New Mexico, south of Santa Fe, centered in 1755. This place was the answer to the long ago homeseekers' prayer, and it was at that time, according to José Librado Arón Gurulé, David Trujillo, and Patricio Gallegos, that their forefathers built houses and cultivated the land in Las Huertas, and their family tradition is confirmed by Archive No. 88, U.S. Public Survey Office, which also gives the names of the first families who registered "The tract of vacant public land commonly called Las Huertas and located at the foot of the Sandías at the North end and opposite the place Bernalillo." Juan Gutierres and eight other families represented, they all had large families and he (Juan Gutierres) was compelled to sell the ranch which supported them all to the Pueblo of Santa Ana in order to enable him to pay off some debts. The families were: Andrés de Aragón, (one of his sons called José),

Javiel Gutierres, a half-breed, José Antonio Rael, Antonio Archibeque, Miguel Gallegos, Matias Gutierres, José Gonzales. There is no account of these families receiving the San Antonio de Las Huertas Grant, but in Archive #88 U.S. Public Survey Office there is a record of the settlers of Las Huertas petitioning his Excellency, Tomás Valdéz Cachupín, in 1765 to bestow upon them, in the name of the King, the land whereon they had settled and cultivated. This record seems to confirm the family traditions of the descendants of the people who founded Las Huertas, that the people did live in Las Huertas many years before they applied for the Grant of San Antonio de Las Huertas. Twenty-one families are named in this record: Andrés de Aragon, Vicente Sena, Antonio Calban, Matias Gutierres, Pedro Gutierres, Miguel Gallegos, Nicholás Montoya, José Chávez, José Antonio Valencio, Serefino Gurulé, Juan Maise, Francisco Lobera, Antonio Archibeque, Antonio Gurulé, Juan Valdéz, Alberto Montoya, Juan García, Pedro García Jurado, and José García.

Governor Tomás Valdéz Cachupín died before the grant was completed and the decree was declared by "Pedro Fermín de Mendinueta, of the Order of Santiago, Colonel in the Royal Armies, Governor and Captain General of this Kingdom of New Mexico do declare that I do make this grant on condition that they make the settlement in accordance with the provisions of the Royal Laws." The foregoing is quoted from Archive #88, U.S. Public Survey Office. The same source discloses that it was not until the month of January in the year 1768 that Bartolomé Fernández, Chief Alcalde and War Captain, got around to going to the spot and informing the settlers of Las Huertas of the decree and the provisions and conditions thereto. Aforesaid Archive #88 records the visit of the Chief Alcalde and War Captain, Bartolomé Fernández who caused the citizens of San José to be called together on the spot of Las Huertas to learn of the decree and conditions. This mention of San José further corroborates the family traditions of the descendants of the Las Huertas founders, that they lived in Las Huertas many years before 1765. On the old grant maps, location of ruins are marked just west of the ruins of the old Plaza of Las Huertas. The Alcalde found, so says Archive #88, that the people had already divided the land and had it cultivated and were satisfied with the division, so—"I designated to them the unimproved lands. I took them by the hand and led them over said lands and they all plucked up weeds and cast stones and we all exclaimed three times, Huzza for the King and may God preserve him." Then the Chief Alcalde and War Captain set about laying out the settlement in accordance with the Royal Laws. He measured off a plaza and allotted each family sufficient ground for his house and a corral for his livestock. The houses and corrals must be made of adobes and built in such a way that the plaza would be enclosed on its four sides with only opening at the corners. The plaza was large enough to permit street opening in case of increase in population; for no one was permitted to live outside the walls. They must stand together in case of hostile invasions. Also they must plant and cultivate corn and wheat and garden edibles, and they must plant fruit trees. The remaining ruins of the old plaza clearly indicate that the plan of building was carried out.

And here the first families of Las Huertas lived and supported themselves. The tales that have come down from them stress their hard times. Indians raided their fields at harvest times. If the Indians won the battle, the Las Huertas citizens lost their crops and faced a bare winter. The Indians raided the mountains. If they won, they drove off the goats, which were the chief source of supply of food and clothing and household furnishings for Las Huertas. There were grasping officials who exacted toll in the way of wheat and corn. And there were drouths. According to José Librado Arón Gurulé and David Trujillo and Patricio Gallegos the people went down the cañón to the vicinity of Algodones for aid in seasons of distress, for they say the people who settled Las Huertas also at the same time settled Algodones on land they bought from the San Felipe Indians, and that they were all members of the twenty-one families who received the grant of San Antonio de Las Huertas. It is true that to this day, the descendants of the first families in Algodones and the descendants of the Las Huertas settlers now living in Placitas and Ojo de la Casa (House of the Spring) are related.

According to David Trujillo, the people living within the walls of old Las Huertas never had a church nor a priest. They made themselves a saint and had him named and blessed by the priest at the San Felipe Pueblo. The people kept their saint in their houses. They carried their dead on ladders (made to bear the dead) to the San Felipe Pueblo and buried them in the cemetery there. The way between Las Huertas and the pueblo was dotted with crosses and stone monuments where they had rested the dead on the sad journeys. Many there are yet living who found such markers.

According to José Librado Arón Gurulé, the people in Las Huertas did some mining. The old Montezuma mine is at the North end of the Sandías and there is the ruin of a smelter in Las Huertas. Many years ago he said a bar of bullion was plowed up in a field in Las Huertas Cañón. He believed, as did David Trujillo and Patricio Gallegos, that the old workings in the mine have long ago been lost, either filled up or caved in by mountain floods or the Indians. And from David Trujillo came the statement that the older Trujillos, born before the year 1800, said that Las Huertas became a town of one thousand people.

And so the people of Las Huertas lived within their walls, worked, prayed, and fought with the Indians until the fateful Order of 1823. "The order in the archive of the government of this province relative to requiring the settlements scattered through the mountains and valleys to attach themselves to the body of settlements situated on the Río del Norte." The foregoing information is found in Private Land Claims, Volume 3 pp. 993-999, in the Library in the Palace of Governors, as well as the following: "I direct that without loss of time you appoint a committee of the corporation in your jurisdiction who by virtue of this order will cause the inhabitants of Las Huertas to remove to your jurisdiction, and with the corporation you will provide lands for them to cultivate which said corporation will see is done, informing me of its receipt and execution. God & c April 23, 1823."—Communication from Governor Don José Antonio Visearrar to San Carlos de Alameda, regarding the circumstance of protecting citizens against hostile Indian invasions.

Thus the inhabitants of Las Huertas were forced to abandon their walled town, their fertile cañón, and plentiful pasturage for their goats. Calletano Chaves, who died in Ojo de la Casa in 1913, lived in Las Huertas at the time of the evacuation. His nephew, Patricio Gallegos, related the following story told by Calletano many times for it had made a vivid impression on his memory. "I was fifteen years old. I well remember the people putting their things together to leave the place. I went with some other boys to take the goats to the mountains for feed. Our fathers told us when we brought the goats in they would be gone and for us to drive the goats down the cañón to Algodones. They would be there looking for us. When we brought in the goats the houses were all empty and nobody was there, so we drove the goats down to Algodones."

Source of Information: José Librado Arón Gurulé, age 88, a direct descendant of one of the twenty-one families who received the San Antonio de Las Huertas Grant from the King of Spain in 1765. David Trujillo, age 47, the son of David Trujillo one of the descendants of the Chaves family among the twenty-one families who received the San Antonio de Las Huertas Grant. Patricio Gallegos, age 60, son of Juan María Gallegos a descendant of one of the twenty-one families who received the San Antonio de Las Huertas Grant, and who settled in Ojo de la Casa (The House of the Spring).

La Madera "The Timber"

by Lou Sage Batchen

La Madera (The Timber) or Madera, as the forest maps call it, is located on the old La Ceja del Camino de San Pedro (Road of the Mountain Summit of San Pedro) about five miles South and East from the place where the Loop Drive crosses the Hagan Road at the East end of Placitas in Sandoval County. La Ceja del Camino de San Pedro in times gone by was the main highway through the Sandías from points around Bernalillo and Placitas to La Madera, Tijeras Cañón (Scissors Canyon), and San Pedro Viejo (Old San Pedro), the site of an ancient pueblo now excavated by a government project. This old road was made by Dame Nature and Father Time through Perdizo Cañón (Partridge Canyon) which opens into Las Huertas Cañón (Canyon of the Gardens) at Ojo de la Casa (House of the Spring).

In 1839 Ramón Gurulé and his daughter Josefa petitioned the Mexican Government for the land grant of San Pedro Rancho, which was the land of the ancient pueblo. They stated that they were descendants of the people who settled Las Huertas and received the San Antonio de Las Huertas Grant from the King of Spain in 1767, and that they had no lands whereon to live or to cultivate and no pasturage for their livestock. They received the Grant in 1840 and they with other descendants of the settlers of Las Huertas went to live at San Pedro Viejo. Five years later they sold the grant to José Ramirez. The information in the above paragraph is contained in Vol. 111 Private Land Claims in the library at the old Palace of Governors.

These people from San Pedro Viejo became the founders of La Madera, though the exact date is a guess. It is thought to be around 1850, though it was probably before that, according to Rumaldita Gurulé, whose mother was born there some time after her grandparents came there from San Pedro Viejo. Among those first families were: Benerando Gutiérrez, Manuel Baros, Francisco Gurulé, José Gonzales, Marco Maestas, and a Lucera. Ramón Gurulé may have been one of the new settlers, along with his son Francisco. These people built their new town in a clearing on a thickly wooded mountain slope not far from the source of Perdizo Cañón. Most of the houses were built of logs and chinked with mud, for the local soil was not adaptable to the making of adobes. But a few of the new settlers were ambitious and industrious enough to bring in adobes with which to build their homes. On this mountain slope, rainfall and not irrigation determined the harvests. In rainy seasons the bean crop was heavy and corn grew abundantly. Vineyards and kitchen gardens were almost nil. Pasturage for their goats was sufficient.

The Good Samaritan of La Madera

As Told by Rumaldita Gurulé

by Lou Sage Batchen

*F*ate played a prank on Manuel Baros when she wove La Madera into the pattern of his life. By virtue of his fairness and wise counsels and his worldly goods, which he turned to charitable account, he became El Jefe (The Leader) of the community. He was a lover and tiller of the soil. He owned several spans of oxen and good wooden plows. Every spring he generously parceled out his precious hoard of seed and offered the use of his oxen and plows to anyone desiring them; but his seeds were neglected in the ground, or not planted at all, and his oxen grew fat and lazy for want of work. The heavily timbered area made haulers of wood of his people and not tillers of the soil. El Jefe was always at hand to relieve cases of distress and sickness; but it seemed that most of their illness and suffering required the incantations or brewed herbs of the witches to cure them. Manuel Baros sought to teach thrift and honesty. He fought witchcraft with reason not switches, or tried to do it. For all he sought to do of good to his fellow men his reward came to him through his son Perciano Baros, who became one of the early Presbyterian missionaries in the vicinity.

From *La Madera "The Timber."*

La Cita de Las Brujas "Rendezvous of the Witches"

As Told by Rumaldita Gurulé, Teresita Gallegos de Baca, and Catalina Gurulé

by Lou Sage Batchen

*L*a Madera, built in the woods, was isolated and although only four miles from San Pedro Viejo, a spooky old place. There was a weirdness about the whole location which made one shiver and think of ghosts and witches. La Madera had always been the rendezvous of witches. They simply abounded thereabouts in little houses higher in the mountains. Witch doctors, witch nurses, and just witches played their evil tricks upon those they envied or hated. In La Madera outdoor gossip must be conducted in low voices, for none could tell who might be listening from behind the trees. But it happened that all the witches did not live in houses far up on the mountainside. There were some right in the village who practiced the arts of the evil ones. There was Pepe, for one, who had a slight cast in his left eye. They must lock the doors to houses where babies were being born. If he chanced to enter a room and look at a newly born baby, for certain that baby would die. If he entered a kitchen and looked at a cake about to be set in the fireplace to bake, nothing could prevent that cake from falling and being unfit to eat.

And at night when the wind was blowing and the pale moon was just a crescent, balls of light would jump about through the woods and around the houses of the witches. The balls of light would hop and run forward then backward, just as in a dance. It was the witches. Then the people clustered about their doorways in the dark to watch but no one ventured abroad. None but those named Juan had any power over the witches. If a witch had cast evil spells upon any of them, they set a Juan to catch her. The Juan would go out into the night and watch. When he saw the witch coming he would jerk off his shirt, turn it wrong side out and fling it in the witch's path. She would never see it. She would fall over it and for the life of her she could not move. Early in the morning the people would come and take her to the houses of the ones she had put an evil spell upon. They would make her cure them. They threatened to kill her if ever she bewitched them again. Then they took switches and lashed her out of the village.

From *La Madera "The Timber."*

El Misterio "The Enigma"

As Told by Catalina Gurulé

by Lou Sage Batchen

Refrigia lived at the edge of La Madera with her old mother. She was very pretty and had large eyes and long lashes that hid them, and she put her hair high upon her head and made herself look very beautiful. Who would ever have thought that she was a witch? But none of them ever saw her eyes when she thought of Quita. Then they were balls of fire like cats' eyes and her fingers reached out like cats' claws that wanted to tear the flesh of someone. Refrigia hated Quita because of Felipe. Refrigia loved Felipe. Quita loved him also. But Refrigia felt that she could not live without him. One night she sought him out and confessed her love for him. Felipe was very gentle with her, but he told her he loved Quita and they were soon to be married.

Very soon after that their padrinos (godparents or attendants) went with them to the priest and they were wed. No sooner was the service ended than Felipe seemed queer. He ran around Quita and laughed and pulled at the wedding veil as a child would do. When they came home he cried at the wedding feast and would not eat of it, but asked for a tinaja (pottery bowl) of atole (a drink made from milk and roasted and ground blue or pueblo corn) just as a child might do. All the wedding guests thought the handsome bridegroom was making a clown of himself for their amusement. But he did not change as time went on. Always there was a pain in his head. More and more he became like a small child. To satisfy him his people made him a crib. Quita must always be playing with him. She tried to hide her grief and do what he wished to please him. Her youth and charm faded. Refrigia never showed her face anymore. Some said they thought they saw her go up into the mountains. "Could it be possible that Refrigia had brought all this misery upon Felipe and Quita?" The moment Quita heard of the suspicion she ran to the house of Refrigia, but she found only harshness and a command to be gone as Refrigia shut her door in Quita's face. Then one day Felipe suddenly became himself again. Quita, too, looked as she did on that fateful wedding day. What of Refrigia? They ran to her house. There on her floor she lay dying and beside her was her witch doll and in her fingers was the big thorn she had pulled from its head. She had relented when death struck her and freed Felipe from the spell she had cast upon him.

And to this day there are those who believe that witches cause them to suffer or become demented by thrusting a thorn or a pin into their witch doll wherever they wish to cause suffering to the ones they envy or hate or to whom they wish to do harm.

From *La Madera "The Timber."*

El Hombre Alegre "The Jolly Man"

As Told by Rumaldita Gurulé

by Lou Sage Batchen

But life in La Madera was not all made up of the goodness of El Jefe (or Manuel Baros) and the wickedness of the witches. There was Marcos Maestas, the jolly man, who was born to gamble. Should two of his neighbors go for a load of wood at the same time he hunted someone to lay a bet with him as to which of the men would return first with his wood. He made a race course for the young men. Exciting foot races were weekly events and betting was heavy. A burro race is almost impossible, but he accomplished them. And that was something to bet on! Anything constituted legal tender when it came to offering bets: corn, beans, wood, goats, and some money, but money in hand was scarce. What difference did it make what they bet? The fun was in betting. And Marco liked to see his neighbors enjoy themselves.

He reserved one room in his house for the playing of betting games. The favorite and most often played game was Cañuto (Pipe or Flute). For this game a pile of sand was placed in two corners of the room diagonally opposite and upon the mud floor. Navajo blankets were hung as drapes to conceal these corners. The game was played with four hollow sticks or reeds and a slender stick which could be inserted in the hollows; all the sticks being about eight inches long. The hollow ones had distinguishing marks upon them and each had a different value. The highest was called Mulato (Tawney) and scored four points. The next was called Cinchado (meaning to grip or cinch). Its score was three points. Dos (Two) was next with two points and Uno (One) was the lowest, scoring one. The slender stick placed in any of these hollow sticks doubled the score of that reed. Two leaders chose sides; each side had four players and each side possessed one of the corners. When the game was on, everybody in the village who could leave his house was there to watch and bet on the side that would score the most points during the evening's game. The side that was to start the game repaired behind the blanket in their corner. The slender stick was inserted into one of the reeds and the four sticks buried in the sand pile. The drape was pulled aside and the other four rushed in to the draw. They had but one draw. If the reed pulled from the sand pile contained the slender stick they were entitled to a second draw, if not they retired with the score given them by the one reed they did draw, and with all the reeds which were now to be hidden in their own sand pile. And so it went, with betting and drinking on the outside. Each time the players rushed to the draw everybody sang:

  Paloma Lucida (Beautiful Dove)
  Lucido Palomar (From Beautiful Dove House)
  Vengan Atinados (Come Ready to Win)
  Vengan a Jerrar (Come Ready to Lose)

Sources of Information: Rumaldita Gurulé, age 67, of Placitas, New Mexico, born in La Madera, New Mexico is a descendant of the Gutiérrez family among the settlers of Las Huertas who received the San Antonio de Las Huertas Grant from the King of Spain in 1767. Terecita Gallegos de Baca, age 32, a daughter of Patricio Gallegos, a descendant of one of the twenty-one families to receive the San Antonio de Las Huertas Grant from the King of Spain in 1767. She resides at Ojo de la Casa. P.O. address is Placitas, New Mexico. Catalina Gurulé, age 45, of Placitas, New Mexico, daughter of Pedro Gurulé, a descendant of one of the twenty-one families who received the San Antonio de Las Huertas Grant from the King of Spain in 1767.

From *La Madera "The Timber."*

Luxuries Come to La Madera

As Told by Rumaldita Gurulé

by Lou Sage Batchen

*I*t was in the late Seventies that the last teams of oxen and wagon left La Madera for Kansas City, that great market at the other end of the Santa Fe Trail, with the usual excitement that accompanied the preparations for the six-months trip. But it was not the trip or the preparations for it that was the big event this time; it was the happy homecoming of Rumaldo Candelaria who had made several trips before this one for his patron, taking wool to market and bringing back precious cargo of merchandise. He had always gone with empty pockets. This trip he had some money of his own to spend. For this the pick of his flock of goats had been sold. He had brought back goods like those bought for his patron. When he arrived with his treasure, his neighbors crowded about his door to see what he had brought. They looked on breathlessly as he unwrapped the bundle. There was a whole bolt of muselina (muslin) and two large copper kettles! And last and most glorious of all was a bolt of calico! At sight of that the women opened their eyes in surprise and sighed aloud with pleasure. What a present for Rumaldo to bring home to his wife and daughters. Señora Candelaria could scarcely believe the evidence of her eyes. When she was a girl, calico brought over the trail from Kansas City sold for ten dollars a yard in Santa Fe. Even now it was so expensive that only the rich could afford to buy it. And the snowy white muselina! The first bride in the family should have a dress and a veil of it.

And that first bride did wear a dress and veil of it. The veil was fastened to her hair at one side of her head and had wildflowers pinned on it where it touched her skirt, as well as where it was fastened to her hair. This dress and veil were borrowed and worn by other brides who preferred it to the merino outfits woven at home from the wool of their goats.

Source of Information: Rumaldita Gurulé, age 67, of Placitas, New Mexico, a descendant of one of the twenty-one families to receive the San Antonio de Las Huertas Grant from the King of Spain in 1767. From *La Madera, Part II.*

Ojo de la Casa "House of the Spring"

by Lou Sage Batchen

Ojo de la Casa is a quarter of a mile South and thence a short distance East from the point where the Loop Drive crosses the Hagen Road at the East end of Placitas in Sandoval County. It is an area of about one hundred fifty acres in Cañón de las Huertas (Canyon of the Gardens) and it is divided into approximately two equal parts by the Las Huertas arroyo, or as the forest maps call it, Las Huertas Creek. The South end of Ojo de la Casa extends into the Cibolo Forest. On the East a high ridge of the Sandías delays the hour of sunrise almost an hour and the high mesa on the West completely hides it from the Loop Drive and cuts off another near-hour of sunshine. In good seasons fruit is abundant in this fertile area and once the inhabitants supported themselves from their corn and wheat and goats, for then there was virgin pasturage for livestock. The soil is noted for its production of chili and in all the generations it has yielded chili no disease has ever attacked it. It is not definitely known when the first people came to this place to build homes, for the area is but two miles up Cañón de Las Huertas from the settlement of Las Huertas which had its beginning about 1755, from information given in Archive 88 relative to San Antonio de Las Huertas Grant, which states that there was a town and cultivated land in the place called Las Huertas before 1765, when the citizens of the town petitioned for the land grant on which they had settled. It could be possible that these settlers cultivated this land, as it has a fine spring and there are evidences of another one.

The following story of Ojo de la Casa was told by Patricio Gallegos, Predicondo Chaves, and Teodosio Chaves:

The first families known to settle in Ojo de la Casa came about 1858. They were: Valentino Zamora, Feliciano Archibeque, Marcelino Archibeque, Juan Archibeque, Pedro Sarna, Nicholás Mora, Rumulo Maestas, Julian País, and Cornelia Archibeque. They called their new town Cañón de Las Huertas (Canyon of the Gardens). Within a few years additional families augmented the population. They were: Cassimiro Gallegos and his wife, Gertrudes Archibeque de Gallegos (and not of the same direct family as the families of Archibeques who came with Valentino Zamora.) Upon their heels came Calletano and Juan Pedro Chaves from the vicinity of Santa Rosa. All of the other families now settled in the cañon were either from Algodones or Tejón (Badger). And then there was Santos Lovato who kept all his secrets to himself—even the place from which he came and when and where he was going.

The tale of Ojo de la Casa is one of those "short and simple annals of the poor" until, later on, the tale was embellished a bit by the advent of a young prospector with his gold pans and spoons late of the Black Hills, South Dakota and Leadville, Colorado.

Valentino Zamora and his wife Juanita Gurulé de Zamora had a large family, so large they say that two of the girls received the name of María. The oldest and youngest of the family. When the padrinos (godparents) were told what they had done they laughed and said, "Nobody could remember the names of Juanita's children." So to meet future use of the name, they added a suitable name to the one given the child, making her María de Los Angeles. The older María had been frightened once by a bolt of lightning which felled a tree near her. She was immediately called María de Rayo, and so were the girls called throughout their lives. María de Rayo married Calletano Chaves and her sister wedded his brother Juan Pedro Chaves. This sister was Paulita. Rosalie Zamora married Nicholas Mora and Marcelino Archibeque took Florentina Zamora to wifehood. These daughters were married at the time they settled Cañón de Las Huertas. María de Los Angeles had not reached her teens. And then she fell in love with Juan María Gallegos, son of Cassimiro. He was sixteen years of age. It was the first love affair in the new settlement. But María of The Angeles was much too young, they all said. The husband to be was far too young. The affair became the issue of the day. Cassimiro Gallegos and the two Chaves brothers, the last comers, had something aside from the youthful lovers on their minds. In all communities the life-giving water is of first importance. Here the spring and its abundance of pure water was open to people and animals alike. The spring gushed into a hole made hard with adobe mud. The place was bemuddied by the hoofs and feet of every animal about and it was utterly unfit for the women to walk upon, and the water was filthy and needed to be settled after it was in the tinajas (pottery vessels). Something must be done. So the meeting was called to discuss the matter. As a result, the community built an adobe house which enclosed the spring. The name of the place was changed from Cañón de Las Huertas to Ojo de la Casa and María of The Angeles and Juan Mařa became the first bride and groom of Ojo de la Casa, for they demanded the right to marriage and an adobe house and land of their own. By now the girl was thirteen. She wore the merino wedding dress other brides of the family had worn, and padre (father) Cassimiro Gallegos, who was the owner of a carreta and a pair of oxen, drove the wedding party to the priest at San Felipe Pueblo. They left Ojo de la Casa about three o'clock in the morning and it took until nearly eight o'clock for the oxen to plod down the cañón to Las Huertas and up the Camino Real (Royal Highway) and across the Río Grande to the church in San Felipe. While they were gone the village of Ojo de la Casa hummed with festive activities. The wedding feast was prepared and a room made ready for the baile (dance). Then the wife of thirteen years and the husband of sixteen set about the business of building a house for themselves, a task which was lightened by community aid, for the whole settlement were so closely related as to be as one big family. The house that they built is still occupied, though the builders of it lie in the little city of the dead, at the foot of the Sandías a short distance from the house she helped build; for in those days it was the woman who practically built the house.

    Cassimiro was a progressive spirit of his time, a trader by nature and somewhat of an adventurer. His stout carreta he made himself without tools, except an axe. The clumsy thing was a load in itself for his oxen but it never broke down. It was lined inside with tough hides. He had dreams of gain. Eagerly his neighbors gathered about him to hear of these dreams. He would build another carreta, he would use his young oxen and they would gather piñón nuts to fill the whole inside of the two carts. It was a good piñón year, the task of filling the carettas would not be too hard. He set to work and by the time the piñóns were ripe for gathering he was ready for the trip. He said, "Fill my carreta with piñóns and I'll take my boy and some men to help keep off the Indians and we'll go down to

Chihuahua and trade our nuts. We'll bring cloth for the women and things for the houses." With that golden promise they set to work. They carried their tijanas all over the mountains and soon the small caravan rolled out of Ojo de la Casa. They were gone a half a year. There is a brass kettle left in the house of María de Lo s Angeles which is supposed to be a relic and reminder of this long ago trip.

But there was an aftermath to this glamorous trip into a far and exciting land. Cassimiro Gallegos could no longer content himself in the Cañón de Las Huertas, where mountains hemmed him in on every side. The hidden village lost its charm for him, the adobe house he had helped build over the spring, the many roomed house he and Gertrudes had built and dwelled within so many years, all irked him, so he loaded his belongings into his carreta and moved to Tejón where there was an immense vista and a winding road where men and wagons and oxen went on their way to Estados (the states, particularly Kansas City).

Time marched on. Valentino and Juanita Zamora were no more. The Archibeque families, craving more of life and people, moved to Albuquerque. Others drifted away. Santos Lovato went silently on his trip from Ojo de la Casa leaving or selling, no one knows which, his property to the gringo, the young prospector. The older ones in Ojo de la Casa shook their heads, cursed Lovato roundly to each other and predicted that the gringo would never be satisfied until he had others of his kind around him and that in time they'd have the fertile Cañón de La Huertas. The prophecy was not an idle one. An American owns about half of Ojo de la Casa today.

The descendants of the families who settled and named Cañón de Las Huertas and who afterward with newcomers built the adobe house enclosing the spring and renamed the settlement Ojo de la Casa, fell to wrangling over the waters that came down from the mountains in the acequia madres (mother ditches) that were built and used in peace before them. They disputed boundaries and use of the spring, a general hegira ensued until more than half of the adobe houses stood ghost-like on the deserted slopes overlooking the fertile fields. One, it is said, picked up his axe and ruthlessly destroyed a fine orchard he could not take with him, others removed the vigas from their houses (the heavy pine timbers which support the ceilings and mud roofs) and put them in other houses. Some of the old dwellings were rebuilt and one or two have remained intact: one the old school room where Juan P. Chávez, the first teacher in the settlement, taught the children of Ojo de la Casa to read and write. Before that, Pedro Sarna, one of the first settlers, taught the boys of Placitas and Ojo de la Casa who were ambitious to write their name and tell their letters. He went with them to the mountains where they herded their flocks and there held open air classes. His one surviving pupil today is José Arón Librado Gurulé, age 88, of Placitas. But to this day, the name of Pedro Sarna is spoken in tones of deep respect by the descendants of the men whom he taught.

And out of old Ojo de la Casa has come a story of a mother's ingenious way of solving a problem which world-wide caterers to the appetites of small children solve today. There was but one food for the children: atole. This atole is a drink of milk and meal made from roasted and ground blue or Pueblo corn. The little children had to drink it whether they liked it or not and this mother overcame their reluctance by making a bit of paste of bright red chili powder and the milk, and floating tiny bits of it in the small tinajas (pottery bowls) of atole. She told the children that the red flecks were birds floating on the little lakes and that they must drink all the atole away from the birds so they would not drown. It became a game to drink off the atole and leave the little red birds in the tinajas.

Also this story came out of old Ojo de la Casa. Old Miguel and his wife Juana lived in a little house on the point of the hill. Their field down in the cañón grew high in weeds and the corn had a hard time to come up. Old Miguel said he was sick and what could a sick man do? Juana bent over her chili melga (bed) and weeded it and scratched up the hard adobe with sharp sticks and faithfully watered it, so they had chili. Juana somehow found strength to keep her house and climb the mesa and gather wood for the little corner fireplace where she did her meager cooking. Old Miguel seemed never to be sick when the dinner was in the tinaja. All the friends and family of Juana wondered what to do. Then one night someone rapped sharply on the tiny high window of Miguel's house. He woke up. Juana woke up. He told Juana to ask who knocked like that on their window in the dark of the night. "I cannot call, so afraid am I," said

Juana. Miguel cried out, "Who knocks at my window and what do you want?" A strange voice answered, "I am the Angel come for you because you are so sick." Old Miguel shook with fear. "No, no, Angel, I am not sick. It is Juana. She is so sick she cannot call to you." After that old Miguel attended his field religiously and brought the wood for the fire.

Sources of Information: Patricio Gallegos, age 60, Ojo de la Casa, P.O. address Placitas, New Mexico, son of Juan María Gallegos and María de Los Angeles Zamora de Gallegos, descendants of the settlers of Las Huertas who applied for the San Antonio de Las Huertas Grant from the King of Spain in 1765. Predicondo Chaves, age 64, Placitas, New Mexico, son of Juan P. Chaves and Paulita Zamora de Chaves, descendants of the settlers of Las Huertas who applied for the San Antonio de Las Huertas Grant from the King of Spain in 1765. Teodosio Chaves, age 74, Santa Barbara, New Mexico, son of Calletano Chaves and María de Rayo Zamora de Chaves, descendants of the settlers of Las Huertas who applied for the San Antonio de Las Huertas Grant from the King of Spain in 1765.

From *Ojo de la Casa "House of the Spring."*

El Inocentón "The Innocent"

As Told by Teresita Gallegos de Baca

by Lou Sage Batchen

One day Lucas and Tomás and Juan sat in the shade of a piñón tree eating the roasted corn they had brought from home for their lunch. Their goats were grazing nearby. All at once Juan caught sight of an Indian. He was so frightened for a moment he could not speak, then he said, "Look, the Indians!" The boys scrambled off on all fours to the nearest arroyos. Not for just one arroyo. No, their parents had told them never, never to hide in the same arroyo, but for each boy to hide in a different arroyo and then it might be that the Indians could not find them all. So into different deep arroyos jumped the young shepherds, and sat very still.

Three Indians circled the herd of goats and hunted for the shepherds. Alas, they found Lucas and dragged him from his hiding place and started off with him. One boy would have to do, for there were no others in the arroyo. Poor Lucas fought and tried to get away but they dragged him along with them. Tomás in his joy at being missed by the wild Indians, jumped up and down and shouted, "Tú no mi hallarse! Tú no mi hallarse!" (You did not find me! You did not find me!). But his joy was short lived. The Indians returned and routed out the poor simple one from his refuge and carried him off with Lucas into slavery.

Source of Information: Teresita Gallegos de Baca, age 32, of Ojo de la Casa, daughter of Patricio Gallegos and granddaughter of Juan María Gallegos, descendants of the settlers of Las Huertas who applied for the San Antonio de Las Huertas Grant in 1765. From *Ojo de la Casa "House of the Spring."*

El Ojo "The Eye"

As Told by Teresita Gallegos de Baca

by Lou Sage Batchen

It happened many years ago. Tules took her young baby and went on a long hard trip with her husband to visit her sister Rosalie, who was ill. While on the brief visit a strange old woman came to the house of Rosalie. "Ah," said she, "what a pretty baby." She looked at the infant with longing eyes; she half held out her arms to it but the young mother ignored her. The old woman went her way and soon Tules and her husband started for home. All the day as she jogged along on the burro Tules tried to quiet her fretting baby but it only cried the more. It was dark when they came to their home in Ojo de la Casa. At once Tules called to her mother, "Come quick. See my baby, what shall I do?" "Who saw your baby while you visited your sister?" "A strange old woman," Tules told her. "She wanted to hold my baby and love it but I did not let her." "Alas, my child, you should have let her hold your baby — if only for a moment. Now a spell is upon your baby — only that woman could undo it and you do not even know who she was. The journey back to try to find her is too hard for the baby." And she shook her head, "There is nothing we can do. When someone looks longingly with their eyes at your baby and for some reason they do not take it in their arms and caress it, the look in their eyes casts a spell on the baby and it will die — unless you can find the person and he will sprinkle the baby with water from his mouth, that will take away the spell. You do not heed what we older ones tell you." And so to this day, some say, many babies die from the spell cast upon them by the unrequited look in the eye.

Source of Information: Teresita Gallegos de Baca, age 32, of Ojo de la Casa, daughter of Patricio Gallegos and granddaughter of Juan María Gallegos, descendants of the settlers of Las Huertas who applied for the San Antonio de Las Huertas Grant in 1765. From: *Ojo de la Casa "House of the Spring."*

Luz de la Luna "Moonlight"

As Told by Teresita Gallegos de Baca

by Lou Sage Batchen

*A*ntonia's baby was born. "God have mercy," cried out the midwife, "his little feet have no legs but grow out from his knees." Everybody came in for a peep at the unfortunate baby before Antonia knew anything of what was going on in the house. "She should know better," wailed the old grandmother, "and be careful. How often have I told these young mothers to watch and never let the moonlight fall upon them in their beds when they are carrying their babies. Now Antonia has caused her baby to be born without legs. When the moonlight falls upon a mother in bed before her babe is born she must not blame anyone but herself if it has some part missing. And listen, if she allows the shadow to fall upon her when the moon has an eclipse, her baby will be very sickly or die—unless she is wise enough to wear a string around her waist with keys upon it." And so they think it is to this very day.

Source of Information: Teresita Gallegos de Baca, age 32, of Ojo de la Casa, daughter of Patricio Gallegos and granddaughter of Juan María Gallegos, descendants of the settlers of Las Huertas who applied for the San Antonio de Las Huertas Grant in 1765. From *Ojo de la Casa "House of the Spring."*

Old Houses of Placitas

by Lou Sage Batchen

The old houses like the old villages were unique. The old villages still remain so where no modern highways have cut through them and robbed them of the charm of primitive simplicity and their narrow lanes which zigzagged about as if to touch every doorstep in them. Placitas is one of those villages to escape the modern touch; the highway went around it, and its winding main street is, as always, the only road through it. But the old houses of Placitas are gone with its past. They have been remodeled, expanded about patios, or zaguans, and another wing added until the characteristics of the original houses have disappeared.

There was both art and utility in these old houses and their uses were manifold. At once they were home, sanctuary, fortress, storage and factory. They were the dwellings. They were the places where the patron saint of the village was kept; for there were no churches in the villages in those early days. They were the walls within which the people fortified themselves in cases of hostile invasions. Everything the families possessed in the manner of supplies must be stored in their houses, and everything the families wore was made there, and everything the families ate was prepared there.

In Placitas the old houses were built mostly of rocks, any size and any shape. They were joined together and held intact in a wall with adobe mud, quantities of it, until the walls were as much adobe as rock. The houses were low and the walls from twenty to thirty inches thick. The ceilings were supported by vigas, the trunks of pines peeled and dried, as they are today, and the ceilings were slender saplings laid evenly and close together crosswise of them. On these saplings was spread a layer of tough, dry grass and over that was spread a layer of adobe mud. The thick mud roof was laid up on top of that. The width of the houses was determined by the length of the pine trunks they could get. In those early days few, very few, possessed beasts of burden. Men and women must bring in their own building material with their own hands or on their own backs. Usually the houses contained two rooms. The windows were small, not much more than peep holes perched high in the thick walls, and the doors were for dwarfs or children, for no others could go through them without doubling over. The floors were adobe mud, made hard by proper drying, and they were not cut into by heels of shoes for then the people had only tewas (moccasins) to wear or else they went barefoot. The door and window frames were made of pine logs split into boards by stone axes and stone wedges; for such were all the tools they possessed at that time. The doors were made of these boards put together with wooden pins. If there were any shutters for the tiny windows they were made in the same way. The house inside and out was plastered with adobe mud. There was left no trace of the rock, and so long as this mud was kept in good condition on those walls the rocks and adobe underneath were unaffected by time or weather.

But it was the inside of the old houses that was quaint and different. The kitchen was the living room. In one corner was a commodious fogon compaña (family fireplace) and adjoining it on one side was the tapanco (porch). Strange to say this word belongs to the Philippines and means awning. The tapanco was a replica of the porch outside carried out in lesser dimensions, being about two feet from the wall, which would constitute its width, and between four and five feet high. The length depended upon the available space from the fogon compaña to the corner of the room. The columns of the tapanco formed its front and the even, smooth mud roof made a place to store tinajas (pottery vessels), for these vessels were used for every conceivable household purpose, and also were the only cooking utensils and dishes and containers they possessed. Most of the tinajas in the old houses at Placitas were carried there from San Felipe Pueblo. On the tapanco roof were pottery receptacles of varying sizes—the large ones in which meat was cooked, meat in great chunks, the large ones in which the fat parts of animals were rendered into lard, and pottery bowls for cooking beans and peas and the blue corn meal; all sizable bowls, and there were small ones for individual use, and there were the tall ones for carrying water, and the low wide ones for carrying food materials.

On the floor of the tapanco the great tinajas were stored. These vessels held food supplies. One was filled with blue meal, another held the lard, another wheat flour if such there happened to be. Another held the cheese made from the milk of the goat, and this was an important food and was an ingredient of many of their dishes. Here also was stored the large smooth slab of stone and the thick hand-sized ones (the metate and manos for grinding the corn into meal). In fact the floor of the tapanco was the storage place for the household possessions too valuable to be left outside the house. At certain times of the year dried meat was kept there in tinajas. And there was the precious salt. Each year the men made trips to that salt region in the vicinity of Estancia of today, to bring home salt. It was a trip of around ten days and large bands of men went together, most of them on foot.

On another side of the room in the kitchen of these old houses a low adobe wall was run about two feet from the wall of the room and parallel to it. Adobe petitions were put in at desired intervals, thus forming bins for the storage of corn, beans, peas, onions and whatever else they may have harvested. These bins were tragically empty in drouth years or in times when the Navajos raided the fields and reaped the harvests.

The center of the floor was the living room and the feasting place. There were no chairs nor tables and the clean, smooth adobe floor must be used in their stead. The room adjoining the kitchen was the sleeping room. On one side of this apartment was a long, slender pole extending the length of the place and the ends imbedded in the walls; for the pole was placed there as the walls were built. On this pole was hung the blankets, Mexican blankets they were, woven by the women of the family from the wool from their goats, upon the looms which were a vital factor in the lives of the people in these old houses. A loom was in every kitchen. At night these blankets were taken from the poles and made into beds for the family; if the nights be cold they were folded into snug sleeping bags; if the nights be mild they were simply made into pallets and laid on the floor. These floors of adobe laid at least eight inches below the threshold were warm as no wind could possibly creep in to chill them. These blankets and the pole on which they hung in the daytime and a crude hand-made wooden chest were the furnishings of the sleeping room.

The older inhabitants of Placitas say that these old houses were built before 1840, amid the ruins of an unknown pueblo of an unknown date. There were little if any changes made in these dwellings until the Eighties, though some articles of furniture were introduced to make living in them more comfortable. There is still to be seen some evidence of the style of these old houses. In the house of José Trujillo the old forms one corner of a newer house built around a patio and it is readily distinguished from the later addition by its construction. The old one was bought by Francisco Trujillo in 1854 from one whose name has long been forgotten. But José said the house was an old one when his father purchased it. A one-room house of the early type, belonging to José Baldonado is still intact. Aside from these, old houses have been lost in the rebuilding and additions and their quaint interiors are but a memory.

Source of Information: Rumaldita Gurulé, age 67, of Placitas, New Mexico, a descendant of one of the twenty-one families to receive the San Antonio de Las Huertas Grant from the King of Spain in 1767. Christiana Baros, age 33, of Placitas, New Mexico, a descendant of one of the twenty-one families to receive the San Antonio de Las Huertas Grant from the King of Spain in 1767. Catalina Gurulé, age 45, of Placitas, New Mexico, a descendant of one of the twenty-one families to receive the San Antonio de Las Huertas Grant from the King of Spain in 1767. José Trujillo, age 47, of Placitas, New Mexico, a descendant of one of the twenty-one families to receive the San Antonio de Las Huertas Grant from the King of Spain in 1767. Conception Archibeque, age 67, daughter of Francisco Gonzales, a Civil War Veteran from Placitas who came from Alameda prior to 1850.

Tejón "Badger"

by Lou Sage Batchen

Tejón is located on the Hagan Road about four and a half miles from the point where the Hagan Road crosses the Loop Drive at the east end of Placitas in Sandoval County. While the name Hagan is a comparatively new one, the road now bearing the name is an ancient and an historic one. It is a natural roadway and the only opening through the mountains from Placitas to Tejón and Hagan. It is a part of the main road from Bernalillo to Golden.

The story of Tejón is not merely a story of the people of Tejón. It is a story typical of the dramas enacted or lived in most of the old Spanish and Mexican Grants given to the early native people and their descendants.

It was on November 17, 1840 that Salvador Barreras appeared before Citizen Antonio Montoya (who signed his name Antonio Montolla) at the place of Angostura, Jurisdiction of Sandía, to request for himself and others that their certificate of possession of the tract of 12,801 acres given them by the Mexican Government and called the Tanque and Tejón Grant be judicially executed and placed upon record. And by virtue of the authority vested in him as Constitutional Justice of the Peace, Antonio Montoya granted the request and gave copies of the papers into the hands of Salvador Barreras.

By 1846, Tejón was a flourishing town. On June 21, 1860, the Tanque and Tejón Grant was examined and confirmed by the Congress of the Unites States, which meant that the government gave a quit claim deed for the grant to the people of Tejón. On February 11, 1882, Congress approved the grant, calling it the Town of Tejón Grant.

The first families who settled Tejón built their town on a flat, fertile, well watered tract not far from the place where Tejón Cañón suddenly emerges from the mountains. A ridge of the Sandías rises a short distance to the south of the place, and off to the north is San Pedro Mountain. A wide arroyo-scarred area stretches west to join the lands of the San Felipe

Pueblo, which forms the boundary of the Tejón Grant. The town was built according to the old Spanish law, which decreed that the house and corral of each family be built in such a manner as to form a wall about the large plaza and with openings or gates left only at the corners offering protection against hostile invaders, just as their ancestors had been compelled to do when they built Las Huertas. That deserted walled town was less than five miles away, and a well defined road, through cañóns and arroyos, joined them.

Tejón had an abundance of pasturage for goats, and less than two miles away was Uña de Gato (Cats' Claws), an old watering place. There was plenty of water for irrigation and for many household purposes, but this water was salty and unfit for drinking or cooking. In the early days of Tejón, before there were any beasts of burden, the women carried in tinajas on their heads all the water used for drinking and cooking, bringing it from the spring at San Francisco, which was nearly two and a half miles up Tejón Cañón. This was not accounted a hardship; it was merely one of the things necessary to be done that life might go on. There was plenty of water for their fields—that was of more importance than having drinking water at hand. That could always be carried from somewhere.

Time passed, the village population increased. Their flocks of goats multiplied. Burros and oxen now lifted body-breaking work from both men and women. Homes were built outside the walls, for there was no more room inside the walls. Then, on a hill not far from the place where the road entered the town, they built a church. It stood like a sentinel outside the walls. Over at the foot of the Sandías they now buried their dead, instead of carrying them to the cemetery in San Felipe, a long hard journey away. Now they placed an old hand-carved San Juan on their altar and held their own fiesta days. Life teemed with interest in the little town. Oxen and heavily laden wagons on their long trips to Estados (The States) plodded their way along through the village, for there was the highway, and the gates of the town now were always open. The gold fever struck the section, and prospectors and burros, with their backs loaded with "grub" and picks and shovels, wended their way through the town, bound for San Pedro and the hills around Tejón. This gold excitement around Tejón spelled the beginning of the end of that quaint little walled town.

About this time, M. S. Otero, a wealthy sheep and cattle man became interested in the grant. That much land would naturally interest a sheep man. Then gold was found in the San Pedro Mountains. There was the possibility that much of the grant might be rich in minerals. The Town of Tejón Grant had been confirmed by Congress but it must also be approved by Congress. That act required money. More money than the people of Tejón could ever pay, for the grant must be surveyed and the boundaries fixed, and legal services must be engaged to make out all the papers and prepare the case and present it to Congress. Such services meant a large amount of money, a small fortune in fact in the eyes of the people of Tejón. But the Grant of the Town of Tejón was approved by Congress in 1882.

Life went on in the village. In the year 1890, March 28, M. S. Otero filed suit in the District Court at Albuquerque against Luis Chaves, José Antonio Zamora, and others for possession of the Town of Tejón Grant. That meant that every owner of the grant was in court and his lands and home at stake. But it required money to go to court. More money than the people of Tejón could possibly raise. Besides, M. S. Otero was a banker. The thought of all his money, and of the strange and unaccountably mysterious ways of the gringos and their courts bewildered them and left them in a state of apathy. José Librado Arón Gurulé of Placitas made frequent trips to see his kinsmen at Tejón to advise them and do all he could to stir them to action. "Fight, fight for your homes and your land!" he would shout at them. "There must be something you can do!" But he failed to arouse their long-sleeping spirit of aggression, that paradoxical trait in his people which caused them to endure unspeakable privations and hardships with true heroism, yet caused them to shrug their shoulders and say, "No podemos remediarlo" (We can not help it) whenever calamity overtook them!

It was on May 23, 1893, that the final decree in the case of M. S. Otero vs. José Antonio Zamora and the other citizens of Tejón was handed down by the second district court, which gave M. S. Otero the Town of Tejón Grant except "The claims of Individuals of the Town of Tejón as a corporation, its successors and assigns. But this exception in this decree is not to be construed in any manner as affecting the findings by this court.

There is not now or ever has been any such corporation as The Inhabitants of The Town of Tejón."

And so the people of Tejón found themselves with nothing left but the plaza and the houses in which they lived. They were duly notified of the owner's intention to close the land to them. But for a time they did plant their fields and garnered their harvests. Two or three families saw the handwriting on the wall and moved away to seek other homes and start life over again. The rest of them remained obstinate. Then small sums were offered for their homes. One man, Luicio Barreras, son of Salvador Barreras, accepted twenty dollars for his holdings. This, said José Librado Arón Gurulé and Ramón Nieto, as far as we know, is all the money ever paid for the whole of Tejón.

Then the first of a series of decisive blows fell upon the heads of the people of Tejón. An order came demanding them to remove their flocks of goats from the land of the grant. The grant was closed to them for that purpose. Some of them sold their flocks, some placed their flocks in the keeping of people on other grants and divided the increase, a few sought public land whereon to pasture their flock. Then one day old Juan Antonio Barreras called the men together to tell them that hereafter they must go a long way for their wood. They had been ordered to take no more off the grant. They discussed the order, shrugged their shoulders. Their ancestors had lived through years of dangers, hardships, and privations in this town; surely they could go on supplying themselves with wood to burn, even if the grant was closed to them. But the next order was a visitation of doom to them. No longer could they plant the fields. Those fields were a part of the grant. The grant was closed to them.

Now the wall around Tejón became indeed a wailing wall. The path outside the wall to the little church became more beaten than ever from the constant pounding of feet of the black-shawled women going there to implore aid of the patron saint San Juan, praying for the restoration of their lands, praying in their time of need as all their people did, to something in which they had faith.

On September 28, 1904, death called M. S. Otero. His two sons shared in the Town of Tejón Grant, in the distribution of his estate. They had been reared in luxury; the tragic side of life had been no part of their experience. They were visionary. Tejón became a part of their vision. They carried on the work of emptying the town. What a perfectly splendid layout it was for a museum! They were right, but born thirty years too soon for the scheme. Here was a walled town in the manner of 1690. Just outside the wall, depicting the march of time, was the little church and the houses nearby built to accommodate the increase in population. The narrow road through the town, the gates—all so picturesque and so reminiscent of the days of the Conquistadores. The houses of adobe and the adobe corrals adjoining them, all facing the plaza they enclosed, striking reminders of the days when, for the sake of protection against hostile invaders, a family and their livestock lived side by side. For a never-to-be-forgotten image of the towns of the long ago, here was Tejón! The church and all the things in it; the old hand-carved San Juan and all the other old handmade wooden saints kept there for occasions other than Tejón's own feast day; the fine altar cloth with its handmade lace; the quaint old candle holders and candelabra made by the hands of the people in Tejón, all now belonged to the new owners of the grant. They bought the church, they said. This story of their vision of Tejón as a museum was told by Frederico Otero, one of the owners of the Town of Tejón Grant.

Old Salvador Barreras and his wife, Victoriana, were the last to leave the town they had helped to build. No one seems to remember where they went. The new owners now hired old Antonio José Gallegos to watch the place. He was installed in the house on the left-hand side of the south gate, which was the gate nearest the church. But the gates of Tejón could not be closed! Too long—since the early Forties—the road through the town had been a part of the highway. The watchman found it impossible to protect a wide-open town and he could not be at the church all the time to guard it. His eyes were keen and his limbs nimble enough, but somehow somebody looted the church of all that made it desirable as a museum feature, or as anything else, for that matter. The heavy timbers supporting the roofs of the houses mysteriously disappeared, as did doors and windows.

In time the walls crumbled, whole houses fell in ruins, but it did not concern the Otero heirs. The Town of Tejón Grant had slipped through their hands and into the hands of their lawyer, Neil B. Field, who also had a dream, a vision for Tejón. He saw it as a mineral grant, and an elaborate prospectus exploiting the grant was written. The above information was also given by Frederico Otero.

Today Tejón is fast crumbling into the dust from which it was raised. Its people are scattered far and wide. Its fields lie brown and barren beneath the summer suns and the winter snows. The waters which were once turned into irrigation ditches to flood those fields, flow down through an arroyo and eventually reach the Río Grande. The name of M. S. Otero is but a memory, and Neil B. Field sleeps beneath the dust. But the story of Tejón will live, just as the stories of old battlegrounds have lived.

Sources of Information: Frederico Otero, age 58, of Albuquerque, New Mexico, son of M. S. Otero, cattle and sheep man and banker, one time owner of Town of Tejón Grant. José Librado Arón Gurulé, age 88, of Placitas, New Mexico, a descendant of one of the twenty-one families to receive the San Antonio de Las Huertas Grant in 1767. Ramón Nieto, age 76, of Placitas, New Mexico, a descendant of one of the twenty-one families to receive the San Antonio de Las Huertas Grant in 1767. Patricio Gallegos, age 60, of Ojo de Las Casa, P. O. address, Placitas, New Mexico, a descendant of one of the twenty-one families to receive the San Antonio de Las Huertas Grant in 1767. Predicando Chaves, age 64, of Placitas, New Mexico, a descendant of one of the twenty-one families to receive the San Antonio de Las Huertas Grant in 1767. Adelida Chaves, age 55, of Placitas, New Mexico, wife of Predicando and descendant of the Armijo Family who came to Placitas before 1870, from Alameda, New Mexico.

The Fury of 1869

by Lou Sage Batchen

It was in the year 1869 that the young scholar, Arón, made his last stay in the Pueblo of San Felipe. He lived in the house of Juan Bustos where he earned his board and keep, but he pursued his rudimentary education under the tutelage of the good priest, Father Baron. So it was that he had access to whatever books were to be found in the church or the house of the priest. That was the one great privilege the youth craved.

Arón was ambitious. He craved to be able to write letters and to read books. But he was not selfish in his ambition. He earnestly desired to teach others to read and write—in Spanish, of course. That was the only language he knew. It was the language of the world as far as he was concerned.

Arón did teach the small children at the pueblo. The chili, the corn, the beans which he was paid for his services, the compensation he gave Juan Bustos for his board and keep. But no reading and writing was required in the daily schedule. Rather, his energies were spent in the teaching of religious songs and verses. In prayers, in adoration of the saints, in reverence for the church, and respect for their elders. If there was a stress laid on any particular thing taught, it was the respect, which included implicit obedience, the children must pay their elders.

In his pursuit of learning, young Arón often entered the church. There were some books there—mostly records. Those books intrigued him. He had a longing to find the entry of his own baptism. He wanted to be certain that his parents had remembered the exact date of his birth. He knew many parents who never knew the dates of their own birth and in as many instances they were not certain of the dates of the births of their children. Dates made little difference in those long ago days of the pre-1860 days. Events were what counted.

But Arón found it most difficult to do the desired research in the record books in the church. Whenever he went there, he either found a few Indians who watched his every move as if they were guards, or he was followed there and his every move noted. It were as if they divined his intention and were there to prevent it.

After a lengthy period of watchful waiting he found the opportunity for which he had actually prayed. An Indian event from which he was excluded left him to his own devices. He stole to the church, got the book upon which he had cast his longing eyes so many times, hid himself and started the search for the entry of his baptism. He found it. But he also found something else. A lengthy entry and not easy to read. He must have time to make it all out.

What he planned to do was not exactly honest, yet his intentions were good. He wished to learn of what was in the book. It was clear that he could not do it in the pueblo. There would be neither time nor privacy. He must take the book and go to his home in Las Placitas. He would guard the book, see that no harm came to it, and he would work out the meaning of all the words in that long record. He would waste no time and would be back with the book before anyone had a chance to miss it.

So it came about that he reached the house of Juan Bustos with the record book and hid it. That night he would go to visit his mother at Las Placitas. He would make it known that he was to go home for a short time, that no one would give the matter a thought.

That portion of his plan he carried out with precision. He arrived at the house of his father, Nicolás Gurulé, and his mother saw to it that he was not disturbed in his studies, for such she thought his request to be left strictly alone meant.

Thus without hindrance, Arón set about reading and copying the stirring entry. He found no date which he could decipher. But he found, later in his life, things which led him to believe that the recorded event took place many, many years before the American Occupation. Perhaps as many as fifty.

The recorded event as Arón copied it was in his possession for many years, and then one day he went to his desk and found that his papers had been disturbed. He knew someone was trying to get the story he would never tell. He had expected that very thing to happen, and had hidden the copied record. The secret was guarded through the years.

The old priest at San Felipe Pueblo fell ill. He raved day and night with a tormenting pain in his head and his body was covered with sores. The Indians said he was stricken with leprosy. At times a paroxysm of pain shot through the body of the poor old priest, and seemed to come from every sore on his body and settled at the very top of his head. There was nothing he could do to bring relief from his suffering.

Another priest came to care for him and look after the mission. He knew the malady was not leprosy, and was much puzzled by the nature of it, but did what he could for the old priest and said nothing of what he thought.

All the servants about the house of the priest were Indians. One youth lived in the house. His duty was to run errands and be on hand at all times, and particularly at night. It so happened that the new priest had need of him one night and called him. There came no answer. The priest went to the Indian's sleeping place. There was no sign of the youth. The priest made sure that the Indian was nowhere in the house before he gave up the search.

The next morning the priest found the young Indian in his bed and aroused him. He demanded of the youth where he had spent the night. The boy did not hesitate to speak. He spoke truthfully, too. The old priest had taught him that it paid to tell the truth. He told the padre that he had sat up watching two Indians burying something just outside the cemetery. He also told the good padre that the Indians were saying that the old priest would die before night.

Leaving the young Indian to his chores, the padre took two Indians and started the work of finding the place the boy had told him about. A place where he saw two Indians burying something. It took only a short time to locate the spot. The padre gave orders to dig and see what they could find in the hole. Without hesitation the Indians set to work. It was clear to the padre that they were not in on the secret of the burial place. As the Indians dug into the loose earth, the padre kept his eyes upon the spot, fearing to lose any clue of what deviltry the Indians were up to—for he felt that such was the case.

He heard a stick strike something. He bent down low and watched the Indians drag out a soil-covered object.

The priest stared at it. It was a perfect image of the sick priest. The robe was a copy of the one the good old father wore. But there was a perfect network of strings coming out the top of the head of the image. The visiting priest closely examined the strings. He found that each string was threaded through the eye made in each of the cactus thorns driven into the body of the image. The thorns thus were controlled by the strings coming out the head of the image. When the mass of strings projecting out the top of the head of the image were jerked about, the thorns scraped the body of the image. The new padre gasped. He was not slow in realizing the awful truth. The old priest was bewitched. Everywhere one of the horrible thorns were thrust into the body of the image, the priest had one of those terrible sores. Whenever the strings on the head of the image were pulled, the good padre suffered death with the sores as well as the head, where all the pain concentrated. They had buried the image and willed that the sick priest die.

Without loss of time the priest hastened to the bedside of the dying priest. He washed each sore upon his body with ashes. Immediately the old priest was healed.

And then came the retribution. The pueblo was combed to find the evil witches. Punishments were meted out until the two witches were identified. Then a great heap of dry grass and sticks was piled up and the image placed on top of it. The whole was crowned with the two Indian witches, bound head and foot. The dry grass at the bottom was set ablaze. The fire ate its way rapidly upward, it became the funeral pyre of the two Indian witches.

Arón had no sooner finished the copy than he hid it away and prepared to carry the book back to the church at San Felipe. It was at that very moment that an ear splitting, blood curdling yell from Indian throats fell upon the ears of the citizens of Las Placitas. The next thing they all knew, an invading mob of angry Indians came marching into the village. They carried clubs and shook them violently. No sound could be heard above their angry shouting. They demanded to see Arón. They marched on to the house of Nicolás and his wife, Catalina. Fearful that the Indians meant harm to Arón, some of the men of the village sought to break through the ranks of the mob to reach the house of Nicolás and warn him. But these men were roughly held back. Some of the Las Placitas men sought to reason with the mob, only to be brusquely pushed aside.

What was it all about? None in the village knew. Why should those friendly Indians from San Felipe turn against them in this way? It all seemed very mystifying and very serious.

It was most serious to the angry Indians. Their sacred place had been robbed. They were the zealous guardians of their church and all the holy things in it, whether it meant anything to them or not. The church and everything belonging to it was their own. No one should molest it. The leader among them had worked them into a fury over the desecration of their holy place, the place the priest called holy. The missing book to them was a place where the padre wrote down the facts of their births and baptisms and deaths. No one had a right to touch it, outside the padre, let alone steal it. Religiously awakened zeal recognized no limits. It is often cruel. This Indian mob at the height of an awakened religious emotion was ready to kill—if need be—for their righteous cause.

Lucas Gurulé could not stand idly by. He fought his way to his brother's house. He was determined that whatever Arón had done, he would save the youth from the fury of those Indians.

The Indians, shouting and shaking their fists and their clubs, were coming on. Lucas stood at the closed door of his brother's house and faced the mob defiantly, courageously.

Behind him he felt the door being removed. From the opening came Catalina. In her hands she carried a book. With upraised head and with a firm and determined step she advanced to meet the oncoming mob.

There was but little distance between her and infuriated Indians. But she showed no fear of them. Why should she? Her son had committed no crime. He was a good and smart and obedient son. They dare not touch him.

Perhaps the keen eyes of the leader read the face of Catalina Bustos de Gurulé. And whatever it was he saw there caused him to halt the mob. She approached him, addressed her greeting to them all as she laid the book into the hands of the now much becalmed leader.

With the precious book in their possession, the leader had little difficulty in swaying the mob to the cause of peace. They had won! Back to San Felipe they went, to restore the book to its honored place.

But not for long did it rest there. That is, not for many years. One eventful Sunday as the good padres of San Felipe took their usual Sabbath recreation, a walk into the nearby mountains, a sudden rain storm came up. One of those furious, beating, sheet-like rains which seems bent on destruction. When the padres reached the pueblo, they found the walls of the church badly washed out. One place where the adobe wall connected with the roof was washed out was directly above the niche which held The Book. It was smeared with adobe mud and was water-soaked, as were other books kept there. The books were sent to the Pueblo of Sandía for safety. No one in Las Placitas now knows the whereabouts of that book which holds so many entries of the baptisms of the long ago babies of old Las Placitas.

Source of Information: José Gurulé, age 90, Las Placitas, New Mexico. Descendant of one of the twenty-one families to receive the San Antonio de Las Huertas Land Grant from the King of Spain in 1767. His family have never left the grant. He is the Arón of this story.

The Panic of 1862

by Lou Sage Batchen

*T*he aged ones in Las Placitas still recall their own particular panic which befell them in the spring of 1862. It was a hectic week which followed the return of the Perea Family from Colorado, where they had fled before the advance of the victorious Texans up the Río Grande Valley.

The Perea Family were rich and influential. Their power extended throughout the length and breadth of the extensive region then known as Bernalillo County. A small army of natives at and around the town of Bernalillo were practically in bondage to Don José Leander Perea, head of the family. To them his word was the equivalent of the law of the land.

La Hacienda de Perea (the landed property of Perea) was just north of the small village of Bernalillo, and lay between El Camino Real and El Río Grande. The house was a large adobe building containing huge living rooms, sleeping rooms for the family and Navajo slaves, and a large store room. In fact the room was a store, which supplied the needs of the Perea household, and at which every peon round about had a charge account.

The peons lived in little adobe houses of their own, on land outside the Perea estates or in the native villages in the vicinity. Those who labored on the Perea estate walked to and from their long days' work and what they earned was applied on their accounts at the Perea store. Eight dollars a month was standard wage for the men.

Yet in spite of the ease and grandeur (for that time) in which the family lived they had their fears and worries; fears for their lives and worries over their property, personal and real, just as the poor natives feared for their lives and their possessions. Only there was a difference. The poor natives feared the cruel Navajos who preyed upon them, and never had the courage to steal from the rich and powerful, nor attack them, while the rich and powerful feared the raids of Los Tejanos (the Texans) who were just as ruthless as the Navajos, but were far more ambitious;

they were out for big stakes. But then the Texans were hated and feared by all New Mexican natives: The rich for what they had suffered at the hands of the Texans; the poor for what they had heard of the Texans. Texas raiders had taken a heavy toll on the rich.

In the very early days the Tejanos built up a reputation for lawlessness all up and down the Río Grande Valley and on the Santa Fe Trail. The upper class New Mexicans called them meddling foreigners, who had taken Texas from the republic of Mexico and who wished to join the department of New Mexico to Texas. The New Mexicans blamed the Texans for their internal troubles of 1837 when the government at Mexico supplanted a native of New Mexico governor by a governor from Mexico, who tried to install a system of taxation. They did not like the idea of the taxes, nor the interfering Pérez, who was the new governor. Under the leadership of General Armijo, Pérez was routed and beheaded. Then followed a catastrophe. General Armijo did not have the courage to seize the government himself and the victorious mob, made up of the followers he could recruit from anywhere, elected José Gonzales, a Taos buffalo hunter, as governor. Armijo quickly reorganized his forces and overthrew Gonzales and executed him because he had threatened to call the Texans to his aid, or so it was charged. Anyhow, the desired result was obtained and hatred of the interfering Texans flamed anew.

In 1841 an armed band from Texas raided the village of Mora and killed five citizens of New Mexico. In the spring of 1843, Colonel Jacob Snively, with a band of one hundred eighty Texans, attacked the spring caravan on the Santa Fe Trail.

Even after the conquest of New Mexico by the government of the United States, the native New Mexicans continued to hate and distrust the Texans. The rich feared them, the poor took up their quarrel and to this day the natives in the villages refer to the Civil War in New Mexico as the war with the Texans.

In 1861, Captain Baylor with his Texas army invaded the southern part of New Mexico and occupied Mesilla and other villages. In 1862, they won a glorious victory at Valverde and completely routed the Union forces of New Mexico. Then they started their march north.

News of their victory and march spread like wildfire up the Río

Grande Valley. The whole territory was thrown into confusion. It was February; the great spring caravan of wool was on its way to Los Estados (the states) and it was time to start the spring work.

At Bernalillo, Don José Leander Perea viewed the coming of the Texans with alarm. The victorious Texans would rob them of all they had and take the men as prisoners of war. He knew other heads of noted families would be forced to protect themselves just as he must do. They must flee the territory. They must go to safety in Colorado. There was no time to lose. He told his family to prepare themselves for the journey.

The peons were rounded up and set to work to expedite the preparations. Carretas were packed with clothing and valuables and supplies. The fine horses and carriages were made ready for the flight of the family with their Navajo slaves. The great house was barricaded and orders issued right and left by the patron, Don José.

Two youths were left to guard the house and adjoining property. They were to stick to their duties, no matter what. The boss of the peons was to start the spring work and see that the peons "kept their places." And with that, the Perea family, slaves, bag and baggage were off with a flourish and a dash. Bound for Colorado, where they would remain until they had the word that all was quiet along the Río Grande.

At the very time that the Don's carriages were traveling the route of the caravan into Kansas in order to avoid the heavy snows and almost impassable mountain passes on the shorter route to Colorado, the Colorado army, Pike's Peakers, were braving their way over those deep, snow-covered mountains to aid the New Mexico army men, Indian fighters, and volunteers to repel Baylor and his Texas army.

By the last of April, all danger of further invasion by the dreaded Texans was past. They had been driven steadily down the Río Grande to finally make their escape.

It was really springtime in the Río Grande Valley when the Perea Family returned to their house at Bernalillo. The house was reopened and the work of cleaning inside and out was started. But a few days had passed when "the devil broke out," in Bernalillo.

Without warning the youths left to guard the house were dragged into the fearsome presence of the Dons, José and his son Pedro. They were scared half to death and in their minds connected whatever was happening to them with the dread Texans, for at once both the men accused the boys of theft, of digging up the earth in the old chicken house yard.

The boys declared their innocence, begged for mercy and vowed that no Tejanos had been around the place and that the army had just marched up El Camino Real. But that was not the answer the Dons wanted. They threatened the youths with floggings if they did not confess—and it would have been floggings if they did. The men demanded of the fear-crazed boys, who had dug up the chicken yard if they had not done it.

The boys saw their way out. So, it was not El Tejanos, it was somebody else? They had not done it themselves—but someone who knew the place had done it. To save themselves they named some peons who worked around the place. After that they were told to go.

With little loss of time, the men they named were summoned, accused, and in spite of their protests of innocence, were flogged. The flogging brought no confessions. The men evidently had nothing to confess.

This happening threw the vicinity into a panic. Word of it was carried to Las Placitas, where the panic spread. Nearly all the men there were Perea men. What would happen to them? Lucas Gurulé pointed out that most of the men of Las Placitas took care of the Don's sheep, and all during the time of his absence were away up in the Jemez Mountains. The others in Perea's service who lived at Las Placitas had been busy at Cerro Pelón with their own herds and had not gone to Bernalillo, or were gone with the caravan to Los Estados.

But the flogging of the men did not end the affair, but rather was but the beginning of it. The boys were again called before Don José and Don Pedro. Again they were accused of the crime of digging in the chicken yard. Then they were asked what they did with the treasure they dug up. Again the boys cried out their innocence. Trembling with fear anew, they begged not to be flogged. Once more they were commanded to name the guilty ones. Again to save themselves they gave the names of three men, ones they knew to be none too honest.

Forthwith the men were ordered to appear before the Dons, and Perea aides went to hasten them on their way. But the three men protested their innocence and no amount of accusations by the Dons could force them to change their minds.

Don Pedro was fast losing patience. The treasure had been dug up from the chicken yard. He would find out who did it. He had a pillory built. When it was completed, the people round about eyed it with fear in their hearts. It meant that the Dons were not through with them yet. Again they blamed Los Tejanos. They were the ones who had stolen the treasure. Los Tejanos were always robbing the great Dons.

The boys were forced to give more names when they were again dragged into the presence of the Dons. By now they had learned that the one sure way to keep the wrath of the Dons from their own heads was to name probable guilty ones. They grew generous in the manner of giving lists of suspected ones; they even named a few against whom they had a grudge.

All those named were rounded up and brought before the patron and his son. All were punished; some were flogged, others put in the pillory where they remained at least two days when they denied the accusations of having a part in the theft of the treasure from the yard of the old chicken house. The panic-stricken people knew not what to do. They could not flee; it would only be the worse for them. So they grimly waited their turns, praying the saints to save them from the dire punishments for things they did not do, or for crimes which they did not commit, and all the time living in terror of being called next into the presence of the Dons. The orgies endured through the week at Bernalillo.

Then one morning the worst spread to Las Placitas. Into the village walked seven of the Perea aides demanding that Manuel and José Chávez accompany them back to Bernalillo. Don José Perea commanded it.

There was a loud protest from the villagers. There were no more honorable men among them than Manuel and José. The Chávez Family were one of the families who built old Las Huertas and received the San Antonio de Las Huertas Grant. There was a loud wailing went up from the lips of the Chávez women, who knew that their men had not been near Bernalillo during the absence of Don José from Bernalillo.

Lucas Gurulé knew that, too. He decided that it was about time that someone besides the Pereas took a hand in their inquisition, and that somebody might as well be himself. He sent for the Chávez men, he called Nicolás Gurulé, and then announced to the Bernalillo delegation that the four of them would accompany Don José's men back to Bernalillo and to the presence of the Don. And so it was.

When they were all conducted into the place where the Dons held their secret sessions, the Dons scowled upon the intruders and made it plain to Lucas and Nicolás that they were not wanted. The two men stood their ground and remained with their friends, the Chávez brothers. Lucas could have it so. He had never had his name on the Perea account book.

But Don Pedro did not allow the presence of Lucas and Nicolás to delay the matters at hand. At once he turned his attention to José and Manuel and accused them of the crime of digging up a treasure from the chicken yard. He informed them that they had been named as the guilty ones and now demanded their confession.

Before they could make reply, Lucas demanded of the Dons that they send for the alcalde at Bernalillo and give the men a lawful hearing. He told his two friends to save their statements until the arrival of the alcalde.

The Dons were speechless for the moment. Perhaps they had never before been defied by the lowly, and had no special and immediate remedy in mind for the unprecedented act. Without apology or explanation the four were dismissed. Lucas's inspiration had saved the day for his friends. As well the courage of him and his subtle threat to invoke the law brought an end to the panic of 1862 in Bernalillo and Las Placitas.

It was some time before the Perea secret leaked out, and the cause of the panic of 1862 was really known.

When the Perea Family fled before the advance of the Texas army, they did not desire to carry all their gold with them. Perhaps they thought it would be safer at home. So choosing a time when they believed they were absolutely unobserved, Don José and Don Pedro buried two leather bags, each one containing three thousand dollars in gold. They were buried in widely separated spots. After their return from Colorado they had gone out secretly to dig up the gold. They discovered that there had been much digging about the yard. To their sorrow they were able to find only one of the bags.

Then it was that they started in to find the thieves in any way they could. Strange to say, and in spite of the lash and pillory, they were never able to wring a confession from any of the accused. And never were they able to find a clue outside their own domain. They never found the gold.

Source of Information: José Gurulé, age 90, Las Placitas, New Mexico, son of the Nicolás of this story and nephew of the Lucas Gurulé of this story. Twitchell, Vol. 2, John Vaughan, *History of New Mexico*.

Tiempo de Pascua "Easter Tide" 1863

by Lou Sage Batchen

*I*t was late February in the year of 1863. The Lenten season had begun. Likewise had the sacrifices of the zealous penitents, who garbed themselves in flowing robes, called themselves Sirvientes de Dios (Servants of God), and sought to make their flesh pay for the sins on their souls. And while they were about it, to make such sacrifices as would bring purification to their families and friends, and to the whole world, just as the Master had done when he prayed and fasted in the wilderness.

They were not members of Los Hermanos de Luz (Penitente Brothers), who were outlawed by the Catholic Church. They were a small group of religious fanatics who desired fervently to do penance the hard way—and did. Only by the Grace of God did they survive. But only at Eastertide did this religious zeal possess them, a zeal which found release only in a sojourn in the mountains, where they fasted and prayed.

They carried nothing whatever with them. God would protect them from the wild beasts. God would direct them to caves where they would be safe and warm. God would lead them to places where they would find nuts and edible roots. They had nothing to fear; for as Servants of God, he would care for them.

Thus it came about in that long ago Eastertide, that two of the religious fanatics paused at Las Placitas on their way to the mountains. There was none in the village who sympathized with their cause, or thought it anything other than pure insanity. No one in the village sought to stay them from their mission, for they knew such efforts would be futile. So they watched the two men continue their way.

Soon the wayfarers came to Ojo de la Casa. There they rested at the friendly house of Valentino Zamora. As they spoke of their assumed duties of sacrificing themselves for others, their zeal-inspired courage proved to be infectious. It was Señora Juanita Zamora who felt the moving power of it. The idea grew within her mind and would not let her rest. She had many children, and many times that number of grandchildren. She grieved over their sins, as well as her own. As the days passed she felt the courage rising within her to go into the mountains to fast and pray, and through bodily suffering redeem herself and loved ones from their sins.

Holy week was approaching. Father Gaspari came to Las Placitas from Bernalillo. He wished to select several boys to play the part of angels in an Easter pageant at Bernalillo. Everyone in the village was brim-full of excitement. Never before had boys from their own families been chosen to take part in the pageants at Bernalillo. Mothers anxiously awaited the good padre's decisions. Thirteen year old José Gurulé was one of the fortunate ones. When they were ready they walked to Bernalillo with Father Gaspari. There they would remain the eight days until Easter Sunday, and prepare for their parts, and have their robes made for them. Very fancy clothes they were to wear in the role of angels.

All this happening served to fan the flame of fanaticism in the mind and heart of Señora Zamora. She felt that she must escape her family and go to the mountains to fast and pray. And she did. She went empty handed, with only the clothes upon her back for warmth. She fairly ran to put as much distance between her house and her destination as she possibly could, before her family should discover her disappearance.

Her family, thinking she was visiting at some neighbors, did not become alarmed until the darkness fell. When calls about the village failed to reveal her whereabouts, the family were alarmed. But Señor Zamora realized then where they must search for her.

She had confided in him her earnest desire to do penance in the mountains. He had rebuked her and forbidden her to do such a rash thing. But now she was gone, without food nor proper bodily clothing to protect her from the cold and freezing weather of the mountains; for it was yet the month of March.

So into the mountains went Valentino and his sons. They searched all through the night and came home exhausted. Señora Zamora had not been found. After refreshing themselves, they set out again. But the day's search was as futile as had been that of the night. The next day the search was resumed, and other men joined the party. Still no sign of the missing Juanita Zamora did they find.

Holy Week was at hand. On the first days much cooking must be done. Food must be prepared for the week, for after Wednesday, there would be no time to cook. Festive food, they must prepare with eggs. All the good housewives had saved as many eggs as possible for the Easter celebration. Eggs and quelites (a tender leafed plant of early spring; the word is probably an Indian word). This green was boiled and served in the manner of spinach. It was served with chili when desired. The favorite egg dish for the Easter celebration was forejas. This required bread. The bread was slicked and cut into small squares and dipped into egg batter. The squares were then fried in fat on both sides, then boiled in a syrup. As sugar—which they made from cane—was very scarce, the syrup was made largely from raisins—which they made from their grapes. For flavoring they used anise and cilantro (coriander) seeds, which they raised. This was a very festive dish and caused a few eggs to go a long way. Eggs symbolized the Resurrection, therefore eggs formed a very important part of the feast. Sopa (pudding with bread as the foundation), a fiesta-day favorite, was also made and served at the Easter feast. In those old days, the bread was unleavened. In every household could be heard the sound of the mano on the metate. There was need for much ground dried peas. From it was made the "coffee" of which everyone partook in abundance. This drink was second to vino, the home-made wine of the grape. Also, the women spent time and work in the making of many candles to be used in the little chapel. And all through the labor preparation, men and women thought with gladness of the boys in Bernalillo, and with sadness of the tragedy of Juanita.

But at last the cooking and baking was over. The food was ready to be served. Early Thursday morning entire families, except the smaller children, arose early and went to fast and pray at the little chapel. All morning they prayed. The chapel, so tiny it was, that only a few could enter at a time. So there was one continual procession in and out of the door.

Then came noon. Every woman hastened to her house. Throughout the hour, or perhaps more, people were hurrying about the village bearing gifts of food and drink to bestow upon one another. Food was exchanged; food was sent to those who were old and not able to attend the services. There was a general feasting until the time came to return to the little chapel to pray.

Then dawned Good Friday. Early and without food the people went again to the chapel to pray. Now they prayed at the stations. In bright-colored pictures spaced about the wall was told the story of the betrayal, arrest, trial, crucifixion, and burial of Jesus. Each picture was a station. These pictures became real to those who agonized before them. They became so real that the emotional almost broke under the strain of their own agony. And thus they went through the morning. Then again the people retired to their homes and again they gave gifts of food or exchanged food with one another and feasted until the hour to return to the chapel, where the procession to the stations continued.

At length it was finished and they were all gathered together for the velorio. They would watch until the dawn.

At just about dawn it was when the weary and almost broken Valentino with a few faithful searchers came upon the exhausted body of Señora Zamora. She was famished and nearly frozen. She could not speak and was only half conscious. She had found a secluded cave much off the beaten trails. But hunger and cold had driven her out. She had lost her way. She prayed as she had never prayed before for her sins and the sins of her family to be forgiven, but mostly she had prayed to be led safely to that family for whom she so eagerly sought to sacrifice herself.

And on that long ago Easter morning there was a loud rejoicing over a risen Savior. But there was also a rejoicing over the living Juanita, the good mother, wife, and friend, whom they had mourned as dead and who seemed resurrected on that Easter morning.

No longer do the people of Las Placitas keep the Eastertide in the old and gracious way. No longer do they sacrifice to bestow upon one another gifts of any kind. In those old days, food was all they had to give, and they sacrificed and gave liberally of what they had at Easter. There are only a precious few yet alive who remember those old days of Eastertide—agonizing, feasting, and fanatical sacrificing of the body to win forgiveness of sins.

Sources of Information: José Gurulé, age 90, Las Placitas, New Mexico. The José Gurulé of this story. Rumaldita Gurulé, age 68, Las Placitas, New Mexico, who had the story from her mother. Benino Archibeque, age 74, Las Placitas, who remembered the story of the long ago Easter. Conception Archibeque, age 68, Las Placitas, who remembered how the Easters of long ago were celebrated. She had the story from her elders. Patricio Gallegos, age 63, Ojo de la Casa, New Mexico, the grandson of the Juanita of this story. Terecita Gallegos de Baca, age 34, Ojo de la Casa, New Mexico, great granddaughter of the Juanita of this story.

PLACE

"When the Indians fully understood he would die before uttering one word of enlightenment to his tormentors, they decided to keep him. For four years he was held captive but finally escaped and returned to San Augustine."

From "San Augustine" by Lester Raines

Alto Huachin

by Lorin W. Brown

On the road to Córdova after one turns East off Highway #64 at Puye, recently known as Riverside, and reaches that part of Chimayó known as La Plaza del Cerro, one takes the left hand road, not the one which leads to the Sanctuario, and continues along this road which winds through the foothills ever climbing towards the up-lands at the base of the Truchas peaks. About one mile after one leaves the Plaza del Cerro one reaches Río Chiquito, a small village to the right of the road, whose inhabitants are engaged in the peaceful pursuits of weaving and chile raising.

Here the grade of the road becomes definitely much steeper and it is necessary to use second or low gear. The first breathing spell is reached when you have topped a high hill from which you can see the village of Truchas sky-lined against the eastern horizon, some five miles away and mostly up.

This spot may be identified by the many mounds on each side of the road, which form a rough circle enclosing a small plain some six acres in extent. No vegetation except cactus and a fuzzy growth of Russian thistle, which never seems to grow beyond the incipient stage, is to be seen on these hills or mounds. This height or the site of these mounds is about three-fourths of a mile from the spot where one leaves the ridge road to Truchas on the left and descends into the valley in which Córdova is located. This site may be identified also by a cross which stands on a mound on the eastern edge of the circle. This cross was made and erected there by the late Don José Dolores López, well known wood carver of Córdova, remembered by many for his hospitality, graciousness and keen sense of humor.

This is the Alto Huachin, the site of an Indian pueblo of long ago, inhabited by Tano Indians. Its location lent itself, admirably, to freedom from surprise attack guarded as it is on the North and West by steep slopes and on the South by the steep rocky gorge of the Río Quemado. These ruins should be of interest to the archeologist since they have never been excavated except for the tentative test holes dug by amateur seekers of curios.

However, if you are headed for Córdova drawn there by the unique attractions of this typically New Mexican adobe village, you will be interested in the connection between these ruins and the history of the settlement of Córdova.

Alto Huachin, or Huachin Height, was so named after the last chief or governor of the ill-fated pueblo. These Tanos dwelt here, continually harassed by the Navajos, Apaches and other predatory tribes as they tended their scant crops in the valley below or hunted small game in the rocky outcroppings of the surrounding hills. To the North and West of Alto Huachin and across a sandy arroyo there is a high butte which to this day is called La Sentinela or The Sentinel. This was a look-out point on which a watchful sentinel was posted to signal the approach of any band of enemies which he might sight.

How many attacks the pueblo survived we do not know, but we can imagine that they were many and unrelentingly fierce. We do know that some time previous to the year 1751 the enemies of the pueblo on the Alto Huachin finally prevailed, killing most of the inhabitants after which they set fire to the buildings, for at this time the site of the erstwhile pueblo was known to the settlers of Santa Cruz de la Cañada by the name "El Pueblo Quemado" or The Burned Pueblo. This fact is established by a document dated as above, in which document a group of settlers of Santa Cruz petition the viceroy for permission to re-settle the lands of El Pueblo Quemado. The word re-settle argues that they had previously settled on these lands and whether they had been driven out or had abandoned them for other reasons is not touched on in the petition.

However the settlement which sprung up in the valley of the Quemado river was henceforth known as El Pueblo Quemado and was not known as Córdova until a United States Post Office was established there in 1913. The name Quemado was not permitted by the United States Postal Department because there existed another town of that name in the southern part of the state, so that the name Córdova was selected, honoring the most prominent and progressive family of the village.

A few of the surviving Tanos from Alto Huachin took refuge in a small valley about two or three miles above where they lived a miserable and fugitive existence. Here they finally died out and the pitifully small ruins of the last stand of a one time flourishing community may be seen today. This valley is still known as La Cañada de los Tanos.

The Salt Traffic from the Estancia Salt Lakes to Mexico

by Lorin W. Brown

"Salt traffic from the Estancia salt lakes to southern Chihuahua flourished two and a half centuries ago.

A bit of interesting history crops out in ancient Spanish documents of the year 1668 which refer to a long forgotten traffic between New Mexico and the south. The Conquistadores having forced the Indians of southern Chihuahua into working their newly opened mines, needed salt for the smelting of their silver ores. Doubtless the product from the Estancia lakes had been used for centuries as a medium of trade among the Indians of the Southwest and had found its way far into the interior of Mexico. At any rate the Spanish seem to have sought out the source of supply without delay, for soon there was a steady stream of burro trains to and fro over the long trail, seven-hundred miles or more between the Salines and the mines of Parral."

Source of information: *El Palacio, Vol. 1, #3, 1/1914.*

Manzano

by Jean Cady

The quiet little town of Manzano (apple) lies encompassed by verdant fields at the foot of the dark Manzano mountains. The picturesque little village is so apart from our modern world that it appears to have always been a part of this sun warmed land. The settlers straggled back to this region of forgotten cities years after they had been driven far to the south by the attacks of nomadic plains tribes and by the great Pueblo rebellion of 1680. The newcomers found an ancient apple orchard, from which they chose the name of their settlement and built their little adobe homes, tier upon tier on the hills around a lake, so beautiful in spring with its myriads of water lilies. This lake is fed by an underground channel from a wonderful spring of clear cold water which bears the unique name of "Ojo del Gigante" (Giant Spring). The brilliant green algae that grows over the sandy floor of the basin shines through the transparent water till it glistens like an emerald, while the surface reflects the tall dark pines that stand about its rim.

At Manzano, there is a Spanish tower or Torreon, from which the early settlers could keep watch for the hostile bands of wandering plains Indians who always menaced this outpost of Spanish colonization.

Sources of Information: Paul A. F. Walter, *The Cities that Died of Fear*; Mary Orr, *New Mexico Magazine*, July 1935; Bandelier, Final Report.

Gallegos: Quay County

by Genevieve Chapin

...Some time about 1840, the original tract of land which became the nucleus for the immense Gallegos holdings was homesteaded by Don Gallegos y Sánchez. This pioneer, with his bride of but a few days, made a visit to Bosque Redondo in 1840, where they found, held in captivity and awaiting sale, a beautiful and intelligent Indian girl, apparently about 23 years of age. She was purchased for the new bride, and taken with the Gallegos to the ranch home. By the time the slaves were emancipated by the proclamation of President Lincoln, this girl had so endeared herself to the family that she seemed as one of them, being known as Rafaela Gallegos. She stayed on at Gallegos, serving one generation after another of the Gallegos family until her death early in 1936, at which time she must have been, at the very least, 110 years of age.

At the death of Don Jesús María Gallegos, the ranch came into possession of his son, Don Francisco Gallegos, during whose management it continued to expand and increase in value. The Gallegos family operated a thriving general merchandise business, and a Post Office, during the lifetime of Don Francisco Gallegos.

It is related that during this time, on one occasion when Don Francisco Gallegos was away on business, the store was left in the care of his wife. Early one morning a band of seven bandits rode up to the store, and made several purchases, the Señora Gallegos supplying all their demands except that for whiskey. That evening, toward sundown, the same gang, having found that Don Francisco was away, rode back and attempted to loot the place, but the brave woman in charge locked the doors against them, and then, with the aid of the Indian servant woman before mentioned, and her two young sons, of about twelve and fourteen years, she returned shot for shot throughout the night, wounding two of the gang. With the coming of day they fled, apparently under the impression that help was coming to the besieged women in the store. From Gallegos they seem to have gone almost directly to the García store, near what is now the Zurich ranch, in Union County. Here, they found the place also in charge of two lone women—García himself being also away on business. Señora García refused to allow them to enter the store, but, yielding to the entreaties of her mother, who was with her and feared the men might be really hungry, this plucky little woman, with a gun in a holster at her hip, carried out to them such supplies as they demanded, even the bandages to dress the wounds inflicted at the hand of another brave woman. Of such stern stuff were our pioneers made.

With the death of Don Francisco Gallegos in 1898, the Gallegos holdings, still increasing, passed into the hands of his two sons—Eufracio and Filiberto Gallegos, and their sister, Sarita Gallegos—now Mrs. Nestor T. Baca.

Sources of Information: Elmer Elkins, Clayton, former sheep inspector; Mrs. Hamm, Clayton, old resident and frequent visitor at the ranch; Mrs. Libby, Clayton, daughter of F. C. de Baca, of this manuscript; John Tixier, merchant of Clayton, grandson of J. B. Tixier, of this mss.

Mountains and Peaks: Rabbit Ears

by Manville Chapman

The Story of the Rabbit Ears, as told by one who had heard the ancient Spanish lore, concerning one of Union County's scenic attractions. (By Col. Jack Potter.)

This mountain was not only a guide for Santa Fe trailers but also for the trail drivers. The first caravan on it from the Missouri River to Santa Fe learned the name of this mountain, Orejas de Conejo "rabbit ears," from the Indians.

Furthermore, I believe that two great battles were fought there more than 200 years ago. History will tell you that an expedition left Santa Fe in 1717 headed for the Orejas de Conejos to meet the Comanches in battle in order to get them to release the Spanish prisoners. As the Spaniards knew this mountain by name, it must have been named before that date, for the great Cheyenne Chief, Orejo de Conejo, was killed in a battle and buried on top of that mountain that bears his name.

Do you know that the first mountain seen by people coming from Texas and elsewhere in the south on this great highway #385, are the Rabbit Ears?

While I don't believe much in this book history, this is my kind of history—handed down from one generation to the next—and you will find it authentic. You can ask any old, gray-headed Spanish-American in this country about Rabbit Ears, or Orejas de Conejos, and he will tell you that his father's father told about the great battle of the Rabbit Ears, and of the great treaty made between the Comanches and the Spaniards not to fight anymore.

To further explain the matter I have some data furnished me by George Fitzpatrick of Albuquerque.

Amado Chávez, first public school superintendent of New Mexico, in a monograph published by the Historical Society of New

Mexico in 1906 described the defeat of the Comanches in 1717, probably the bloodiest slaughter of Indians in western history.

At the time the lives of Spanish settlers were in constant danger, and finally it was decided to put an end to the raids. Representatives in all parts of the province met in Santa Fe and began organization of a volunteer army.

Don Juan de Padilla, Don Carlos Fernández, and Don Pedro Pino were chosen to command the army, and within a short time 500 young men, all well armed, mounted, and with pack mules, had been assembled for the expedition. Many carried fire arms, others machetes, lances, and bows and arrows.

The army camped the first night at the Pueblo of Pecos, then moved by way of Anton Chico to the plains in what is now northwestern Texas, finally coming to a valley in which they met scouts who had preceded the main band. Here they learned the Comanches were camped a few leagues ahead. Preparations were made to attack at daybreak.

When they came upon the tepees of the Comanche camp the order was given to charge. The Comanches at first thought it was another Comanche party returning victorious from a campaign, and before they collected their senses the slaughter was on.

Hundreds were killed and 700 taken prisoners. The Spanish prisoners were liberated.

So severe was the punishment of the Spanish punitive expedition that the Comanches never again went on the war path against the Spaniards.

The expedition ended the wars between the Spanish settlers and the Comanches for all times.

Whenever the young bucks wanted to start a war against the Spaniards the gray-haired old men would take them to las "Orejas de Conejos" where in former times that great battle took place and show them the pile of bones and skulls and repeating to them the story of that famous fight and the fact that so many of their ancestors were lost never to return, and that would cool their desire to fight.

Points of Interest in Taos County: The Las Trampas Mission

by B. C. Grant

*T*he Las Trampas Mission of the Twelve Apostles dominates the old town of Las Trampas in its valley far up in the Sangre de Cristo mountains in the southern part of Taos County and is reached by following the highway. As settlers were in the country by 1795, the church was undoubtedly begun soon afterwards. The dignified building of warm, slightly pinkish adobe is approached through a gateway in an adobe wall. Within a desert yard to both the right and left is used as a cemetery where colorful crosses of odd designs catch the eye. The church entrance, near which, on the left, hangs a bell, is a large decorated door set in under an upper balcony with a railing which stretches across from the two heavy abutments or uncompleted towers on the front corners of the building. The long, flat roof-line runs back to join the higher walls of the transept.

Within the building, the walls are hung with old paintings, artificial flowers and fine old tin work. A well-carved pulpit is a special feature. On the right of the nave is a latticed door through which may be seen a Penitente room or morada where are stored a cross, an empty coffin used in their Good Friday procession and a large cement stone in which is embedded a shallow copper dish. There is also an old "death cart" where, on a block of wood, supported by large solid wooden wheels, sits a gruesome figure in black representing Death. Its elongated up-tilted face has pale lavender eyes painted behind oval bits of glass; its legs are crossed and the arms with wooden skeleton hands are raised to hold the bow and arrow of straw. A room with such equipment marks the building as the most unique in all New Mexico.

Source of Information: Interview with Majel Claflin, Taos.

Las Vegas

by Bright Lynn

Río Gallinas, or Las Vegas, was a prominent point on the Santa Fe Trail. The place was not known by the latter name until the 1830's. Here the first waters of the Río Grande watershed were reached. In 1832 Dr. Gregg found, where the city of Las Vegas now stands, only a little hovel at the foot of a cliff. This was the first house built in Las Vegas. It was definitely colonized in 1835 and ten or eleven years later the place had over one hundred homes.

Las Vegas then was only a small town of scattered population when Kearny came to take possession in the name of the United States government. He came from Bent's Fort, arriving here on August 15, 1846. His proclamation was made from the roof of what is now known as the Dice apartments on the North side of the Plaza, but at that time it was occupied by an old settler by the name of Frank G. Kihlberg. He absolved the people from allegiance to Armijo, the governor at that time, and promised protection to life, property and religion. Tradition has it that his camp was pitched on what is now the Normal Hill—the old trail below to the south.

". . . On the 20th day of March, A.D., 1835, Juan de Dios Maes and others, citizens then living in the vicinity of what is now the Town of Las Vegas, petitioned the proper authorities representing the government of Mexico, for a grant of land, bounded on the north by the Sapello river, on the south by the boundary of the grant made to Don Antonio Ortiz, on the east by the Aguaje de la Llegua, and on the west by the boundary of the grant to San Miguel del Bado, binding themselves to receive possession of the same in the name of the Federation, and urging its adoption and concession because it would tend to the advancement of agriculture and the well being of several families without occupation.

"This petition was on the same day presented to the corporate authorities in the Town of San Miguel del Bado.

"... On the 6th day of April, 1835, the said justice proceeded to establish on the Gallinas river, at the present city of the Town of Las Vegas, a town, then named and known as Nuestra Señora de los Dolores de Las Vegas, and now known as the Town of Las Vegas, the said original town being founded and established about that portion of the present town of Las Vegas known as the Plaza of Las Vegas."

Source of Information: From an address delivered by Judge Luis E. Armijo at The Las Vegas Historical Society Centennial Celebration of 1935.

Lea County Plains—Once a Hunting Ground

by Mrs. Benton Mosley

The Indian's Buffalo Hunting Days here have been depicted elsewhere, see Our Predecessors (part 2) under topical paragraphs: Indian's Buffalo Hunting, Foot Indians, Buffalo Traps, Hunting on Horseback, Woman's Work and Buffalo, a Livelihood.

"Ciboleros" or Mexican Buffalo Hunters which Gregg so colorfully describes as coming leather-clad and with betasseled lances to the Llano Estacado, on fleet and highly trained lance horses—forerunners of the cow pony—doubtlessly did some hunting here. A few Mexican or Spanish relics found at watering spots, faint traces of cart roads, and the fact that the early Anglo-Americans found Mexican hunters who knew the country so well as to make excellent guides, together with early Spanish place names of the few landmarks—mostly of lakes on the Texas side—indicate the ciboleros' having hunted here.

Such hunting parties—social as the Mexican ever is—were made up of fifteen, twenty-five, or as many as fifty Mexicans from the Pecos or Río Grande settlements, or from Old Mexico, who came in "the time of Lakes" and spent a few weeks killing "winter meat." A few such lancing parties were seen by the earlier Anglo hunters, a little farther to the north.

The cibolero's method of killing the buffalo was to dash, mounted, into an unsuspecting herd, and riding close beside a racing buffalo, stab him just behind the shoulder with the lance, then on to the next, and on as long as the lance horse was able to keep close beside the buffaloes. The swiftness and skill demanded of both horse and hunter—along with the danger entailed—made such hunting something supreme in Mexican sport. Something akin to the modern rodeo, polo, and the Spanish bullfight, yet more thrilling than either of these. The horses ridden were sometimes gored fatally, and occasionally the lance would injure or be driven back through the hunter or his mount.

Buffalo meat and hides so taken were cured and packed either on burros, pack-mules, or carretas (carts) drawn by burros or oxen. If the weather was warm the meat was sliced thin and dried into "charqui"—often slightly barbecued to hasten the drying process. Unlike the nomad Indian, the cibolero had a home elsewhere and left his family there during the hunt. . . .

Los Torres

by L. Raines

Name: Los Torres, (the towers), named after the twin, tower-shaped mountains on the southeast

Altitude: 5,341

Population: 70

Location: Southwestern San Miguel County, on the lower Gallinas River. On New Mexico Highways 20 and 67; 28 miles southwest of Las Vegas

History, Growth and Development: Los Torres was settled in 1866. The original houses were built close together for protection against the Indians, all facing the south. The community has many Penitentes, who during Holy Week climb the twin mountains, scourging themselves as they go. In their morada are many old santos and crucifixes of wood.

August 10 is the feast day of the village. The night before, the population retire to an appointed spot in the mountains, where they pray during the night, returning in the morning for mass.

Source of Information: Information provided by Lucy Lucero.

San Augustine

by Lester Raines

Name: San Augustine, after the patron saint, Augustine of Hippo
Population: 100
Location: Central San Miguel County, directly east of Tecolote, shut away from the outside world by the steep canyon walls of the Río Gallinas. Reached over U. S. Highway 66 from Romeroville

Early History, Development, Points of Interest: One of the treasures of the village is a diminutive wooden image of St. Augustine, which occupies a place of honor in the church. The church is the center of interest in the community, both for what it stands for and for the protection it afforded during the Indian attacks. Beyond the 12 or 15 adobe houses of the little settlement are ancient walls, representing an Indian culture of many years ago. Due to the washing of water through countless ages, the cliffs above the walls are marred with holes and dents. The weathering elements of time have unearthed hundreds of shards of Indian pottery, predominantly orange and black. Some of the larger shards are so beautifully turned and grooved that it is evident these particular Indians were unusually skilled in workmanship. The common belief is that there is a buried Indian village in the vicinity of the walls.

When cleaning an irrigation ditch Juan Gonzales noticed a place in the soil that sunk even more than was necessary for his purpose. His curiosity aroused, he threw out a few shovels of dirt and discovered innumerable human bones, presumably of Indian burial. At another time he discovered, under a thin layer of soil, the bones of an Indian kneeling in the corner of one of the oldest dwellings. All the discoveries indicate that before the San Augustine canyon was populated with Spanish-Americans there was an Indian civilization of comparatively high culture.

There is very little information concerning the date of first settlement in the canyon by the Spanish, but it is evident that four or five generations have lived there. A time-honored tradition that people of San Augustine now have of their ancestors is the extreme cruelty of the Indians and the constant menace of attack. Toward the north and west of the village, towering above the other cliffs, is a rocky, peaked rise known as Sentinel Hill. Indians chose Sentinel Hill as a strategic point to place spies and scouts. In this way they were able to keep the little village constantly under observation, knowing just when to swoop down on the people, to steal their horses and goats, and to burn their dwellings. If the Spanish had sufficient warning of an attack, the entire population would congregate on the top of the church, where they kept an ample supply of rocks with which to stone the marauders.

Another signal point of the Indians is located directly above San Augustine under a huge, jutting cliff. Called Cueva María (Cave of Mary), it has been given in recent years the more appropriate name of Yellow Cave, as everything in and about the cave is yellow.

Isidro Romero was kidnapped by Indians while tending his flocks a short distance from the village. Taken to the Indian camp, he refused to tell where his people had hidden their gold. The Indians heated a cowhide over the fire, then swathed Romero in the fiery hide. Surviving this torture without betraying his people, he was severely beaten and dragged behind a running horse. When the Indians fully understood he would die before uttering one word of enlightenment to his tormentors, they decided to keep him. For four years he was held captive but finally escaped and returned to San Augustine.

Around a bend in the canyon, 2 miles from San Augustine, is the remains of an improved farm. A few straggling trees remain of a once bountiful fruit orchard. Reputedly haunted, the place can find no owner to convert it into a paying farm. Fifty or sixty years ago a man lived there with a beautiful 16 year old daughter. The Indians attacked the family and carried off the girl. Now, so runs the story, if one rides by at midnight, one hears the pitiful cry of a wretched woman and sees a mysterious radiance illuminating the spot.

Present day San Augustine is much the same as other little villages throughout New Mexico. The citizens are indebted now to the government for aiding them through the depression, as they were for governmental aid in times past during Indian trouble. A few years ago an irrigation system was worked out from the Río Gallinas flowing through the canyon, which enables them to water crops and make a little soil return a good yield of beans, oats and corn.

The church is and always has been of great importance in the village. The bright spot is the monthly coming of the priest. The women spend days cleaning the church and making it attractive, and in flower season they decorate it with flowers carefully raised for the purpose.

There is a little adobe schoolhouse where the children are given the foundation of an education.

The villagers are now attempting to make their homes more accessible to the rest of the world by constructing a road up one side of the canyon wall. The work of throwing rocks and clearing away stumps and trees has been both difficult and tedious. They have succeeded in clearing enough of a trail to permit wagons and a few daring car-drivers to traverse it. Generally speaking, they are happier to stay in their own little domain and live their daily lives as did their ancestors before them.

Source of Information: Information supplied by Juanita M. Bottorff through interviews with Victoria Buenavilla, Margarito Gonzales, and Fidel Saiz of San Augustine.

San Miguel del Bado

by L. Raines

Name: San Miguel del Bado (St. Michael at the crossing), after the patron saint of the village and after the crossing of the Pecos River, later a point of entry on the Santa Fe Trail

Altitude: 6,000

Population: 500

Location: On the Río Pecos in southwestern San Miguel County. Reached over U. S. Highway 85 and a country road joining the highway 1-½ miles east of San Jose

History, Development, Points of Interest: The small Spanish-American village of San Miguel was settled around 1750 by Indians cast out from their own tribes because of their conversion to the Catholic faith. Before the American occupation of the territory of New Mexico it was regarded as the center of the surrounding settlements. Most traders crossed from Cimarron to the Canadian and went on through San Miguel and Pecos, entering Santa Fe from the south. During the Mexican regime a small detachment of troops was maintained at San Miguel, and here the Texans were imprisoned when they made their ambitious invasion of New Mexico for conquest. It was the county seat of San Miguel County until county affairs were removed to Las Vegas.

Before 1805 San Miguel was administered by the Franciscan Fathers of Nuestra Señora de Los Angeles (Our Lady of the Angels) near Pecos. As the congregation grew, the Bishop of Durángo was petitioned to give San Miguel a resident pastor. Further, bad roads and hostile Indians made the journey from Pecos hazardous. The Franciscan Fathers continued their work among the first settlers along the Río Pecos until in 1820 Spain secularized the Franciscan order in all her dominions. Padre José Francisco Leyba remained in San Miguel as a Catholic priest. The parish at this time extended as far west as the Texas boundary. The territory had to be covered on horseback and many dangers had to be met on the trip. Father Leyba died in November, 1853 and was buried on the gospel side of the altar within the altar railing in the San Miguel church.

The church was built in 1806 by Indians of the parish under the direction of the Franciscan Fathers. Unlike most churches of the period it is not of adobe but is of solid rock. The walls are about 20 feet high, 3 feet in thickness. Above them rise two towers, each 36 feet high. Originally a mud roof crowned the structure but it was replaced in 1881 by a more permanent one. In the towers there used to hang two old bells, "María del Carmen," cast in 1830 and "María Miguela," cast in 1851. They were cast in San Miguel and into their metal went gold and silver jewelry donated by people of the parish. Because of the weakened condition of the towers and to insure greater safekeeping they were removed, and are now in the care of the parish priest. Another large bell, still in use, stands on a large platform in front of the church. A solid rock wall 5 feet high, built in 1806, surrounds the church.

The first floor in the church was laid in squares, under which the wealthier inhabitants of the village were buried. The present floor has been laid on top of the old one. The wooden pews are elaborately carved and there are a number of beautiful statues.

Interest in the little village centers around the church, the convent, and the school, conducted by the Sisters of the Sorrowful Mother. The Franciscan Fathers, from 1806 to 1820, and their successors, the secular clergy, have carefully preserved the parish records, which are remarkably detailed and complete, being an important record of history, both religious and civil, of the Southwestern territory.

Sources of Information: Information supplied by Margaret Herrera, through interviews with residents of San Miguel: Reverend John P. Moog, Sandoval Francisco, López Faustine, and Mrs. Ortiz Alfredo; also by Estella Ortiz.

Starvation Peak

by Lester Raines

*H*istorical landmark located 17 miles southwest of Las Vegas on the old Santa Fe Trail. Highway 85 passes within a mile of its foot. The summit is 7,000 feet and the climb from the road may be made in an hour. Legends declare the old mountain to have been the scene of an Indian raid in which 120 Spanish men, women and children fled to the high mesa top, where they were surrounded and starved to death.

Source of Information: Information supplied by Arthur Gump.

Tecolotito

by Lester Raines

Name: Tecolotito (Tay-koh-loh-te-to), little owl
Population: 150
Location: On the southern border of San Miguel County, the Río Pecos dividing it from Guadalupe County. Reached over U. S. Highway at Romeroville, turning off on the road to Anton Chico
History: Originally settled by a band of Spanish-Americans who believed in witchcraft. They used to gather on certain nights along the banks of the Pecos to talk to the spirits and become versed in witchcraft. The group gradually dispersed, and the settlement was taken over by the Lucero family, who built homes and extended the village. They planted orchards along the banks of the river and built a two-room stone schoolhouse.
Industries: Fruit and vegetables

Source of Information: Adelle Velásquez.

Roswell

by Georgia B. Redfield

*T*he Spanish-American settlement—"Chihuahua"—a district of twenty-two blocks located within the city limits of the southeastern section of Roswell, is rich in folkways and folk-lore of the Spanish-American people.

This district incorporated as a part of the city with a population of one thousand Spanish speaking people, has the colorful atmosphere of a Spanish village. The people living here, in a world all their own, cling to old customs and live in quaint adobe, mud roofed houses, the exteriors made gay in the autumn with garlands of bright red chili. Chairs in the cleanly swept "patios"—yards—are usually occupied, afternoons, by the old men and women of the different households, who enjoy mid-day "siestas" in the sun.

On many of the premises the little burro or a milk goat may be seen, tied with a long rope, which permits a contented cropping of salt grasses growing on the sides of the narrow "caminos"—streets.

The inhabitants of the settlement sing the old folk-songs and dance the Spanish fandangos and quadrilles at celebrations and wedding parties. The songs are usually soft slow, and of romantic nature such as "La Chaparita"—The Little One—"La Golindrina"—The Swallow—"La Paloma"—The Dove.

At the valoria, (similar to the Irish wake) singers gather around bonfires in the patios and sing sad songs and chants, in praise of the dead.

Folk-dances are intricate and unusual. The dancers move through the figures in a graceful earnest way.

Independence day, 16th of September is begun with cannon salutes, and later there is a barbecue at which Spanish dishes, chili, tamales, and enchiladas are served. In the evening there is a carnival and street dancing.

There is a Catholic church in Chihuahua, a Catholic and a public school with 125 children enrolled.

Estancia in Tradition

by N. S. Rose

The question has been asked: "When and why was Estancia named and for what or who was it named?"

Well, that was a good while ago and none of us here today can lay claim to being eye witnesses to the naming ceremony. All we have to go by at this late date is pretty well founded and authenticated tradition.

From ancient Spanish writings, and word of mouth, we learn that this was on the direct trail from Chihuahua to Santa Fe, and that it was the regular practice of the caravans going back and forth between these two places, to halt here by the spring to rest and let their weary footsore stock recuperate on the rich grass that grew around the spring. From this fact the name, Estancia, which means a resting place, was given by these early travelers to the spring and soon began to be applied to the plain surrounding the spring.

Within the memory of some now living, this name was used for the spring and the plain, then much later came the building of the Santa Fe Central Railroad, together with the locating of the town, and other towns along the line of the railroad. Then the organizing of Torrance County and locating the county seat at Estancia. During those years, from 1901 to 1904, the settlement of the plain by homesteaders began, and the plain became valley. We believe it was John W. Corbett, one of the leading characters in the early development, who proposed the name "Valley" and his suggestion became a regular usage.

During those formative years there was much life and action in this region, and the name seemed doomed to be a misnomer, but gradually the spell of its magic overtook the people and their business interests until now the peaceful valley has lulled these interests to sleep, and it remains a resting place as in the days of the early Spanish travelers.

History of Arroyo Seco, New Mexico

by Simeon Tejada

*T*he history of Arroyo Seco begins in the year 1804. Arroyo Seco is located nine miles to the northwest of Taos and two miles to the east of Highway No. 64.

Cristóbal Martínez and José Gregorio Martínez were the first settlers in Arroyo Seco. These two men came to plant here from Río Arriba County for three years and after harvesting their crops they would go back to their homes in Río Arriba County with their produce.

In 1807 they made an adobe house enclosing a plaza or patio, having no doors or windows in the outside walls for better protection from attacks of the Indians. The only entrance into the inside square was a narrow opening flanked by blank walls. The ruins of this house are still very evident today.

The name of Arroyo Seco was given this site in 1807, for since they did not have the acequia or irrigating ditch which they have today and which brought water from the Lucero river and since in that year they experienced a severe drought so that the arroyo, their only source of water supply dried up, they called the place Arroyo Seco (dry arroyo).

Today they irrigate with water from the Lucero river, this name having been given to this river after a Mercenary by the name of Lucero de Godoy who, having asked the Crown of Spain for a grant of land, was given this grant on the Lucero river. He erected a house but abandoned it after a few years.

Then Antonio Martínez asked for and was given this grant and today it is known as the Antonio Martínez grant.

Arroyo Seco is a picturesque village at the foot of the Sangre de Cristo range. Two miles east of it are many caves, many of which have not been explored.

There are also close by, three water falls. In one the water falls 150 feet and in the smaller one it falls 60 feet in every case disappearing into the earth.

Between Arroyo Seco and the San Geronimo pueblo of Taos a very tragic happening took place in the years between 1810 and 1812. It so happened that nine natives called "llaneros" or plains indians came with the intention of stealing horses belonging to the Indians of the pueblo of San Geronimo. They hid on a small hilltop from which they could watch the horses which they meant to steal that night. Eight of them slept after placing the remaining one as a sentinel to guard them. This sentinel went to sleep on the stone where he was seated.

The pueblo Indians as was their custom had gone out at sunset to scout around and seeing the sentinel asleep on the hilltop fired their rifles at him and killed him. The noise of rifle fire awoke the other eight and they were killed also by the Pueblo Indians.

The plains Indians were so called because they lived on the plains; they were the Comanches, Arapajos and the Kiowas.

The people of Arroyo Seco hired a man to teach their children reading and writing. He taught them in Spanish.

The first school was erected in 1876 and the first teacher was a Frenchman by the name of Du Carlos Lavarta.

The first settlers had no church until the year 1834. The first mass was celebrated by Padre Martínez in the shade of a pine tree.

Source of Information: Antonio Pacheco, Taos County Senator, Arroyo Seco, New Mexico; Lorin W. Brown, translation.

La Capilla de San Juan "The Chapel of St. John"

by Thorp and Adams

(U. S. Highway 66, one and a half miles north of Seboyeta).

Near a little town called Juan Tafoya, (whan-ta-foy-a), and close to a small hamlet called Marques, is a huge cliff of red sandstone with, as seen from a distance, a contrasting snow-white streak at its base. A closer view shows the entire white streak at its base. A closer view shows that the entire white streak is a wall built of rock and painted white with haspe (native gypsum). Entering by one of the two doors in this wall, you find within a little capilla, or chapel, with an altar, candles, and Santos. This is the Capilla de San Juan. The old attendant, or sacristan in charge, will tell you that on the twenty-fourth of June, "San Juan day," of a certain year, the Navajos attacked the little village of Juan Tafoya. The people fled to the shelter of this cliff, where they successfully repelled the Indians' attack. Out of gratitude they built the chapel by walling up the cave, and dedicated it to Saint John.

How Apache Creek Got Its Name

by Clay W. Vaden

According to Mr. H. C. Graham, pioneer resident, Apache Creek, which runs through his ranch property, very likely got its historic name in the following manner:

The late Epitacio Martínez and his father, who lived on Tularosa Creek 3 miles east of the Graham ranch were cow hunting in early days—in the early 1870's. When they rode along the cut-off of Tularosa and Apache Creek they were fired upon by a band of Geronimo's Apaches who killed the father and badly wounded the son, Epitacio, then a boy about 12 years of age, in one of his legs. The boy fell off his horse and while his father engaged the Indians in a fight, the boy crawled quite a distance and hid near the creek under a pine log, covering himself with pine bark and leaves.

From that day to the present time the creek at the scene of this encounter near Reserve, Catron county was known as "Apache Creek," which is a tributary of Tularosa Creek. The later stream empties into 'Frisco river about 3 miles below Reserve between the Middle and Lower 'Frisco.

List of Illustrations

Photos Courtesy Palace of the Governors
Photo Archives (NMHM/DCA)

COVER: Unidentified wedding group at Santa Fe, New Mexico, 1912, Jesse Nusbaum, NMHM/DCA, #061817

Frontispiece: A. D. Rogers, A. Keith Johnston, Territory of New Mexico, Fray Angélico Chávez History Library, Map Collection (78.9) ca. 1857 .. 22

Chile and corn drying outside home, Santa Cruz, New Mexico, ca. 1910–15, unattributed, NMHM/DCA, #008088. 177

Burros loaded with firewood, Agua Fria, New Mexico, ca. 1925–45, T. Harmon Parkhurst, NMHM/DCA, #005517 177

House and oven, Agua Fria, New Mexico, ca. 1900, unattributed, NMHM/DCA, #056647 178

Chicken pull in Agua Fria, New Mexico, ca. 1900, unattributed, NMHM/DCA, #057659 178

Two Mexican Boys at Agua Fria near Santa Fe, New Mexico, ca. 1911, Jesse Nusbaum, NMHM/DCA, #139519 179

Church bell at Santa Cruz, New Mexico, ca. 1911, Jesse Nusbaum, NMHM/DCA, #013935 180

"Valley and town of Mesilla, New Mexico," 1856, Middleton, Wallace, & Co., NMHM/DCA, #133628 181

Unidentified wedding group at Santa Fe, New Mexico, 1912, Jesse Nusbaum, NMHM/DCA, #061817 181

Interior, de la Peña House, Santa Fe, New Mexico, 1912, Jesse Nusbaum, NMHM/DCA, #015335 182

Rear of church, Córdova, New Mexico, ca. 1900, unattributed, NMHM/DCA), #058847 182

Relatives of artists Eliseo and Paula Rodríquez husking corn, Santa Fe, New Mexico, ca. 1970?, Ed Andrews, NMHM/DCA, #071218. 183

"New Mexican Threshing Machine," northern New Mexico, undated, Philip E. Harroun, NMHM/DCA, #015374 183

Plastering adobe, Abiquiu, New Mexico, ca. 1897, Philip E. Harroun, NMHM/DCA, #012535 184

"Mexican Woman Baking, Santa Fe," ca. 1898–1900, Christian G. Kaadt, NMHM/DCA, #069106 184

Chimayó weaver, Chimayó, New Mexico, undated, unattributed, NMHM/DCA, #013770 185

Birds eye view of Chimayó, New Mexico, ca. 1911, Jesse Nusbaum, NMHM/DCA, #014450 185

Procession at Santuario de Chimayó, Chimayó, New Mexico, 1910, Jesse Nusbaum, NMHM/DCA, #014379 186

Street scene, Truchas, New Mexico, ca. 1925–45, T. Harmon Parkhurst, NMHM/DCA, #011594 186

Cart (New Mexico History Museum Artifact No. 9500/45), undated, unattributed, NMHM/DCA), #011838 187

Acequia Madre, Albuquerque, New Mexico, 1881, Ben Wittick, NMHM/DCA, #015754 188

Interior of McSween Store, Lincoln, New Mexico, undated, Lincoln County Collection, NMHM/DCA, #089733 189

Main Street of Lincoln, New Mexico showing Watson house, site of burned McSween house and Tunstall Store, undated, Frasher, NMHM/DCA, #105473 189

Group in front of Lincoln Hotel, Lincoln, New Mexico, ca. 1890–1900, unattributed, NMHM/DCA), #110991 190

Church at Trampas, New Mexico, ca. 1912, Jesse Nusbaum, NMHM/DCA, #014164 190

Funeral procession, Mora, New Mexico, ca. 1895, Tom Waltom, NMHM/DCA, #014757 191

Home, Manzano, New Mexico, ca. 1900, unattributed, NMHM/DCA, #037438 191

Church, San Miguel, New Mexico, November 14, 1882, Adolph F. Bandelier, NMHM/DCA, #009673 192

Bibliography of New Mexico Federal Writers' Project Documents

WPA—Works Progress Administration/NMFWP—New Mexico Federal Wrtiers' Project
NMSRCA—New Mexico State Records Center and Archives

A Second Ananias, Reyes N. Martínez, August 14, 1936, NMFWP, WPA #234, NMSRCA

A Sheepherd at Work in Taos County, Reyes Nicanor Martínez, December, 1940, NMFWP, WPA #223b, NMSRCA

A Witch Story, Lorin W. Brown, January 9, 1939, NMFWP, WPA #139, NMSRCA

About Billy the Kid As Told by Ismael Valdéz, L. Raines, August 3, 1936, NMFWP, WPA #212, NMSRCA

Alto Huachin, Lorin W. Brown, September 9, 1938, NMFWP, WPA #220, NMSRCA

Billy the Kid, Edith L. Crawford, May 10, 1937, NMFWP, WPA #212, NMSRCA

Billy the Kid Story: Donicino Molina, Edith L. Crawford, June 14, 1937, NMFWP, WPA #212, NMSRCA

Billy the Kid Story: Francisco Gómez, Edith L. Crawford June 1, 1937, NMFWP, WPA #212, NMSRCA

Canuteros and the Death of Colonel Means, Lorin W. Brown, April 27, 1937, NMFWP, WPA #234, NMSRCA

Cooperation, Reyes Martínez, February 27, 1937, NMFWP, WPA #233a, NMSRCA

Don José Miguel Archuleta, A Character of Old Taos: La Bajada de la Santa Cruz, Lorin W. Brown, May 18, 1937, NMFWP, WPA #233a, NMSRCA

Dos Hombres Sabios de Las Placitas "The Wise Men of Las Placitas," Lou Sage Batchen, June 4, 1941, NMFWP, WPA #224b, NMSRCA

Early Days in Lincoln County As Told by Josh Brent, Frances E. Totty, June 1, 1938, NMFWP, WPA #212, NMSRCA

Early Days and Customs in Agua Fria, Lorin W. Brown, August 11, 1937, NMFWP, WPA #229, NMSRCA

Early Life in Questa As Told by Frank V. García, L. Raines, July 25, 1936, NMFWP, WPA #236, NMSRCA

El Adivino Casual "A Fortune-Teller by Accident," Lorin W. Brown, February 7, 1939, NMFWP, WPA #152, NMSRCA

El Hombre Alegre "The Jolly Man" As Told by Rumaldita Gurulé, from La Madera, "The Timber," Lou Sage Batchen, December 17, 1938, NMFWP, WPA #224a, NMSRCA

El Inocentón "The Innocent" As Told by Teresita Gallegos de Baca, from Ojo de la Casa "House of the Spring," Lou Sage Batchen, November 26, 1938, NMFWP, WPA #224a, NMSRCA

El Leoncito, Lorin W. Brown, April 8, 1940, NMFWP, WPA #77b, NMSRCA

El Misterio "The Enigma" As Told by Catalina Gurulé, from La Madera "The Timber," Lou Sage Batchen, December 17, 1938, NMFWP, WPA #224a, NMSRCA

El Ojo "The Eye" As Told by Teresita Gallegos de Baca, from Ojo de la Casa "House of the Spring," Lou Sage Batchen, November 26, 1938, NMFWP, WPA #224a, NMSRCA

El Platero "The Silversmith," Lou Sage Batchen, August 17, 1942, NMFWP, WPA #224a, NMSRCA

Estancia in Tradition, N. S. Rose, October 21, 1940, NMFWP, WPA #237, NMSRCA

Flight to Mexico, Lorin W. Brown, April 26, 1937, NMFWP, WPA #139, NMSRCA

Gallegos: Quay County, Genevieve Chapin, July 11, 1936, NMFWP, WPA #219, NMSRCA

Ghostly Revenge, Genevieve Chapin, September 10, 1936, NMFWP, WPA #227, NMSRCA

Going for Wood, Lorin W. Brown, April 19, 1937, NMFWP, WPA #152, NMSRCA

Hallucinations and a Wildcat Venture, Reyes Martínez, March 20, 1937, NMFWP, WPA #234, NMSRCA

History of Arroyo Seco, New Mexico, Simeon Tejada, October 10, 1938, NMFWP, WPA #233a, NMSRCA

How Apache Creek Got Its Name, Clay W. Vaden, November 25, 1936, NMFWP, WPA #182, NMSRCA

How the Civil War Reached Las Placitas, Lou Sage Batchen, February 26, 1941, NMFWP, WPA #224a, NMSRCA

Interview with José García y Trujillo, Janet Smith, August 26, 1936, NMFWP, WPA #212, NMSRCA

La Capilla de San Juan "The Chapel of St. John," Thorp and Adams, March 10, 1936, NMFWP, WPA #215, NMSRCA

La Cita de Las Brujas "Rendezvous of the Witches" As Told by Rumaldita Gurulé, Teresita Gallegos de Baca, and Catalina Gurulé, from La Madera "The Timber," Lou Sage Batchen, December 17, 1938, NMFWP, WPA #224a, NMSRCA

La Madera "The Timber," Lou Sage Batchen, December 17, 1938, NMFWP, WPA #224a, NMSRCA

Las Huertas, Lou Sage Batchen, October 11, 1938, NMFWP, WPA #224b, NMSRCA

Las Vegas, Bright Lynn, November 21, 1938, NMFWP, WPA #227, NMSRCA

Lea County Plains—Once a Hunting Ground, Mrs. Benton Mosley, September 28, 1936, NMFWP, WPA #208, NMSRCA

Los Comanches, Lorin Brown, April 6, 1937, NMFWP, WPA #152, NMSRCA

Los Torres, L. Raines, June 1, 1936, NMFWP, WPA #227, NMSRCA

Luxuries Come to La Madera As Told by Rumaldita Gurulé, from La Madera Part II, Lou Sage Batchen, January 9, 1939, NMFWP, WPA #224a, NMSRCA

Luz de la Luna "Moonlight" As Told by Teresita Gallegos de Baca, from Ojo de la Casa "House of the Spring," Lou Sage Batchen, November 26, 1938, NMFWP, WPA #224a, NMSRCA

Manzano, Jean Cady, April 27, 1936, NMFWP, WPA #237, NMSRCA

Mexican Boy Captured by Apache Indians, Clay W. Vaden, September 16, 1936, NMFWP, WPA 87, NMSRCA

Mountains and Peaks: Rabbit Ears, Manville Chapman, no date, NMFWP, WPA #189, NMSRCA

New Mexico Folklore: Goblins of Truchas, Manuel Berg, April 12, 1937, NMFWP, WPA #152, NMSRCA

New Mexico Witchcraft: A Magical Cure, Manuel Berg, April 26, 1937, NMFWP, WPA #139, NMSRCA

New Mexico Witchcraft: The Dancing Light, Manuel Berg, April 12, 1937, NMFWP, WPA #139, NMSRCA

New Mexico Witchcraft: The Flying Brujas, Manuel Berg, May 3, 1937, NMFWP, WPA #139, NMSRCA

New Mexico Witchcraft: The Hanging Tongue, Manuel Berg, June 1, 1937, NMFWP, WPA #139, NMSRCA

New Mexico Witchcraft: The Magic Ointment, Manuel Berg, April 5, 1937, NMFWP, WPA #139, NMSRCA

New Mexico Witchcraft: Victims of a Bruja, Manuel Berg, June 14, 1937 NMFWP, WPA #139, NMSRCA

Nuestra Señora de Dolores, Lorin W. Brown, January 23, 1939, NMFWP, WPA #152, NMSRCA

Old Houses of Placitas, Lou Sage Batchen, February 13, 1939, NMFWP, WPA #224a, NMSRCA

Ojo de la Casa "House of the Spring," Lou Sage Batchen, November 15, 1938, NMFWP, WPA #224a, NMSRCA

Old Days in Socorro, New Mexico, N. Howard Thorp, February 25, 1937, NMFWP, WPA #87, NMSRCA

Old Timers Dictionary in Detail: Mrs. Deonicio Álvarez, Spanish Wedding Custom, Marie Carter, April 12, 1937, NMFWP, WPA #197, NMSRCA

Old Timers Stories: Bertha Mandell Candler, Marie Carter, June 27, 1937, NMFWP, WPA #197, NMSRCA

Old Timers Stories: Mrs. Juan Valdéz, Marie Carter, May 24, 1937, NMFWP, WPA #197, NMSRCA

Old Timers Stories: Nemecio Provincio (Wife: Anita Provincio), Marie Carter, May 17, 1937, NMFWP, WPA #197, NMSRCA

Padre Antonio José Martínez of Taos, New Mexico, Luis Martínez, May 21, 1936, NMFWP, WPA #234, NMSRCA

Pioneer Story: Mrs. Lorencita Miranda, Edith L. Crawford, May 5, 1939, NMFWP, WPA #211, NMSRCA

Pioneer Story: Rumaldo Águilar Durán, Edith L. Crawford, November 21, 1938, NMFWP, WPA #210, NMSRCA

Points of Interest in Taos County: The Las Trampas Mission, B. C. Grant, no date, NMFWP, WPA #235, NMSRCA

Ranchos de Taos, New Mexico, B. C. Grant, June 1, 1936, NMFWP, WPA #233a, NMSRCA

Reminiscences of Billy the Kid, Edith L. Crawford, December 27, 1937, NMFWP, WPA #212, NMSRCA

Reminiscences of Billy the Kid As Told by Sam Farmer, Hijinio Salazar, Apolonio Sedillo, Gregorio Ventura, Edith L. Crawford, December 16, 1937, NMFWP, WPA #212, NMSRCA

Roswell, Georgia B. Redfield, December 10, 1936, NMFWP, WPA #186a, NMSRCA

San Augustine, Lester Raines, May 13, 1936, NMFWP, WPA #227, NMSRCA

San Miguel del Bado, L. Raines, June 1, 1936, NMFWP, WPA #227, NMSRCA

Slavery, L. Raines, June 1, 1938, NMFWP, WPA #77a, NMSRCA

Social Life, Reyes N. Martínez, May 13, 1936, NMFWP, WPA #233a, NMSRCA

Starvation Peak, Lester Raines, April 20, 1936, NMFWP, WPA #227, NMSRCA

Story of Billy the Kid, Edith L. Crawford, June 7, 1937, NMFWP, WPA #212, NMSRCA

Tales of the Moccasin Maker of Córdova: Witchcraft, Lorin W. Brown, May 3, 193-, NMFWP, WPA #139, NMSRCA

Tecolotito, Lester Raines, May 13, 1936, NMFWP, WPA #227, NMSRCA

Tejón, Lou Sage Batchen, January 20, 1939, NMFWP, WPA #223b, NMSRCA

The Ambuscade, Lorin W. Brown, May 18, 1937, NMFWP, WPA #233a, NMSRCA

The Bell Marianna, Lorin W. Brown, May 3, 1937, NMFWP, WPA #153, NMSRCA

The Biography of Guadalupe Lupita Gallegos (I), Bright Lynn, October 29, 1938, NMFWP, WPA #227, NMSRCA

The Biography of Guadalupe Lupita Gallegos (II), Bright Lynn, January 5, 1939, NMFWP, WPA #227, NMSRCA

The Fury of 1869, Lou Sage Batchen, June 4, 1941, NMFWP, WPA #223b, NMSRCA

The Ghost of Hayes Ranch (Three Miles North of Cookes Peak), Frances Totty, June 1, 1937, NMFWP, WPA #139, NMSRCA

The Good Samaritan of La Madera As Told by Rumaldita Gurulé, from La Madera "The Timber," Lou Sage Batchen, December 17, 1938, NMFWP, WPA #224a, NMSRCA

The Masons, L. Raines, August 3, 1936, NMFWP, WPA #152, NMSRCA

The Mexican War at Reserve, H. P. Collier, July 30, 1936, NMFWP, WPA #182, NMSRCA

The Panic of 1862, Lou Sage Batchen, March 26, 1941, NMFWP, WPA #224a, NMSRCA

The Salt Traffic from the Estancia Salt Lakes to Mexico, Lorin W. Brown, July 17, 1939, NMFWP, WPA #237, NMSRCA

The Taos Massacre—1847, Luis Martínez, March 5, 1936, NMFWP, WPA #233a, NMSRCA

The Trunk, Manuel Berg, July 26, 1937, NMFWP, WPA #152, NMSRCA

The Weaver of Talpa, Reyes N. Martínez, May 13, 1936, NMFWP, WPA #234, NMSRCA

The Witch of Arroyo Hondo, Reyes Martínez, September 19, 1936, NMFWP, WPA #139, NMSRCA

Tiempo de Pasqua "Easter Tide" 1863, Lou Sage Batchen, June 18, 1941, NMFWP, WPA #224b, NMSRCA

Victorio, L. W. Brown, no date, NMFWP, WPA #87, NMSRCA

Wamsley's Crossing, Reyes N. Martínez, May 13, 1936, NMFWP, WPA #235, NMSRCA

What I Know About Billy the Kid As Told by Francisco Gómez, E. L. Crawford, December 4, 1937, NMFWP, WPA #212, NMSRCA

Names Index

Abreu, Ramón, 114
Abreu, Santiago, 114
Adams, 319, 324
Águilar, José, 109
Águilar, José, 207
Alfredo, Mrs. Ortiz, 312
Alsberg, Henry G., 15
Alvarado, Andrés, 38–39
Álvarez, Cecilia Richards (Mrs. Deonicio Álvarez), 40–43, 45, 325
Álvarez, Cruz Richards, 43, 45
Álvarez, Deonicio (Dennis), 40, 42-43
Álvarez, Edward Richards (Eduardo), 43, 45
Álvarez, Estella Richards (Mrs. Paul Scharman), 43, 45
Álvarez, Joe Richards, 43
Ames, Annie Marie, 49
Anaya, Nieves, 60
Andrés Dol store, 56
Andrews, Ed, 183, 321
Antonia, 261
Antonia, María, 209
Apache Indians, 36, 38, 98, 100–102, 137–138, 294, 320, 325
Aragón, José, 237
Arapajo Indians, 318
Archibeque, Antonio, 238
Archibeque, Benino, 289
Archibeque, Conception, 265, 289
Archibeque, Cornelia, 253
Archibeque, Feliciano, 253
Archibeque, Juan, 253
Archibeque, Marcelino, 253–254
Archibeque de Gallegos, Gertrudes, 254, 256
Archuleta, Carlota, 124
Archuleta, Colonel Don Diego, 120, 122–124
Archuleta, Don José Miguel, 25–28, 323

Archuleta, Ramón, 172
Archuleta, Salvadore, 84
Arellano, Julian, 128
Arguello, Mrs., 170
Arias, 52
Armijo, General Manuel (Governor), 57, 115, 119–120, 216, 279, 303
Armijo, Juan, 233
Armijo, Luis E., 304
Augustine of Hippo, 308
Ávilla, Mrs. Rufujio, 149

Baca, Abran, 132–133
Baca, Captain, 203
Baca, Don Jesús María, 116
Baca, Elfego, 104–106
Baca, Estebans, 131
Baca, F. C. de, 299
Baca, Judge José, 132–133
Baca, Masias, 133
Baca, Onofre, 132–136
Baca, Salomé, 160–161
Baca, Severo, 55, 209–211
Baca, Sotorona, 219
Bailey, May (Mrs. Royal Jackman), 44
Baker, Frank, 195
Baker, Harry, 195
Baldonado, José, 265
Bandelier, Adolph F., 192, 297, 322
Barber, Charley, 196, 198
Barber, Susan McSween, 108
Barela, Pedro, 174–176
Baron, Father, 272
Baros, Christiana, 265
Baros, Florentina, 91
Baros, Manuel ("El Jefe"), 242, 244, 249
Baros, Perciano, 244
Barreras, Gil, 154–156
Barreras, Juan Antonio, 269
Barreras, Luicio, 269

Barreras, Salvador, 266, 269–270
Barreras, Victoriana, 270
Batchen, Lou Sage, 19, 221, 223, 228, 231, 237, 242, 244–245, 247, 249, 251, 253, 259–262, 266, 272, 278, 285, 323–327
Bautista, Juan, 149
Baylor, Captain, 132–134
Baylor, Captain, 279–280
Beaubien, Don Narciso, 117, 121
Beaubien, Luz, 216
Bechtol, 104
Bell, 203–204
Benito, Don, 78–79
Bent, Governor Charles, 117, 120–121
Berg, Manuel, 139, 141, 143–145, 147, 149, 151, 154, 325, 327
Billy the Kid, 108, 193, 195–208, 211–220, 323, 326–327
Bissell, Harvey, 46
Bond-McCarthy store, 25
Bottorff, Juanita M., 310
Brady, Sheriff, 195–196, 203, 219
Brent, Carlotta Baca, 219
Brent, Josh, 219–220, 323
Brooks, J. W., 52
Brown, 134
Brown, Lorin W., 14, 25, 29, 32, 34, 38, 83, 88, 92–93, 100, 157, 159, 164, 293, 296, 318, 323–327
Brown-López, Cassandra, 86–87
Bruges ("Burgess," "Broches"), 38–39
Buenavilla, Victoria, 310
Burns, Walter Noble, 217
Bustos, Juan, 272–273

Cabeza de Vaca, Alvar Nuñez, 13
Cachupín, Tomás Valdéz, 238
Cady, Jean, 297, 325
Calban, Antonio, 238
Canby, General, 235
Candalarias, Pablo, 130
Candelaria, Rumaldo, 251
Candelaria, Señora, 251
Candler, Asa, 46
Candler, Bertha Mandell, 44–47, 325
Candler, Jeff, 44, 46–47
Carolina, 204

Carson, Kit, 87
Carter, Marie, 23, 40, 44, 48, 50, 325–326
Casad, Sara Van Winkle, 47
Casad, Thomas, 44, 47
Cassado, Joe, 151, 153
Cassado, Natividad, 151
Cassidy, Ina Sizer, 15–16
Chácon, Luz, 145–146
Chácon, Vicenta, 145–146
Chapin, Genevieve, 168, 298, 324
Chapman, Manville, 300, 325
Charles Ilfeld Company (Ilfeld store), 132, 210
Chaves, Adelida, 271
Chaves, Calletano, 240, 254, 258
Chaves, Jose, 196
Chaves, Juan Pedro, 254, 258
Chaves, Luis, 268
Chaves, Predicondo (Predicando), 253, 258, 271
Chaves, Teodosio, 253, 258
Chávez, Amado, 300
Chávez, Don Manuel ("El Leoncito," "The Little Lion"), 92, 324
Chávez, José, 238
Chávez, José, 282–283
Chávez, José de la Luz, 165
Chávez, Juan P., 257
Chávez, Manuel, 282-283
Chávez, Mrs. José de la Luz, 165
Chávez, Roman, 92
Chávez y Chávez, José, 217
Chepita (Kit Carson's wife), 87
Chimayó Indians, 209
Chisum, John, 199
Chisum Ranch, 206
Claflin, Majel, 302
Coan, 235
Coe, Frank, 201
Coleman, Pat, 41
Collier, H. P., 81, 104, 327
Comanche Indians, 56, 93–95, 98–99, 300–301, 318, 325
Conklin, A. M., 132, 134
Corbett, John W., 316
Corona, Captain, 97–98
Corralitas Ranch, 46

Crawford, Edith L., 107, 109, 195, 201–204, 207–208, 323, 326–327
Crescencio, 137
Cruz, 212
Cu, Ale, 197
Cuder, Father, 210

de Aragón, Andrés, 237
de Cervantes, Miguel, 17
della Croce, Giulio Cesare, 17
Doke, 196
Dolores, José, 164
Domínguez, Antonio, 30
Dorsey, John, 132
Durán, Aurra, 110
Durán, Enrique, 110
Durán, Fermina, 227
Durán, Isidor, 110
Durán, Juan, 110
Durán, Manuel, 110
Durán, Nestor, 109–111
Durán, Romundo, 110
Durán, Rumaldo Águilar, 109–111, 326
Durán, Salomé, 109, 111
Durán, Santos, 109, 111
Durán, Simón, 110
Durán, Teodoro, 110
Dutchover, Fay, 54

Eaton, Colonel, 133, 135
Eaton, Deputy Sheriff, 135
Elkins, Elmer, 299
Else, Ben, 199
Enríquez, Jesús (Enriques), 48–49, 52
Enríquez, Luz Noriego de, 48–49
Esquibel, 134
Esteco, 196

Farmer, Jim, 207
Farmer, Sam, 110, 204, 206, 326
Farmer, Teodoro, 207
Faustine, López, 312
Felipa, 80
Felipe, 247–248
Fermín de Mendinueta, Pedro, 238
Fernández, Bartolomé (Chief Alcalde and War Captain), 238–239

Fernández, Don Carlos, 301
Field, Neil B., 270–271
Fitzpatrick, George, 300
Frasher, 189, 322
French, Captain, 105
Fulgenzi, Mary A., 80

Gallegos, Antonio José, 270
Gallegos, Cassimiro, 254–256
Gallegos, Don Francisco, 298–299
Gallegos, Don Jesús María, 298
Gallegos, Don José Manuel, 120, 122
Gallegos, Eufracio, 299
Gallegos, Filiberto, 299
Gallegos, Guadalupe Lupita, 55–58, 209–212, 326
Gallegos, J. M., 210–211
Gallegos, Juan María, 241, 254–255, 258–261
Gallegos, Lucas, 195–196
Gallegos, Miguel, 238
Gallegos, Patricio, 230, 237, 239–241, 250, 253, 258–261, 271, 289
Gallegos, Rafaela, 298
Gallegos, Sarita (Mrs. Nestor T. Baca), 299
Gallegos, Señora, 298
Gallegos de Baca, Teresita (Terecita), 245, 250, 259–261, 289, 324–325
Gallegos y Sánchez, Don, 298
García, 299
Garcia, Frank V., 78, 323
García, José, 238
García, Juan, 238
García, Nasario, 17, 21
García, Mrs., 215, 218
García, Tibursio, 138
García, Señora, 299
García Store, 299
García y Trujillo, José, 193, 214, 216–218, 324
Garduño, Teodorita, 164–166
Garrett, Pat, 198–200, 215–216, 218–220
Gaspar Pérez de Villagrá, 13
Gaspari, Father, 286
Geck, Alvino, 54
Genoviva, 18

Geronimo, 320
Gillett, Sergeant J. B., 132–136
Godoy, Lucero de, 317
Gómez, 52
Gómez, Francisco, 202, 208, 323, 327
Gonzales, Francisco, 265
Gonzales, Illario, 58
Gonzales, José, 115
Gonzales, José, 238
Gonzales, José, 242
Gonzales, José (Governor), 279
Gonzales, Juan, 308
Gonzales, Margarito, 310
Gonzales, Onofre, 227
Gonzales, Sabino, 108
Graham, Mr. H. C., 320
Grant, B. C., 302, 326
Gregg, Dr., 303
Gregg, 305
Guerra, 52
Gump, Arthur, 313
Gurulé, Antonio, 238
Gurulé, Catalina, 245, 247, 250, 265, 273, 275–276, 324
Gurulé, Francisco, 242–243
Gurulé, José Librad Arón (Arón), 227, 230–237, 239–241, 257, 268–269, 271–273, 275–277, 284, 286, 289
Gurulé, Josefa, 242
Gurulé, Lucas, 276, 281–284
Gurulé, Nicolás, 227, 235, 273, 275, 283–284
Gurulé, Pedro, 250
Gurulé, Ramón, 242–243
Gurulé, Rumaldita, 227, 242, 244–245, 249–252, 265, 289, 323–325, 327
Gurulé, Serefino, 238
Gurulé de Zamora, Juanita, 254, 256, 285–289
Gutierres, Javiel, 238
Gutierres, Juan, 237
Gutierres, Matias, 238
Gutierres, Pedro, 238
Gutiérrez, Benerando, 242

Hamilton, George, 196
Hamm, Mrs., 299

Harroun, Philip E., 183–184, 321–322
Hayes Ranch, 327
Hearst, Joe, 83
Henry, ("Dutch"), 132
Hern, 105
Herrera, Antonio, 127
Herrera, Chinita, 108
Herrera, Fernando, 196
Herrera, Gregorio, 107
Herrera, Margaret, 312
Herrera, Trinidad, 107
Hidalgo, Candelario, 196
Horgan, Paul, 92
Huff, Emerson, 220

Ignacia, María, 55, 57, 209, 211

J. I. Rael store, 129
Jackman, Royal, 41
Jaramillo, Pablo, 121
Jessie (sister of Bertha Mandell Candler), 44
Jesus, 225
John the Baptist, 225
Johnston, A. Keith, 22, 321
Joseph, Antonio, 83
Joseph, Hon. Antonio, 113
Joseph de Tevis, Don Pedro, 83
Juan, 259
Juan of Tecolote, 235
Juana, 257–258
Jurado, Pedro García, 238

Kaadt, Christian G., 184, 322
Kearny, General Stephen W., 57–58, 116, 119, 303
Kihlberg, Frank G., 303
Kimbrell, George, 197–198
Kiowa Indians, 94, 318
Kosharek, Daniel, 11

Lacy, Ann, 3–4, 14
Lamy, Bishop, 29, 114
Las Cebollas ranch, 138
Laureano de Zubiría, Archbishop Don José Antonio, 113–114
Lavarta, Du Carlos, 318

Lee (General, brother of Louis), 121
Lee, Sheriff Louis (Stephen), 117, 121
Leyba, Padre José Francisco, 311–312
Libby, Mrs., 299
Lincoln, President, 298
Lloyd, George, 134
Lobera, Francisco, 238
López, Don José Dolores, 293
López, Jesusita, 54
López, Julian, 197
López, Nicolás, 29–31
López, Savina, 51
Lorenza, 56-57
Louisianita, 210
Lovato, Santos, 254, 256
Lucas, 259
Lucas ("El Capitán"), 231–232
Lucera, 243
Lucero, Emma, 110
Lucero, Adela, 124
Lucero, Lucy, 307
Luján, Juan, 143
Lummis, Charles L., 92
Lupe, Tía, 159–160, 162–163
Lynn, Bright, 55, 209, 303, 324, 326

Macky, Pedro, 199–200
Madrid, Militón, 137
Maes, Juan de Dios, 303
Maestas, Marco ("The Jolly Man"), 242, 249, 323
Maestas, Rumulo, 253
Maise, Juan, 238
Manzanares, Hon. Francisco, 113
Mares, Mrs. Felix, 170
María (slave), 80
María de la Antilles, 205
María, Doña, 79
Mariana, Doña, 84–86
Márquez, 52
Márquez, Guadalupe, 93
Martínez, Anastacio, 203
Martínez, Antonio, 317
Martínez, Antonio María, 61
Martínez, Antonio Severiano, 112
Martínez, Cristóbal, 317
Martínez, Don David, 100
Martínez, Don Julian A., 125, 127
Martínez, Don Manuel, 118
Martínez, Doña Marcelina, 100
Martínez, Doña Mariana, 125
Martínez, Doña Pabula, 160
Martínez, Erineo, 175
Martínez, Epitacio, 320
Martínez, Escolástico, 69
Martínez, Father Antonio José ("The Presbyter"), 79, 112–-18, 121, 123, 318, 326
Martínez, Francisco, 35
Martínez, Inocencio, 84
Martínez, Isidoro, 110
Martínez, José Gregorio, 317
Martínez, José María, 159–160, 162
Martínez, Luis, 112, 118–119, 326–327
Martínez, Luz, 112
Martínez, Manuel, 112
Martínez, María de la Luz, 112
Martínez, Pedro, 154
Martínez, Reyes N., 14, 20, 59, 63, 70, 73, 76, 125, 128, 171, 323–324, 326–327
Martínez, Salvador, 165
Mascarenas, Anacleto, 95–96
Mason, Epitacio, 130–131
Mason, Jesús, 130
Maxwell, Lucien, 216–217
Maxwell, Mrs., 217
Maxwell, Pete, 217–218
Maxwell Ranch, 216
McCarthy, Charley, 104–106
McNab, Frank, 201
McSween, A. A., 201, 207–208, 220
McSween, Mrs., 220
McSween Store, 189, 322
Means, Colonel, 83–87, 323
Medena, Katy, 49
Meletón, 203

Middleton, Wallace, & Co., 181, 322
Miguel, Don, 196
Mike, 205
Miller, Charley, 41, 51
Miller, S. P., 51–52
Milton, John, 196
Minton, Charles Etheridge, 16

Mirabal, Honorata, 110
Miranda, Emelio, 107
Miranda, Felipe, 108
Miranda, Guadalupe, 216
Miranda, José Dolores, 107–108
Miranda, Lorencita, 107–108, 326
Molina, Donicino, 201, 323
Molina, José, 201
Molino, 134
Mondragón, Juan, 166
Montero, Amado, 109–111
Montero, Nestora (Mrs. Nestora Griego), 109, 111
Montoya, Alberto, 238
Montoya, Ajapita, 151–153
Montoya, Antonio (Montolla), 266
Montoya, Cresencio, 151–152
Montoya, José, 203
Montoya, Lucio, 197
Montoya, María Teresa, 102
Montoya, Nicholás, 238
Montoya, Pablo, 102, 123
Montoya de Martínez, Juanita, 86–87
Moog, Reverend John P., 312
Moore, Charlie, 105
Mora, Juan, 233
Mora, Nicholás, 253--54
Morgan, 134
Morgan, Elizabeth, 131
Mosley, Mrs. Benton, 305, 324
Mote, Billy, 195, 199
Murphy, 219
Murphy gang, 207

Narvez ("Old Narvez"), 228–230
Navajo Indians, 92, 98–100, 209, 231, 264, 278, 280, 294, 319
Navárez, Nellie, 49
Nieto, Ramón, 269, 271
Niza, Fray Marcos de, 19
Nuestra Señora de Dolores, 32
Nuestra Señora de Gaudalupe, 25
Nusbaum, Jesse, 179–182, 185–186, 190, 321–322
Nussbaum, Aileen O'Bryan, 16

O'Hara, Charles, 54

Ochoa, Jesús, 52
Old Miguel, 257–258
Old Weaver of Talpa, 76–77
Ollinger, 203–204
Orejo de Conejo, 300
Orr, Mary, 297
Ortis, José, 137
Ortiz, Don Antonio, 303
Ortiz, Don Tomás, 120, 122
Ortiz, Estella, 312
Otero, Frederico, 270–271
Otero, M. S., 268–269, 271

Pacheco, Antonio, 318
Pacheco, Emilia A., 141, 143–145
Padilla, Don Juan de, 301
Padilla, Felipe, 137
Padilla, Jesús, 137
Padilla, Pascual, 125–127
País, Julian, 253
Paul, Colonel, 235
Parkhurst, T. Harmon, 177, 186, 321–322
Patrón, Juan, 199
Pedro, Don, 34–37
Pepe, 245
Perea, Don José Leander, 278, 280–284
Perea, Don Pedro, 280–284
Perea, Jacinto, 52
Perea Store, 278
Pérez, 279
Pérez, Governor Alvino, 114
Pinal, Father, 55
Pino, Don Pedro, 301
Plasida, 138
Pool, J., 52
Pool, Mr., 51
Pool Ranch, 51
Potter, Col. Jack, 300
Price, Colonel, 121–123
Provincio, Agapito, 50, 53
Provincio, Anita (wife), 23, 50, 54, 326
Provincio, Anita (daughter), 54
Provincio, Emilio, 54
Provincio, Eulogio, 52–53
Provincio, Fidel, 54
Provincio, Henry, 54
Provincio, Louis, 54

Provincio, Nemecio, 23, 50–54, 326
Provincio, Otellio, 54
Provincio, Ramiro, 54
Provincio, Raymundo, 54
Provincio, Victor, 50, 53
Pueblo Indians, 318

Quintana, María de la Luz, 112
Quita, 247–248

Rael, José Antonio, 238
Rafael ("El adivino"), 225–227
Raines, Lester (L.), 19, 78, 80, 130, 213, 291, 307, 308, 311, 313–314, 323, 325–327
Ramirez, José, 242
Ramón, 53
Ramona, Doña, 36–37
Randall, Bill, 132
Redfield, Georgia B., 315, 326
Refrigia, 247–248
Refugia, 80
Refugio Corporation, 48
Roberto, 47
Rodolph, Mr., 213
Rodríguez, Eliseo, 183, 321
Rodríguez, Paula, 183, 321
Rogers, A. D., 22, 321
Romero, Cristóbal, 130
Romero, Hilario, 80
Romero, Isidro, 309
Romero, Vicente, 93–99
Roosevelt, President Franklin Delano, 13, 15
Rosalie, 260
Rose, Mr., 105
Rose, N. S., 316, 324
Rosenwall, 210
Ross, George, 83
Roybal, Andrés, 59
Roybal, Ramón, 20, 59–62
Roybal, Toña, 59
Rymer, Elise, 11

Sais, Jesús, 196
Saiz, Fidel, 310
Salas, Liso, 202

Salas, Octaviano, 108
Salazar, Doña Ana María, 118
Salazar, Hijinio (Iginio), 204–205, 207, 326
Salazar, Igenio, 202
Salis, Juan, 137
San Felipe Indians, 274–276
Sanches, Don Pedro, 196
Sánchez, Major Pedro, 118
Sánchez, Telesfor, 137
Santistevan, María del Carmen, 112
Sarna, Pedro, 253, 257
Scheurich, 83
Scott, 41
Sedillo, Apolonio, 204–206, 326
Selva, Amalia, 147
Silva, 212
Simpson, Captain, 83, 86–87
Simpson, Don Pedro, 104
Smith, Janet, 193, 214, 324
Snively, Colonel Jacob, 279
Snow, Will, 51
Sostenes, 211–212
Stock, 196
Story, Mrs., 41
Story, Mrs. O. C., 52
Swin, Macky, 196–197

Tafoya, Father Sambrano, 107
Tafoya, Pat, 154
Tano Indians, 293–295
Taos Indians, 25, 117, 120–121, 123, 158
Tejada, Simeon, 91, 317, 324
Téllez, 52
Thorp, 319, 324
Thorp, N. Howard, 132, 325
Tingley, Gov. Clyde, 49
Tixier, J. B., 299
Tixier, John, 299
Tomacita, 150
Tomás, 259
Tome, 197, 199
Torres, Gerelda, 107–108
Totty, Frances E., 219, 323, 327
Trotier, Charles Hipolyte (Sieur de Beaubien), 216
Trujillo, David (Dave), 230, 237, 239–241

Trujillo, David (father of Dave), 241
Trujillo, Francisco, 195
Trujillo, Francisco, 223–225, 227, 265
Trujillo, José, 227, 265
Trujillo, Juan, 195, 197, 199
Trujillo, Manuel, 164, 166
Trujillo, Melitón, 158
Trujillo, Mrs., 170
Trujillo, Toña ("Tía Toña"), 171–176
Tules, 260
Tunstall Store, 189, 322
Turley, Simon, 122
Twitchell, 235, 284

Ulibarrí, Mercedes L., 124
Ulibarrí, Santiago, 55–58
Unamuno, Miguel de, 21
Urdemalas, Pedro de, 20

Vaden, Clay W., 137, 320, 324–325
Valdéz, David, 49
Valdéz, Ismael, 213, 323
Valdéz, Josefita, 86
Valdéz, Juan, 238
Valdéz Jr., Juan, 49
Valdéz Sr., Juan, 48–49
Valdéz, Juliana ("Mrs. Juan Valdéz"), 48–49, 326
Valdéz, Magadelena, 49
Valdéz, Marcos, 173–176
Valdéz, Mrs., 45
Valdéz, Robert, 45, 47, 49
Valencio, José Antonio, 238
Valley-Fox, Anne, 3–4, 14
Vaughan, John, 284
Velásquez, Adelle, 314
Ventura, Gregorio, 204, 206, 326
Victorio, 38–39, 137, 327
Vigil ("El Coyote"), 115
Vigil, Don José Gabriel, 25–26
Vigil, Don Melitón, 157–158
Vigil, José Antonio ("El Capitán Vigil"), 96–98
Vigil, Prefect Don Cornelio, 117, 121
Vigil y Alarid, Don Juan Bautista, 119
Visearrar, Governor Don José Antonio, 240

von Schmid, Christopher (Cristóbal), 18

Walter, Paul A. F., 297
Waltom, Tom, 191, 322
Wamsley, Mr., 128
Washington, George, 203
West, Jim, 132
White, A. L., 200
White, Jim French, 196
Wilson, Charley, 199–200
Wittick, Ben, 188, 322

Yrissari, Jacobo, 216
Yrissari Ranch, 217

Zamora, Florentina, 254
Zamora, José Antonio, 268
Zamora, María de Los Angeles, 254–256, 258
Zamora, María de Rayo, 254, 258
Zamora, Paulita, 254, 258
Zamora, Rosalie, 254
Zamora, Valentino, 253–254, 256, 285–286, 288
Zurich Ranch, 299

www.ingramcontent.com/pod-product-compliance
Lightning Source LLC
Chambersburg PA
CBHW021336230426
43666CB00006B/315